Special Economic Zones

Issues, Laws and Procedures

Volume I

Edited by

K.R. Gupta

ATLANTIC

PUBLISHERS & DISTRIBUTORS (P) LTD

Published by

ATLANTIC

PUBLISHERS & DISTRIBUTORS (P) LTD

B-2, Vishal Enclave, Opp. Rajouri Garden,
New Delhi-110027
Phones : +91-11-25413460, 25429987, 25466842

Sales Office
7/22, Ansari Road, Darya Ganj,
New Delhi-110002
Phones : +91-11-23273880, 23275880, 23280451
Fax : +91-11-23285873
web : www.atlanticbooks.com
e-mail : info@atlanticbooks.com

Chennai Branch
5, Nallathambi Street, Wallajah Road,
Chennai-600002
Phones : +91-44-64611085, 32413319
e-mail : chennai@atlanticbooks.com

ISBN 978-81-269-0884-4 Vol. 1
ISBN 978-81-269-0885-1 Vol. 2
ISBN 978-81-269-0886-8 (Set)

Printed in India
at Printman (India), Delhi

Preface

Special Economic Zones are specially delineated duty-free enclaves deemed to be foreign territories for the purposes of trade operations, duties and tariffs. A scheme for setting up the SEZs in the country was announced in the EXIM Policy in March, 2000 with the objectives of developing integrated world-class infrastructure for exports including carrying out manufacturing of goods and rendering of services. Components of SEZs include roads, airports, ports, transport system, generation and distribution of power, telecom, hospitals, hotels, educational institutions, leisure and entertainment units, residential/industrial/commercial complexes, etc.

The concept of Special Economic Zones was given by the People's Republic of China which set up SEZs as early as in 1970 as a measure to attract capital, technology and managerial expertise. Riding high on the phenomenal success of its Special Economic Zones, China's economy started registering a robust growth on a consistent basis. During the last 30 years China has come from nowhere to become the epicentre of global economy. Today, it is impossible to imagine global economy without China. The country has made itself completely indispensable by making almost everything affordable to middle-class population of the world through gigantic production machinery of Special Economic Zones which make these products on a large scale, leading to a drastic reduction in cost price.

Encouraged by the grand success of China's SEZs—particularly Shenzhen and Shantou—both of which have become huge urban agglomerations, the Indian Government has envisaged SEZs as the new mantra for export-oriented economic activity. Much has been said and discussed about the Special Economic Zones Act, 2005. From politicians to businessmen, from journalists to activists—all have expressed different points of view thereon. Some favour it vehemently, others accept it partially, while the government is keen to promote the establishment of large, self-contained areas supported by world-class infrastructure oriented towards export promotion.

The overwhelming enthusiasm to set up Special Economic Zones is accompanied by several controversies—the major ones being over the likely benefit to the economy in the wake of a plethora of tax and tariff concessions being dished out to the SEZs; the future of existing export-oriented units, Software Technology Parks and Hardware Centres; grabbing the land of poor farmers for setting up SEZs without adequate compensation; the impact of taking away arable land, for industrial purposes, on agricultural production; the absence of proper rehabilitation package for the displaced families, etc.

The present book *Special Economic Zones* in two volumes studies in detail the various aspects of policy relating to Special Economic Zones. Different problems relating to people's apprehensions about these models of growth, including displacement of a large number of landowners, environmental pollution likely to be caused by a large number of huge industrial units being set up in the SEZs, the inter-Ministerial differences over some issues—principally the unprecedented concessions, incentives and sops being given to the SEZs, etc.—have been discussed in the four analytical articles written by economic experts making valuable suggestions. Besides, there are documents containing foreign trade policy; notifications on income tax, central sales tax and customs duty, etc.; circulars and orders of related ministries, government departments and Reserve Bank of India, giving rules and regulations governing the SEZs; laws and subsequent amendments thereto within the ambit of Special Economic Zone policy of the Government of India. Also given in this book are documents containing the policy framework of States where a number of SEZs are being set up. The Land Acquisition Act, 1894 containing the highly controversial principal of eminent domain which is still being used to divest the landowners of their land has been given as Appendix-I, while the National Policy for Resettlement and Rehabilitation of Project Affected Families, 2003, and the National Rehabilitation Policy, 2006 form Appendix-II.

Such wide coverage makes this book a unique treatise on Special Economic Zones—the newest and most significant models of development meant to showcase India's manufacturing prowess, its burgeoning services sector and its world-class enterprises.

I am sure it will prove highly useful for multinational companies, SEZ developers, policymakers, parliamentarians, lawyers, and businessmen for whom it will serve as a reference book. The students of Economics will find it inculcating, and the general readers interesting and informative.

K.R. GUPTA

Contents

VOLUME I

VOLUME II

Special Economic Zones

1

A Special Economic Zone (SEZ) is a specifically delineated duty-free enclave and shall be deemed to be foreign territory for the purposes of trade operations and duties and tariffs. Goods and services going into the SEZ area from Domestic Tariff Area (DTA) shall be treated as exports, and goods and services coming from the SEZ area into DTA shall be treated as if these are being imported. The SEZ may have areas demarcated as:

(a) Processing areas for setting up of unit for production of goods and rendering of services; and

(b) Non-processing areas, if any.

An SEZ may be set up in the public, private or joint sector or by State Government. In case of privately developed Zones, the investors could be either Indian individuals, NRIs, Indian or foreign companies.

A scheme for setting up the Special Economic Zones in the country was announced in the Export and Import (EXIM) Policy on 31st March 2000. The scheme has the following objectives:

(a) Development of integrated world-class infrastructure for exports, including carrying out manufacture of goods, rendering of services in connection therewith and would include industrial, commercial and social infrastructure. Components of a Special Economic Zone shall include roads, airports, ports, transport system, generation and distribution of power, telecom, hospitals, hotels, educational institutions, leisure and entertainment units, residential, industrial/commercial complexes, water supply, sanitation and sewerage system, and any other facility required for development of the Zone;

(b) Undertaking new infrastructural works such as construction of standard design factory building, etc. and operation and maintenance of infrastructure in the Zone through private/joint/state sector in the Export Processing Zones (EPZs) converted into SEZs.

SEZs go beyond the concepts of industrial concentration as they have a mix of both industrial and human settlements and have much wider flows of goods and services within the enclave as well as their transfer to domestic economy, besides exports to other nations.

Conceptually, they are similar to Free Trade Zones (FTZs) which also offer similar incentives and benefits of trade and commerce within the regions, but they are also different from them in the sense that they normally involve laying down of huge infrastructure and development-oriented townships comprising both industrial settlements and human habitations.

The SEZ enclaves are meant to showcase the country's manufacturing prowess and its burgeoning services sector, especially its world-class enterprises in the areas of Information Technology, Computer Software and Hardware skills.

Although the first Export Processing Zone or Free Trade Zone (as they were known earlier) in Asia was built more than four decades ago near the western Indian port of Kandla, the concept of Special Economic Zones as engines of growth of such high magnitude were not envisaged in any country, leave alone India.

The Special Economic Zones are considered a highly visible component of former Chinese Premier Deng Xiaoping's economic modernization programme. The original four SEZs—Shenzhen, Zhuhai, Shantou and Xiamen—were established in 1979 and have been a source of much discussion and inquiry ever since.

Encouraged by the grand success of China's SEZs particularly Shenzhen and Shantou, both of which have become huge urban agglomerations, the Indian Government has envisaged the SEZs as the new mantra for export-oriented economic activity.

The Government of India introduced the SEZ policy in the year 2000 and brought the Special Economic Zone Act, 2005 with a view to providing an internationally competitive and hassle-free environment for exports. Units may be set up in SEZ for manufacture of goods and rendering of services. The units have to be net foreign exchange earners but they shall not be subjected to any pre-determined value addition or minimum export performance requirements. Sales in the DTA by SEZ units shall be subject to payment of full customs duty as per import policy in force. The policy also provides for converting the existing Export Processing Zones into Special Economic Zones. Till now a number of EPZs located at Kandla and Surat (Gujarat), Cochin (Kerala), Santa Cruz, Mumbai (Maharashtra), Falta (West Bengal), Madras (Tamil Nadu) Vishakhapatnam (Andhra Pradesh) and Noida (Uttar Pradesh) have been converted into SEZs.

Unlike China, which has developed only six large export oriented-industrial areas, the Indian Government has approved the establishment of 237 SEZs in sectors across petrochemicals, auto parts, Information Technology, biotechnology, gems & jewellery and electronics. Out of these, 63 have been notified of which 23 have become functional. Investments of nearly Rs. 11,200 crore have been made in these SEZs. Apart from these, over three hundred applications are pending for consideration of the Board for Approvals, of which about one hundred have land in possession. Hundred per cent Foreign Direct Investment is allowed in Industries under automatic route. The States of Andhra Pradesh, Maharashtra, Haryana and Gujarat lead in the proposed SEZ commitments.

India's Special Economic Zones are scattered around the country—from Surat- to Kochi- to Noida near New Delhi. They are at their initial stages—the infrastructure is being created around them, the policies relating to various issues relating to approval, tax concessions, land acquisition and rehabilitation of Project Related Families (PRFs) are being clarified.

Criteria for Approval

The proposals for setting up SEZ are required to meet the following conditions:

(i) Minimum size of the SEZ shall not be less than 1000 hectares. This, however, would not apply to existing EPZs converting into SEZs as such, or for notifying additional area as a part of such SEZs, or to product-specific SEZs or port/airport-based SEZs on a case-to-case-basis;

(ii) The SEZ and units therein shall abide by local laws, rules, regulations or bye-laws in regard to area planning, sewage disposal, pollution control, etc. They shall also comply with industrial and labour laws and such other laws/rules and regulations as may be locally applicable;

(iii) Such SEZs shall make adequate arrangement to fulfil all the requirements of the laws, rules and procedures applicable to them;

(iv) Only units approved under the SEZ scheme would be permitted to be located in these SEZs. At least 50 per cent area of the SEZ shall be used for developing industrial area for setting up of such units.

Benefits of Setting Up SEZs

The Foreign Trade Policy (2004-09) clearly enunciates that Special Economic Zones are growth engines that can boost manufacturing, augment exports and generate employment. The Government has designed the SEZ policy to give an impetus to the private sector to overcome India's massive infrastructure problems which are widely acknowledged as an impediment to investors. Emphasising the need to develop infrastructure, a recent *Financial Times* article stated, "while manufacturers are attracted to India's low cost environment and burgeoning domestic market, they are worried about moving their goods—be it cars, mobile phones or textiles—through the country's poor network of roads, overburdened airports and clogged ports. Power cuts can force business to a grinding halt."[1] That is why the predominant objective of development of SEZ is to create infrastructure which would facilitate setting up of industrial area for units therein. India's export growth which is already on an upswing can get a further boost if adequate infrastructure is developed through SEZs.

India introduced economic reforms way back in the early 1990s, and has harnessed its economy well for globalization and economic liberation. As compared to China and the East European counties, India has few policy, political and ideological problems in the adoption of the SEZs. The country has always maintained excellent relations with the countries in South-East Asia, South Asia, Middle East and Africa, and hence can find sizeable markets for its exports. India has trade relations with all the major trading blocs and all the geographical regions of the world, viz. West Europe, East Europe, CIS and Baltic States, Asia and Oceania, Africa, American and Latin American countries. The SEZ experiment in India may, therefore, serve as a good succession to the economic reforms programme, the economic conditions having been well laid out, and conducive atmosphere created for investments into and exports from the country.

The market processes are not new to India. The country is a founder member of World Trade Organisation (WTO) which provides for a rule-based, transparent and predictable multilateral trading system which protects the member countries from the pressure of stronger trading partners. WTO rules envisage non-discrimination in the form of National Treatment and Most Favoured Nation (MFN) treatment to India's exports in the markets of other WTO members. There are also contingency provisions in WTO rules that enable member countries to take care of exigencies like balance of payment problems and situations like unfair trade practices. Under the umbrella of WTO, India can march ahead in its policy of stimulating greater economic activity through exports and making foreign trade an effective instrument of economic growth. The SEZs are supposed to provide an internationally competitive and hassle-free environment for exports and are thus expected to give a further boost to the country's exports.

India's exports were US$ 105,152 million for the year 2005-06 while the imports stood at US$ 156,993 million showing a trade deficit of US$ 51,841 million. The provisional figures for India's imports and exports for 2006-07 (April-September) as given by Economic Survey 2006-07 are US$ 60,550 million and US$ 95,691 million respectively, which means that the trade deficit is likely to grow to US$ 35,141 million in the first six months of the current Financial Year. While exports grew by 34.2 per cent of the GDP during 2005-06, the imports grew by a whopping 48.2 per cent of the GDP. The trend of imports growing at a faster rate than the growth of exports continued during the fiscal 2006-07 being 25.9 per cent of the GDP for imports as against 22.9 per cent for exports. With a burgeoning trade deficit, primarily on account of rising oil prices, the reversal from current account surpluses witnessed between 2001-02 and 2003-04 to a current account deficit in 2004-05 is continuing into 2006-07 also. India's share in world export is merely 1 per cent as against 7.8 per cent of China. The value of India's exports is US$ 99.5 million as against US$ 762.0 million of China.

The data clearly shows that India has not been able to increase its exports in proportion to the growth of its imports. The policy of setting up Special Economic Zones is a step in the right direction to increase exports at a faster rate so that the trend of trade deficit is reversed. India is a country endowed with rich resources in ores, minerals, chemicals and geo-biodiversity. Its climate is conductive to the growth of nearly every type of crop. Besides, the country has well-established industries in plantation products, agriculture and allied goods, marine products, leather goods, gems and jewellery, engineering and electronics, textiles, handicrafts, cotton and several unclassified items. There is a huge human resource capital in the form of engineers, business managers, entrepreneurs, traders, skilled and unskilled workmen. All these positive factors can be garnered by the SEZs to boost exports.

According to India's Foreign Trade Policy, the SEZ units may export goods and services including agro-products, partly processed goods, sub-assemblies and components except prohibited items of export in ITC (HS). The units may also export by-products, rejects, waste scrap arising out of the production process. Export of Special Chemicals, Organic Materials, Equipment and Technologies (SCOMET) shall also be undertaken, though subject to fulfillment of the conditions indicated in the ITC (HS) classification of Export and Import items. Further, SEZ units, other than trading and service units, may also export to the Russian Federation in Indian Rupees against repayment of State Credit/Escrow Rupee Account of the buyer, subject to RBI clearance, if any. The huge resources of the country shall provide abundant raw material to the SEZs to manufacture various items for export.

Employment to Women

In many countries like China, Sri Lanka and Poland the SEZs have given large employment to women. The Indian SEZs are also likely to do the same as there are several thousands of women workers in India and they will earn salaries that they would not be able to earn outside the Zone. As the difference between the wage of men and women is not too different in the SEZs, they may well become the harbingers of women's improved socio-economic condition, at least in the areas around the SEZs.

Multinational companies (MNCs) have established their factories in the Special Economic Zones in most of the South Asian countries and they employ thousands of women workers. Their work, however, is mostly repetitive in nature like sewing, knitting, fixing small parts, etc. As a result, women often suffer from chronic illnesses. They also have other problems related to night shifts. They are not given proper contracts and are hired and fired easily. No health benefits are usually given to women workers, and with marriage and pregnancy, their contracts are often terminated. However, in a country like India where there is rampant unemployment, if the women did not work in factories, they would have no income at all which would push them back into poverty and vulnerable situation. The setting up of SEZs in

India is likely to improve the socio-economic condition of women. Thus, the social benefits of establishing SEZs can be seen as the by-products of the larger economic benefits.

Agri Export Zones

The Government of India has laid special emphasis on export of agricultural products in the Exim Policy announced in March 2001 and decided to set up Agri Export Zones in the country. There is a proposal to set up agri-export-oriented units in the AEZs wherein production and processing will be integrated. Some of these AEZs are now being consorted to SEZs to bring them under the ambit of the new policy and provide them all the benefits and concessions for export.

The producer of the AEZ shall become the developer of the SEZ. He will enter into contract farming with the farmers around the unit and ensure supply of quality seeds, pesticides, micro-nutrients and other materials to the group of farmers from whom the exporter would be purchasing their products as raw material for production of the final product for export. The Reserve Bank of India has directed the banks to provide Packing Credit to the export-processing units under the extent guidelines, for the purpose of procuring and supplying inputs to farmers. The banks may treat the inputs supplied to farmers by exporters as raw material for export and consider sanctioning the lines of credit/export credit to processors/exporters to cover the cost of such inputs required by farmers to cultivate such crops to promote export of agri-products. Thus, the SEZs which are converted from AEZs will not only boost export of agricultural products but also ensure that good quality crops are raised. An AEZ will work out a strategy for end-to-end development of the product. It involves an identification of farmers, ensuring availability of inputs like seeds, fertilisers, pesticides, water, credit, power, etc., determining and extension of pre-harvest technology like grading, sorting, processing and packaging, provision of infrastructure, ensuring logistics and marketing.

Human Resources

India has a large English-speaking population with professional, technical and managerial skills to understand the market dynamics and move strategically in achieving success. All the major cities have sufficient people with diverse educational skills to offer to several kinds of professions. Most of the skills are available at relatively low wages. It is widely believed that the human resources that India possesses are an added advantage and will be instrumental in sustaining high growth of the economy in all sectors and spheres. India's Computer Engineers and Information Technology experts match those of the most advanced countries of Europe and America. The Special Economic Zones for IT and IT-Enabled Services, being set up at Jabalpur, Indore, Jaipur, Kancheepuram, Coimbatore, Madurai, Kharagpur, Hyderabad, Pune, Gurgaon, Noida and many other places will take IT and ITES in India to new heights and earn huge foreign exchange for the country.

What gives India an edge in the expansion process is its wide range of industries and an abundant supply of all kinds of labour at a reasonable price, well below the international prices, which can reduce cost and give a competitive edge in international markets. India's export growth which is already on an upswing can get a further boost if the main problems of infrastructure and supply of labour are solved in these Zones. However, the labour laws of the country will prevail as before in these Zones. But, since most employment is on contract basis, the labour laws will not be enforced, and would be circumvented.

Virtual Special Economic Zones

The Central Government may, on the recommendations of the Board, notify any area as a Virtual Special Economic Zone, if the following conditions are fulfilled:

(a) one or more export-oriented units are situated in the area proposed to be notified as Virtual Special Economic Zone;

(b) each export-oriented unit in the area proposed to be notified as Virtual Special Economic Zone has made an investment of fifty crore rupees or such other higher value as may be prescribed in plant, machinery and building;

(c) every such unit has an export turnover of fifty crore rupees or such other higher value of turnover as maybe prescribed for a class or classes of export-oriented units.

Every export-oriented unit located in Virtual Special Economic Zone shall be eligible for such exemptions, duty-drawbacks and concessions as the Central Government may, by notification specify in this behalf, subject to such conditions as maybe specified therein, which are available to an entrepreneur. Such export-oriented unit shall not be allowed similar exemptions, duty-drawbacks or concessions under any other law for the time being in force.

The export-oriented unit shall, without prejudice to the provisions of this Act, continue to be governed by provisions of other laws for the time being in force, and concessions, duty-drawbacks and benefits applicable to such units under any law for the time being in force.

Alternative Routes in Asia

Many multinational companies have found beneficial options in investing in these foreign territories as the SEZs are called. Prominent among them being Nokia which has set up an SEZ in Sriperumbudur in Tamil Nadu for manufacturing handsets with an investment of US$ 145 million. Samsung and LG Electronics have already set up manufacturing units for mobile phones in India.

Hyundai Motors has chosen India as its base for the Santro, and plans to ship 3,00,000 cars to six countries within two years. Other MNCs in the race include Beyerische Motorein Werke (BMW), General Motors and Intel. Another 'biggy', Tata Yazaski, has set up a unit to manufacture automobile cables. This is followed by a US-company setting up a float-glass manufacturing unit in the Vishakhapatnam SEZ.

Some Indian companies have also succeeded in entering into joint ventures. For example Pasari Silk Mills, a Kolkata-based company has tied up with US-based home textiles retailer, Koplanich for manufacturing high value home furnishings in silk in the Falta SEZ. It is learnt that India's largest company Reliance Industries is expected to invest around US$ 5-6 billion in setting up the country's largest SEZ in the Northern State of Haryana. The Reliance SEZ will occupy an area of 5,000 hectares and the company is already engaged in the task of upgrading the local infrastructure including an airport, housing, shopping mall, etc.

The SEZ is expected to come up near National Highway-8 in Gurgaon and would extend to Jhaffar district. According to the agreement, the Reliance Ventures would hold 90% equity in Reliance Haryana SEZ. The State Government would hold the rest and the new firm would be listed in the stock exchange within a few years. The total cost of the project is expected to be around 400 billion rupees out of which an amount of 150 billion rupees is expected to come from other domestic and foreign investors. According to the original plan disclosed by RIL Chairman Mukesh Ambani, 15 per cent of the Zone would be used to set up a residential township, 50 per cent will be for theme parks, hotels, sports clubs and another 30 per cent will be set aside for shopping malls. However, this plan will have to be re-drafted in the light of the changes made in the SEZ policy that the minimum share of the processing area within the SEZ should be 50 per cent.

It is believed that the SEZ would offer high quality infrastructure facilities besides allowing for the duty-free import of capital goods and raw materials. It would also generate huge employment opportunities for the people of nearby area.

Other companies that are setting up SEZs include ONGC, Mahindra and Mahindra, Infosys Technologies, Wipro, Bio-con, Howlett Packard, Adani Group, Serum Bio-pharma Park, Tata Consultancy Services, ETL Infrastructure Services, Syntel International Private Ltd., M.L. Dalmiya and Company Ltd., Moser Baer Ltd. A list of companies so listed is given in Table 1.1.

Table 1.1: Major Companies and their Proposed SEZs

S. No.	Name of Developer	Location	Type	Area (In Hectares)
1.	Dwi's Laboratories	Andhra Pradesh	Pharmaceuticals	105.496
2.	Wipro Ltd.	Andhra Pradesh	Information Technology	6.48
3.	Apache SEZ Dev. India Private Ltd.	Andhra Pradesh	Footwear	126.90
4.	A.P. Techno Projects Private Ltd.	Andhra Pradesh	Information Technology	10
5.	Hyderabad Gems Ltd.	Andhra Pradesh	Gems and Jewellery	80.93
6.	Chandigarh Administration	Chandigarh	Electronics, Hardware and IT/ITES	31.4966
7.	Reliance Infra-structure Limited	Gujarat	Petroleum and Petrochemicals	440.08
8.	Adani Exports Ltd.	Gujarat	Multi-product	2406.75
9.	Infosys Technologies	Karnataka	Information Technology/ Information Technology Enabled Services	125
10.	Infosys Technologies	Karnataka	Information Technology/ Information Technology Enabled Services	30.99
11.	Wipro Ltd.	Karnataka	Information Technology	6.48
12.	Wipro Ltd.	Karnataka	Information Technology	5.17
13.	Bio-con Ltd.	Karnataka	Biotechnology	35.55
14.	Serum Bio-Pharma Park	Maharashtra	Pharmaceuticals and Biotechnology	23.1793
15.	Flextronics Technologies India Pvt. Ltd.	Tamil Nadu	Electronics, Hardware	101.21
16.	Tata Consultancy Services Ltd.	Tamil Nadu	Information Technology	28.53
17.	ETL Infrastructure Services	Tamil Nadu	Information Technology	10.57
18.	Syntel International Pvt. Ltd.	Tamil Nadu	Information Technology/ Information Technology Enabled Services	11.73
19.	M.L. Dalmiya and Company Ltd.	West Bengal	Information Technology/ Information Technology Enabled Services	48.5623
20.	Moser Baer Ltd.	Uttar Pradesh	Non-conventional Energy	11.9

In addition to the above, Orissa got a nod for starting four SEZs with an investment of over Rs. 12,000 crores in manufacturing, IT and ITES sectors. One SEZ is to come up in Jharsuguda on 347 hectares at an estimated investment of Rs. 5,742 crores with a potential to create 7000 jobs. The second one, for the aluminium industry, is to be developed by Hindalco Industries on 855 hectares in Sambalpur at an estimated investment of Rs. 3,909 crores aimed at creating 8000 new jobs. The third one relates to beach sand and mineral processing to be developed by Saraf Agencies Pvt. Ltd. in Chhatrapur with an investment of Rs. 1,300 crores, creating 2,200 jobs. The fourth SEZ relates to four million sq. ft built-up space primarily for IT and ITES sectors to be developed by DLF on 54 acres in Bhubaneswar at an estimated investment of Rs. 140 crores, creating 6000 jobs. Approvals have also been granted for setting up of the SEZs in Tamil Nadu at Chennai, Sriperumbudur, Coimbatore and Kancheepuram.

Tax Benefits and Other Concessions

The SEZ policy provides for a large number of tax benefits and other concessions to make the package attractive. The SEZs will be treated as though they are foreign territories within India. The units and developers will be given 100 per cent exemption from Income Tax for 5 years, and 50 per cent of their ploughed back profits will also be exempted from Income Tax for five years. In addition, there is a provision for exemption from customs and central excise duties for five years. Other exemptions and incentives are mentioned below:

(i) Income Tax benefit under section 81IA to developers for any block of 10 years in 15 years;

(ii) Duty-free import/domestic procurement of goods for development, operation and maintenance of SEZs;

(iii) Exemption from Service Tax and Central Sales Tax;

(iv) Income of infrastructural capital fund/company from investment in SEZ exempt from Income Tax;

(v) Investment made by individuals, etc. in an SEZ also eligible for exemption under Section 88 of Income Tax Act;

(vi) Losses if any, can be carried forward while computing Income Tax.

Apart from these tax benefits, there are some other incentives and facilities for SEZ enterprises. These include:

(a) A 100 per cent Foreign Direct Investment has been allowed for:
  (i) townships with residential, educational and recreational facilities on a case-to-case basis;
  (ii) franchise for basic telephone in the SEZ;
(b) The developer shall be allowed to transfer infrastructure facility for operation and maintenance;
(c) Generation, transmission and distribution of power in SEZs shall be permitted;
(d) The SEZ units may import or procure from domestic sources, duty-free, all their requirements of capital goods, raw materials, consumables, spares, packing materials, office equipment, etc. for implementation of their projects in the Zone without any license or specific approval;
(e) The duty-free goods imported/procured locally can be utilised over the approval period of five years;
(f) The domestic sales by SEZ units will be exempt from SAD;
(g) The domestic sale of finished products, by-products shall, however, be on payment of applicable Custom duty;
(h) The domestic sale of rejects, waste and scrap shall attract payment of applicable Custom duty on the transactional value;
(i) There will be exemption from any duty of Customs under the Customs Act, 1962 or the Custom Tariff Act, 1975 or any other laws for the time being in force on goods imported into or service provided in the Special Economic Zones or in a unit therein to carry out the authorised operations by the developer or entrepreneur;

(j) Drawback or such other benefits may be admissible from time to time on goods brought and services received from the Domestic Tariff Area into a Special Economic Zone by the service providers located outside India to carry out the authorised operations by the developer or entrepreneur;

(k) There will be exemption from Service Tax under Chapter V of the Finance Act, 1994 on taxable services provided in the Special Economic Zones;

(l) There will be exemption from the Securities Transaction Tax leviable under Section 88 of the Finance Act, 1994 when the taxable securities transactions are entered through a unit of International Financial Services Centre;

(m) There will be exemption from levy of taxes on sale or purchase of goods where such sale or purchase takes place in the course of inter-State trade or commerce, and such sale or purchase of goods shall be deemed to have taken place in the course of export or import of goods for the purpose of the Central Sales Tax Act, 1956 if such goods are meant to carry out the authorised operations by the developer or entrepreneur.

Many people feel that the plethora of tax and tariff exemptions dished out to SEZ developers and entrepreneurs are much more than were necessary and far beyond the limit a developing country like India can afford. These sops, according to the Ministry of Finance, will inflict a loss of Rs. 90,000 crore on the exchequer—an unacceptably large amount for an investment of Rs. 1,00,000 crore. SEZs will bleed the larger economy, feel some quarters. The International Monetary Fund (IMF) Chief Economist R. Rajan has blatantly criticized the huge economic incentives offered to the Zones. He says:

> The concern is if you focus on tax incentives to set up these Special Economic Zones, the incentives diminish and you hurt the revenues of the government. Overall, it becomes yet another give-away which the Government cannot afford.

However, the Commerce Minister Kamal Nath has set aside such criticism, saying that the benefits to the economy, once the production activities of Special Economic Zones gather momentum, shall be many times the amount forgone through tax exemptions.

As a counter-reaction to R. Rajan's attack on India's Special Economic Zones, the Commerce Minister remarked that the concept of revenue loss was imaginary. When there was no levy, the question of revenues loss did not arise.

Business magazine *Frontline* has directed attention towards the Haryana Special Economic Zone Bill, 2005 which gives exemption from payment of any tax, duty, fees, cess or any other levy under any existing State law, to the developer and the exporting units set up under Special Economic Zones in the state of Haryana. But the loss likely to accrue to the State exchequer was not properly assessed, and there was hardly any debate in the State Assembly over the issue.

It has also been pointed out that the exemptions granted are not time-bound, they appear to be in perpetuity. Chapter Five, Section 11 of the Haryana SEZ Act, 2005 exempts from State duties, taxes, fees, cess and levies all the goods exported out of or imported into the SEZ, inter-unit transactions of goods within the SEZs, goods from the SEZ sent for value addition to the Domestic Tariff Area and returned to the SEZ thereafter and services that provide value addition to a product within the SEZ. Sub-section 2 stipulates that all transactions and transfers of immovable property or related documents within the SEZ shall be exempted from stamp duty. Since no time period has been suggested, it may be surmised that these exemptions are in perpetuity.

It is not the case of Haryana alone. Other States like Andhra Pradesh, Maharashtra, Gujarat and Karnataka which are at the forefront of setting up SEZs have similar provisions in their legislations. It can, however, be argued in this regard that as per the provisions under section 50 of the Special Economic Zone Act, 2005 of the Government of India, the State Governments have to formulate an Act/Policy for granting exemptions from

State taxes. If the States do not make laws commensurate with those of the Centre the policy of incentives and initiatives will not only lack uniformity but also give rise to anomalies and controversies. The time frame for each concession, however, needs to be clearly specified so that there is complete transparency in the system.

Expressing its concern over the large number of tax and tariff exemptions, the Ministry of Finance has stated that in the long run all exporters would shift to the Special Economic Zones to get the benefit of tax and tariff exemptions, robbing the government of Rs. 1.75 trillion in revenue. However, it is neither easy nor convenient for all exporters to shift to these designated enclaves. There are certain rules governing the Special Economic Zones and the units therein which prohibit such shifting. The developers of SEZs have to take approval from the Board of Approvals indicating the name and address of the applicant, status of promoter, alongwith a project report covering financial details including investment proposed, mode of financing the project, foreign equity and repatriation, and the specific industries covered under the Zone. Point (iv) of Criteria for approval in Appendix 14-II-N of Guidelines for SEZ Developers issued by Ministry of Commerce and Industry holds special significance here. It reads:

> Only units approved under SEZ scheme would be permitted to be located in these SEZs....

Due to the restriction above, it is difficult to imagine how all the exporters would shift to the Special Economic Zones to avail of the large-scale tax and tariff exemptions. Moreover, the SEZs and the units therein have to abide by local laws, rules, regulations and the bye-laws, industrial and labour laws and such other rules and regulations as may be locally applicable and all this virtually rules out wilful shifting of exporting units in an SEZ.

INTERNATIONAL EXPERIENCE REGARDING SEZs

China

The concept of Special Economic Zones was given by the People's Republic of China. The SEZs were set up by the Chinese Government as early as in 1970s as a measure to attract capital, technology and managerial expertise. In 1987, China permitted the transfer of power to private entities as a result of which land acquisition by provincial and municipal townships to set up Special Economic Zones became the order of the day. By the year 1992, China had set up over 12,000 real estate development companies for the purpose. By the end of the same year, half of Hong Kong's market money was invested in China's real estate market, accounting for nine per cent of the country's foreign exchange inflows.

The Chinese Government adopted special policies and flexible measures allowing SEZs to utilize a special economic management system. Special tax incentives for foreign investment in the SEZs gave greater independence on international trade activities. Apart from above, the political will expressed by the former Chinese Premier Deng Xiaoping and the responsibility given to the local provincial authorities were primarily responsible for the conduct and continuation of SEZ experiment in China.

The economic characteristics on which China's SEZs are based are represented as the following "4 principles":

(i) Construction primarily relies on attracting and utilising foreign capital;
(ii) Primary economic forms are Sino-foreign joint ventures and partnerships as well as wholly foreign-owned enterprises;
(iii) Products are primarily export-oriented;
(iv) Economic activities are mainly driven by market.

According to McKenney, the main objectives of the SEZ development in China were to develop China's coastal area through closed enclaves, attract foreign investment to modernize China, and to bring latest technology, knowledge and management. The location of Shenzhen, Zhuhai, Xiamen, and Shantou Special Economic Zones at China's southeast coastline near the major trading centres like Hong Kong, Macao, Taiwan, and in close proximity to the entire southeast Asia, facilitated easy export.[2]

China's SEZs began to show significant progress within a few years of their setting up. The Shenzhen SEZ located in

Guangdong province in particular started showcasing the economic miracle of China. Its total exports and imports are growing @ 12 per cent to 15 per cent on a year to year basis. China's SEZs are listed separately in their national planning and have provincial-level authority on economic administration. Local congress of SEZs and the Government have legislation authority.

Riding high on the phenomenal growth of its Special Economic Zones, China's economy has started registering a robust growth on a consistent basis. During the last 30 years China has come from nowhere to become the epicenter of global economy. Today, it is impossible to imagine global economy without China. The country has made itself completely indispensable by making almost everything affordable to the middle class population of the world through the gigantic production machinery of Special Economic Zones which make these products on a large scale leading to a drastic reduction in cost price.

The previous decade has seen an unprecedented growth in China's Gross Domestic Products. The country's share in global Foreign Direct Investment which was around 2 per cent in the early 1990s has reached over 8 per cent. The huge influx of FDI has created an enormous increase in employment opportunities and given rise to an affluent Chinese middle class. In terms of Purchasing Power Parity, China's economy is among the top three in the world and has been able to maintain an impressive 10 per cent GDP growth rate for about a decade. Goldmen Sachs in their BRIC report have predicted that by 2050, China will outcompete every other economy to become the world's largest economy with a GDP of US$ 44.45 trillion.

The main factors behind the success story of China's SEZs have been flexible labour laws, adoption of international management practices, low import duties and indirect taxes, measures like tax holidays, abolishing export duties, etc. The most important factor perhaps, has been the provision of extensive infrastructure such as transportation, telecommunication, regular power supply which facilitated manufacturing and trade without any constraint. It also lowered the cost due to economies of scale. Low costs, in turn, have kept the prices highly competitive—

estimated to be 25 per cent lower than those in India—enabling China to capture bulk of the orders in international markets.

Problems in China's SEZs

The Chinese experience of SEZs has not been without problems. The issues relating to changes in land use have been a bone of contention between the people and the authorities. Demonstrations against land acquisition, particularly in the provinces of Guangdong, Hebei and Hainan are common. China's population is increasing every year—the annual additions being around 10 million. Notwithstanding, a large part of arable land is being diverted to non-agricultural purposes resulting in a decrease in food production. Acquiring agricultural land of over 20 million farmers between the years 1992 and 2006 has adversely impacted food security and distribution of foodgrain among the poor masses. Now, even China, where SEZ model was said to be a great success, is worried about the huge economic disparities created by the experiment. According to reports, China is now focusing on broad-based development through the five-year plans.

The SEZs in China showed a robust growth till the end of the 20th century, after which it became difficult to sustain such high growth. Of late, the SEZs have shown trade deficits which have grown as high as the country's total trade deficit. Further, as most of the equipment and spares for infrastructure-laying are imported, the production costs have, at times, risen above the value of exports.

Industrial expansion through Special Economic Zones made necessary the laying down of huge infrastructure such as roads, bridges, large buildings, cables & wires for power and communication, etc. Such large-scale infrastructure financed through public borrowings has resulted in high indebtedness of the central as well as the provincial governments. It has been alleged that the expansion of SEZ concept throughout China has not been commensurate with implementation of appropriate measures to control inflation, fiscal deficit and equitable tax policies. There have been serious anomalies in China's financial banking, foreign exchange and tax collection systems inhibiting the Government from using economic tools to create stable economic conditions. It is also believed that the Chinese SEZ experiment relied heavily on low labour costs, low real estate costs and negligible overhead expenses rather than on transfer of technology on a large scale. Whereas low wages created rifts between the workers and developers of SEZs, the half-hearted technology adoption did not produce the desired level of quality products as compared to those of other countries like Japan, France, UK and the USA.

China is paying a heavy price for rapid industrialisation wrought by SEZs, in terms of heavy environmental pollution. The areas around SEZs are covered with thick clouds of smoke. During the last five years or so China has been consuming 4 to 5 times as much coal and electricity as the USA—itself a major consumer of fuel and power. Many of the companies have set up industries flagrantly disregarding emission rules. Chemicals and effluents are drained into rivers and lakes rendering these water bodies in a grim condition. A recent UN report has disclosed that nearly three lac people die every year in China due to terminal diseases and disorders caused by environmental pollution. With the norms of Kyoto Protocol being strictly enforced from the year 2008, China will have to sharply cut down its greenhouse gas emissions or spend large amounts on carbon trading with countries like India.

There have been some other anomalies in China's growth story through the Special Economic Zones. The provincial Governments of Shanghai and Shenzhen—home to world-class SEZs—often compete in their quest to lure investors to their respective provinces, leading to unnecessary controversies, rivalries and disputes. While coastal China has surged ahead with the flourishing of port-based SEZs, the hinterland has virtually remained outside the ambit of development because of its geographical disadvantage. China's unprecedented growth has been at the cost of an equitable society. However, the Chinese Government has realised this, and now, having the cushion of huge foreign exchange reserves of nearly a trillion dollars, together with an astounding trade surplus of 177.5 billion dollars, China is embarking on a more equitable and all-inclusive reform path. Wen Jiabao has made it clear that economic growth and foreign trade will not be compromised with. In his speech in the Chinese National People's Congress in March 2007 he announced a series of measures aimed at the upliftment of the deprived classes, particularly in the rural areas. The measures include direct subsidies to grain producers, increase in Government expenditure on rural schooling to 29 billion dollars, and a comprehensive rural health insurance programme. He also made it a point to ensure that forceful acquisition of land in the countryside would henceforth be disallowed. These schemes are not for an apparent appeasement of rural populace but a realisation of the importance of equity for faster and equitable growth.

SEZs in Other Countries

Apart from China, some other countries such as Brazil, Kazakhstan, Philippines, Russia, Poland and the UAE have used the concepts of Special Economic Zones, Free Trade Zones, and Export Processing Zones for giving a boost to their manufacturing, exports, and attracting Foreign Direct Investment. Each SEZ in these countries has a different focus and experienced different level of success. Whereas the Chinese model of SEZ aimed at raising the FDI inflow, the SAIF Zone at Sharjah, UAE focused on ready-to-do business facilities, Poland had the primary objective of employment generation, and the Jebel Ali SEZ at Dubai aimed at strengthening the city's entrepreneurial status and diversify the economy. The objectives of each SEZ are governed by the specific conditions and strategic locational advantages.

Even countries like Bangladesh, Pakistan, Sri Lanka and Nepal have tried to promote their exports and also generate employment by establishing Special Economic Zones. Since all these are populous countries, they are into such exports as require cheap labour. Bangladesh and Sri Lanka have done well in garment exports. The countries of South Asia have been able to cut costs by locating their industries in the Special Economic Zones where many tax concessions have been given by their respective governments. In these SEZs, different laws are applicable and a well-functioning infrastructure is available to meet the requirements of different exporting units. Other attractive incentives like repatriation of profits have been given to invite foreign investment.

There are contrasting views on international experience on SEZs. In the early years of reform in China the SEZs played an important role in 'opening China's window to the outside world' and in experimenting with reform initiatives. The high rates of growth, availability of consumer products, increased foreign investment and an improved standard of living drew widespread attention to market economics as a viable alternative to state-owned enterprises and central planning.

Many others feel that the global experience with SEZs is not a happy one. Only a handful of SEZs, of the hundreds that exist, have generated substantial exports.

PROBLEMS RELATED TO SPECIAL ECONOMIC ZONES

When the Government of India introduced the policy in 2000, for setting up Special Economic Zones in the country with a view to providing an internationally competitive and hassle-free environment for exports, there was an enthusiastic response in the shape of hundreds of applications by the prospective developers. The media hailed SEZs as engines of growth, though some quarters criticized the policy on various counts. Since then, politicians, businessman, journalists and activists—all have expressed different points of view on SEZs—some favour them vehemently, others accept them partially, while still others want the SEZ Act to be repealed completely.

While the nation is still divided over the establishment of SEZs, various problems have come to surface regarding the policy and implementation of the SEZs. The problems relate to: forceful acquisition of land through agents and high-level government officials joining hands with corporate houses; large tracts of fertile agricultural land being earmarked for proposed SEZs; giving meagre compensation to landowners/farmers for their precious pieces of land; inflicting huge revenue loss to the exchequer by offering a plethora of tax and tariff exemptions to the developers of SEZs; aggravating the problem of environmental pollution, and harming natural ecosystems by converting green belts into industrial units while still letting the SEZs remain free from environmental laws; causing the problems of resettlement and rehabilitation by displacing thousands of families due to setting up of projects on their lands, etc. All these problems are discussed below:

Land Acquisition

Acquisition of land has surfaced as the biggest problem for setting up of Special Economic Zones. Historian Sumit Sarkar has called the SEZ policy the biggest land grab movement in the history of modern India. The experts feel that the driving motivation behind land grab in India, as was the case in China, has been greed. Bureaucrats and politicians are aware of the soaring value of land the moment the Government announces a permitted land use from agriculture to industry. No wonder that the major corporate powers—Ambanis, Tatas, Mahindras, Kalyanis and many foreign companies are eyeing for this windfall.

While the country is in dire need to address the issues of agricultural crisis, the Government is welcoming the foreign as well as native companies with red carpet to build their enclaves and mansions on the soils of the peasants. However, all over India, the peasants and other sections of population alongwith several organisations have risen against this assault on their rights, resources and sovereignty. In fact, an undercurrent of awareness is spreading through the grassroots of society on an important issue—the protection of property rights.

The land acquisition for SEZs has turned into a Gordian knot. Problems like forcible acquisition of land for the projects, adverse impact on agriculture, inadequate compensation to farmers and displacement and rehabilitation of a large number of people are involved in this complex issue.

The issue of land acquisition in the name of promoting industrialisation or Special Economic Zones shows how deeply entrenched the sense of political patronage continues to be in the influential sections of Indian society.

Liberalisation of the Land Market

If businesses cannot legitimately acquire the necessary land for their purposes then it is the land market that needs to be reformed. Instead, they have sought to eliminate the land market completely by asking the government to act as the middleman and perpetuate the land mafia. It was because of these charges against the Government that the Empowered Group of Ministers has brought the new legislation under which the Government has been barred from acquiring any land for setting up SEZs.

The provision of public facilities or infrastructure sometimes requires the exercise of legal powers by the State under the principle of eminent domain (under Land Acquisition Act, 1894) for acquisition of private property which can lead to displacement of people, driving them out of their land, livelihood and shelter, restricting their access to traditional source bases and uprooting them from their socio-cultural environment.

Social activists like Medha Patkar have stressed the need to abolish the Land Acquisition Act, 1894 as it is an outdated law and makes development and people enemies. She says that the Law, made during the British rule, is still being used in a shameless manner for acquiring not only properties but also the livelihoods of people in exchange for meagre amounts of cash. Providing housing plots and a few civic amenities is preached as resettlement. The fact that this does not address serious economic deprivations and on many occasions does not even consider the impracticality of providing new sites—too far from the source of livelihood, thereby inviting these new sites to be unused or misused—is never considered.

A new policy and Act, therefore needs to be brought in—not just amending the Land Acquisition Act, but by replacing it with a new law that brings the process and parameters of development planning, minimum displacement and actual rehabilitation—all in one fold. The concepts of 'public facilities' and the 'principle of eminent domain' which also figure in the National Rehabilitation Policy (NRP), 2006 need also to be reviewed. The term eminent domain is as outdated as it is anti-democratic. Today, we need to define development not merely in material terms but by including criteria pertaining to democracy, sustainability and equity.

Opinions among social activists range from those who want land to perpetually remain under agriculture or forests, to others who focus more on adequate rehabilitation and compensation package. *Hindustan Times* through an Article by Barun Mitra has drawn attention to the fact that the right to property is being encroached by the Land Acquisition Act. The Indian farmers are placed at an unenvious position vis-à-vis the business class. Whereas the rich business class can survive irrespective of their legal rights, because of their wealth they can buy protection from the people in position and power. The poor remain vulnerable as ever if they are denied their rights. Today, Indian businesses can buy and sell assets, engage in mega mergers and acquisitions, but most Indian farmers hardly enjoy the freedom to buy, sell, lease or rent land. Enforcing a legal right is a difficult proposition for those who are too poor to afford court fee and other charges to seek justice. Rent control, land ceiling and zoning, coupled with weak legal avenues for the enforcement of contracts, have made land in urban India artificially scarce. The land mafia, bureaucrats, politicians and businesses—all have benefited—except the landowner himself.

The Indians have been slowly but steadily made to surrender the right to property since the country's independence. The Ninth Schedule was created in 1951 in an attempt to put land acquisition beyond the purview of judicial review. The populist nationalisation in 1969 greatly diluted the scope of property right protections. The first non-Congress Government went one step further in 1978 and amended the Constitution so that the property right no longer remained a fundamental right.

The way the legislation has been misused in India tells a sorry state of affairs relating to land acquisition. First the State passed legislations undermining the basic principles of law in the pretext of helping the poor. Land was sought to be confiscated from the big landlords and redistributed to the poor. And now the same land is being forcibly acquired through the use of the term 'eminent domain' from the poor to be given over to large private owners.

State as a Land Broker

Until recently, when the Empowered Group of Ministers brought some changes in the SEZ policy that the State

Governments cannot acquire land for setting up SEZs, these Governments had been following the old trend in which the land broker State acts on behalf of private corporations and prevails over dissenting and protesting public. The worst part has been that the administrative machinery did not hesitate to resort to lathi-charge and firing on the protesting public. There was violence in Dadri (Haryana), and, Singur and Nandigram (West Bengal); several persons were killed when the police opened fire to disperse people who were trying to stop forcible acquisition of their land. The State-run urban development authorities like the Delhi Development Authority (DDA) and the Haryana Urban Development Authority (HUDA) went to the extent of pushing out private developers arguing that the latter had brought land for meagre amounts from the original landholders and then made large sums of money by selling the same land to SEZ developers. Now, when the State has been stopped from acquiring land for establishing SEZs, and the SEZ developers have been asked to acquire the land in the proposed SEZ area on their own, the real estate agents will have an unbridled business.

The real estate has always been a big business in India. The elite groups, working through the Government and in the name of the landless have been subverting the use of land as a marketable asset. The Government has been helping them to buy this land at less than the market price against the interests of farmers and other landowners. In the absence of the Government mediating the land acquisition deals, the game is entirely in the hands of real estate agents. Being rich, resourceful and acting in unison, they can always dictate terms to the poor and needy landowners. It is, therefore, doubtful if the exploitation of the farmers and other landowners will be checked even if the Government has preferred to withdraw from the scene. With the land acquisitions already made through the Government for a number of proposed Special Economic Zones across the country, the land market already stands subverted and an active land mafia has already been created. Many of the property agents are closely related to the politicians and other influential people in the area. They will buy land from the farmers and other landowners at a pittance and sell it to the SEZ developers at exorbitant rates, making quick money. Moreover, the Government may not acquire land directly, but it will not stop wielding an influence on the land acquisition deals.

The Government has already circumscribed the use of land for agriculture purpose, thereby preventing the rightful owners from deciding what they could do on the land. The State has, thus, already exercised the power of deciding whether the land for one purpose can be used for another purpose. What is happening in India is the transfer of property of individual owners to private parties in the name of industrial development thought SEZs. It has been argued by social experts and activists that such a framework of private property-based market system does not have any logical footing—neither through the Government nor through the private players. The SEZ lands, they say, are not under public ownership, nor are they urban apartments and commercial shops sold by the State-owned development authorities. Large tracts of land have been acquired by the Government and transferred to other private individuals. The transfer of wealth is evident from the fact that a large number of titles were sold off prior to the actual allotment of property. Such a transfer of wealth from poor farmers to rich business class is against the principles of equity and social welfare. There has been widespread criticism of the Government acting as a land broker. That is why it has decided to steer clear of the business of land acquisition. As a matter of fact, Government intervention into private property-process must take place if there is a strong evidence that clearly establishes that such public action will realise greater value for all. If the Government's policy of acting as a land broker for SEZ developers has been undesirable, its staying away from the land acquisition deals and leaving poor landowners at the mercy of land mafia is also deplorable.

Another critical issue is that in many States some wastelands are also under cultivation, but the farmers have not yet been given any legal titles. In some cases these are ceiling lands under land reform processes but are yet to be distributed to the landless. In Raigarh district where Reliance Industries is planning to build an SEZ on what are known as *dali* lands, the same have been under cultivation by the tribals for many decades now. The regularisation of these lands is still awaited as they fall in the category of forest land. In Jagatsinghpur district in Orissa where the multinational Pohang Steel Company is planning to set up its SEZ, about 300 families are yet to be allotted legal titles. In the absence of these titles or *pattas,* the villagers have virtually no bargaining powers. They get displaced without adequate, at times, no compensation.

Agricultural Land for Industrial Use

As per Commerce Ministry figures, more than 1,20,000 hectares of land will be acquired by more than 200 SEZ projects across the country. A lion's share of this is fertile agricultural land, while the remaining part comprises cultivable wastelands, grazing lands, pastures, scrub forests and urban land around some major cities. As the size of many Special Economic Zones is very large spread over hundreds of acres, the impact on surrounding areas, from geographical and land use point of view will be large.

While none can deny the fact that industrialisation is necessary for a fast economic growth, the important questions that need to be answered are: Why should it come at the expense of agriculture? How far is it necessary, at this stage of development to shift resources from agriculture to industry? At a time when our agriculture sector has not been doing well, why should there be an unchecked and desperate sacrifice of agricultural lands imposing threat to food security?

There have been conflicting answers to these questions. Some experts believe that for the employment-starved, still predominantly traditional Indian economy, where an overwhelming majority of the labour force is struggling to earn a living in agricultural sector, development entails growth of industry and services. There is no alternative other than to shift some resources and labour from the low productivity primary sector to high productivity secondary sector. Globalisation and economic reforms have given a kickstart to the industrialisation process. But it has not yet made a perceptible change in the life of marginalised sections of society. To bring these sections into the mainstream development process, the country needs to embark upon industrialisation on a larger scale. To build factories, townships, roads, airports, bridges—all integral parts of industrialisation—we need land. In India, the land-man ratio is quite adverse because most of the available land is used to grow food for the masses, and any attempt to acquire land to build up industry and infrastructure has to impinge on agricultural land.

The economists see no threat to India's food security because the land requirement for industrialisation is minuscule in relation to the total agricultural land available in the country. For example the 1.25 lakh acres of land which is being acquired in West Bengal for industralisation, constitutes less than one per cent of the total arable land in the State. The situation must not be very different in other States as well.

One of the key indicators of economically advanced countries is that industry, not agriculture, is the major sector of their economies. If we are to reach the level of advanced countries, the shifting of a sizeable part of resources from agriculture to industries is imperative. India cannot continue to protect its farmers if it wants a modern future. Modern countries do not have a large percentage of their workers farming out in the field. The ones who do, find that it is expensive as they divert billions of dollars from industries to farm subsidies. India should avoid such a future.

It can be argued here that industry and agriculture are not, to a great extent, mutually exclusive sectors. Developing industry does not mean that the agriculture will be ignored. The programmes and incentives to boost agriculture like fertilizer subsidy, exemption of agriculture income from income tax, promoting biotechnology in farming, bringing latest farming techniques like dryland farming and drip irrigation, etc. are, therefore, likely to continue and are an integral part of the Eleventh Five-Year Plan.

Industrialisation will help agriculture in many ways. The food-processing industries will create a huge demand for agricultural products; agro-based industries shall bring about modernisation of agriculture leading to higher produce; research centres developing high-quality seeds and manufacturing units of fertilizers, chemicals, etc. shall lead to higher per acre yield. The infrastructure built while setting up SEZs will be used for quick transportation and distribution of foodgrains across the country.

Coming back to the issue of land, the key is to work out how most effectively the land can be used. Most of the proposed SEZs are around major cities like Delhi, Gurgaon, Noida, Mumbai, Bangalore, etc. where farming is not a prime activity. The Union Commerce Minister Kamal Nath has stated that we need to slow down on acquisition of agricultural lands—especially the two-crop lands—and to set up these Zones on wastelands instead. Another suggestion given in this regard is to make it mandatory for the developers of the SEZ to develop a measure of land for agriculture from a piece of wasteland, equal to the one that they have acquired from the farmers.

Those who hold a different view on acquisition of farm land say that it is a micro-economic problem pertaining to those who are losing their land and their livelihood. It concerns the tillers of the soil and others who depend for their daily bread on appropriated land, those owner cultivators, sharecroppers, landless agricultural labourers and even small local traders whose existence had so far been rooted in the plots of land that are proposed to be handed over to the SEZ developers. Giving away prime agricultural land for the sake of industrialisation does not necessarily result in equitable development. The farmers are deeply attached to their land which has been passed on to them by their forefathers. Most of them are not ready to leave their piece of land whatever be the price or compensation package. For people of particular regions who have lived amidst the traditions and culture of that region, it is not easy to move away and find their roots elsewhere. Dispossessing poor farmers, therefore, is an unconscionable social policy.

The Issue of Adequate Compensation

Compensation is a particularly contentious issue. There has been a lot of resentment among the farmers whose lands are proposed to be acquired for setting up SEZs at a price determined by the Government. Various news reports have suggested that the State Governments, under the aegis of Land Acquisition Act, 1894 acquired farm land for "public purpose" at low rates and resold it to developers at a premium. It is such deals that have made the whole issue contentious and showballed it into police-farmer clashes, for example at Kalinganagar in Orissa and Nandigram in West Bengal—following which the venue of proposed SEZ at Nandigram had to be shifted to some other place. According to Vivek Mehra, Executive Director of Price Waterhouse Coopers (PWC) who advises a lot of SEZ developers, the present crisis is a fallout of bad land acquisition policy and politics. The State Governments need to adopt "pragmatic land acquisition policies that do not lead to deprivation among the displaced...."[3]

In land acquisition, the small sellers of land are in a disadvantaged situation as they are not in a position to bargain with the multinationals. The Government, therefore, has to intervene to protect their interest. Moreover, if the investors are asked to acquire land directly from the market, it might lead to speculation, holding up of land in the expectation of higher prices and hence, cause unnecessary delay.

Adequate compensation is, therefore, the most important issue in the entire controversy surrounding the setting up of SEZs. The policy needs some changes so as to make land acquirement equitable. The proper policy would be that the SEZ developers should acquire land at market price itself.

In some cases while some farmers may sell the land to the developers, many others may refuse to do so because they want to remain cultivators. In such cases, the developers should purchase cultivable land in some nearby area and the farmers who are not willing to sell their land to the SEZ developers should be given the land purchased at market rates at other places. Sometimes the land where the SEZ is proposed to be set up is more fertile than the land acquired elsewhere for the cultivators. In such cases the land to the cultivators that is allotted in exchange for their land at the proposed SEZ maybe increased correspondingly. To give a concrete example, if the fertility of land offered to the cultivators is 50 per cent of that land which is acquired from them, they should be offered double area of the land so as to compensate them suitably. In this way the developer would get a compact area of land required to establish the SEZ. This compensation package is also equitable as it allows the affected persons to retain their current living standards. It leaves the farmer as a farmer though at some other place. The cause of agriculture is also not harmed through this policy of industrialisation.

Another way to compensate the farmers whose land is acquired for SEZ would be to give priority of employment to suitable persons whose land has been acquired. The Empowerment Group of Ministers which held a crucial meeting in the first week of April 2007 also said that at least one member of each displaced family be given a job in the SEZ.

As long-term measures Vivek Mehra of PWC has suggested that there should be ways and means to provide education, health and physical infrastructure to the displaced, so that a few years hence, they can aspire to work as engineers and managers in the factories set up on their land.

A sectorial break up of SEZ approvals in India shows that a large number of them have been in the Information Technology sector which employs skilled workers. A report by the investment bank Morgan Stanley says that this trend will further alienate the displaced as they will not find much work opportunities in such specialised sectors. The report therefore recommends a big push to small enterprises and labour-intensive units that will generate jobs and reap the country's demographic dividend.

Aradhna Agrawal, a consultant with the Indian Council for Research on International Economic Relations, who has just completed a Finance Ministry study on revenue implications of SEZs says that the farmers should be paid the market price for their land to ensure that the development takes place with a humane face. She also gives an alternative suggestion that the State Government should create a land bank by acquiring infertile land and developing its infrastructure and connectivity to attract investors.[4]

Another suggestion given in this regard is to create a farmers' investment fund. The Government can levy some taxes on the

SEZs for a period of 25 years and the money should be spent solely to provide necessary inputs to the farmers in the area.

The Government should frame a compensation policy on the basis of suggestions and reports by the experts and implement it in right earnest. It will create a trust in the minds of people about the Government and its policies. Most of the opposition to proposed plans stems from the fears that the affected people will not be adequately compensated. The BCC News has brought to light the instances where the Indian Government has not paid for the land acquired under some statutes. In Kerala, for example, the compensation for land acquired 40 years ago from Brahmins in Palghat, under the Land Ceiling Act, is yet to be paid. It has also been experienced that local politics plays a great role in deciding the amount of compensation, and that particular communities who are in minority in the area are not treated at par with others. These bottlenecks and bureaucratic delays have to be removed if we are to achieve a balanced socio-economic development of our country.

Closely related to the problem of compensation is money management. Most of the landowners seeking compensation are illiterate. They have absolutely no idea of how to properly keep and utilize the money received on selling their land or compensation received from the Government. When the compensations is paid, the sum is often frittered away by families who have never handled large sums. When their land and household are sold or acquired, the money received is their only asset, and their future depends on its proper utilization. Wasting it on social evils and addictions would drive them to poverty and hunger. It is therefore necessary to tell them the ways and means of how to keep it intact or how to convert it into valuable assets which will ensure regular livelihoods for them. They can be taught to put this money in banks where it remains safe and earns interest. The SEZs have provisions for bank branches to be opened within them. These banks can cater to the financial requirements of the landowners whose land has been acquired. There are also suggestions that the landowners should be allotted shares of the SEZ companies on a preferential basis and at lower rates so that they become stakeholders in the company to which they have contributed by selling their land. This will create wealth for these landowners and remove economic disparities likely to be created due to setting up of the SEZs.

Displacement and Rehabilitation

Compulsory acquisition of land for public purpose including setting up SEZs and other infrastructure projects displaces people, forcing them to give up their homes, assets, and means of livelihood. Apart from depriving them of their lands, livelihoods and resource-base, displacement has other traumatic psychological and socio-cultural consequences. The system of extending cash compensation does not, by itself, in most cases enable the affected families to obtain cultivable agricultural land, homestead and other resources which they have to surrender to the State. The difficulties are more acute for persons who are totally dependent on the acquired assets for their subsistence such as landless agricultural workers, forest dwellers, tenants and artisans as their destitution and distress are more severe, and yet they are not eligible for cash compensation. When the entire villages are displaced villagers lose access to local forests, streams and grazing land. They get no compensation for this.

The most consistent fallacy in the debate over displacement *vs* development is the assumption that social engineering is justified if landowners are suitably compensated. It fails to factor that displacement destroys kinships and livelihoods of craftsmen, small traders, fishermen, etc. who subsist on margins of village economy or ecosystem. Then there are the voteless and voiceless nomads whose dependence on seasonal crop cycles is being overlooked in the new scheme of things. For example, a large number of tribals from Purulia and Bankura district of Jharkhand depend on six to eight months' work at Singur's farmland earmarked for the Tata's one lakh rupee car project.

We need a new displacement strategy to sustain equity and justice. The makeshift settlements into which the displaced people are herded—often lacking basic amenities or job opportunities cannot be called rehabilitation.

Some suggestions have been offered by the social activists based on the practices of some other countries. If possible, the residential area in the village should not be acquired even if the surrounding land is. If the homesteads are left intact within the projects, acquisition will not displace people from that area. From their homesteads, they can supply labour and eatables to the project staff. The villages will remain intact as islands within a sea of development.

Resettlement and Rehabilitation Policies

The National Policy on Resettlement and Rehabilitation for the Project Affected Families (PAFs), 2003, was gazetted on February 17, 2004, by the Ministry of Rural Development. The first draft of this policy was brought out in 1993, and it was subsequently revised a number of times.

Although the policy marks a watershed for community activists and groups working on issues relating to development-induced displacement, it does not promise a hopeful future for many communities that will be displaced from their homes and livelihoods in the face of India's march to economic development. Some people believe that the new policy is a regression from the earlier draft—while the earlier one believed in 'total rehabilitation'—the new one does not even give a time frame for rehabilitation. The policy is relevant only for projects displacing more than 500 families in plain land, and 250 families in hilly areas. For a policy to set a lower limit is ridiculous. The clause may be misused as the project authorities may underreport the number of affected families to avoid the responsibility of rehabilitation.

Further, there is no statement placing a moratorium on multiple displacement. There have been instances where a significant number of people have been displaced more than once by dam projects such as Rihand, Koyna and Sardar Sarovar. Many of them have still not been rehabilitated.

Many voluntary organisations and people who responded to the earlier draft of the Resettlement and Rehabilitation Policy had suggested that a development policy was needed which contained perspective plans for regions by looking into the needs, availability of resources and technological as well as management options in order to minimise displacement by development processes.

A large number of Special Economic Zones and Port Projects are likely to displace fishing communities. There is no indication in the policy about where and how they and other such communities engaged in traditional livelihoods will be rehabilitated.

The earlier draft had stated that the displaced communities should be compensated individually and collectively for losses including land, trees, houses, wages, livelihoods, community amenities and services. This policy only talks of providing basic amenities such as water, schools, dispensaries, etc. Some people have also found it surprising that people's participation on such an important issue involving the lives of a large section of people was not sought.

The official circles say that the Government is committed to "putting in place more effective systems of relief and rehabilitation for tribal and other groups displaced by development projects."[5] Prime Minister Manmohan Singh, in his recent speech at the Federation of Indian Chambers of Commerce and Industry (FICCI), declared that the UPA Government is keen to bring out a National Rehabilitation Policy shortly. Let us hope that the new policy addresses the core issues ignored in the earlier policy.

Problems of Coastal Areas

Some Special Economic Zones are being set up in the coastal areas. These areas have their typical problems, and allowing SEZs here often means land acquisition and conversion of land use with no commensurate benefits to the affected population and no retrieval of their loss of livelihoods. Some of the proposed SEZs in coastal areas and their impact on the people are discussed below.

The Goa Government is converting the whole Pernem taluk into an SEZ. As part of this project there are plans to construct an international airport at Mopa village, a cyber city, a film city, an institute, a fashion design centre, a central convention centre, and a jewellery export unit. Once the airport comes up, there are possibilities of growth in tourism, and the State Government is planning to set up a recreation park in South Goa. The land has not yet been acquired for the proposed SEZ. The Chief Minister has ordered the administration to freeze the land so that the owners do not enter into fresh deals with the builders. However, as per changes made in the policy after the EGOM meeting in the first week of April, 2007, the State Governments have been barred from acquiring land for the SEZs. It is not clear whether the freeze on land at Pernem has been set aside in the new legislation.

The Positra SEZ in Gujarat will take up 4,600 acres of land of coastal areas to set up textile, chemical, pharma, metallurgy and IT industries. The area is home to about 18,000 people. On the petition filed by an NGO, the Gujarat High Court has ordered that the villagers are not to be displaced until the Resettlement and Rehabilitation scheme is approved by the State.

In Karnataka, an SEZ is being set up at Tadri, situated on the banks of the fertile and productive Aghanashini estuary. The villagers fear that this would adversely impact their rice fields, salt pans, fisheries, clam collection and mangrove diversity.

Another coastal area is Orissa's Gopalpur where Vizag-Parwada-Anakapalle SEZ is being established displacing thousands of people.

The importance of coasts was legally established when the Coastal Regulation Zone (CRZ) notification was drawn up in 1991 under the Environment Protection Act, 1986. The notification lays down norms for safeguarding the sensitive coastal ecology, recognizing that these areas form the livelihoods base of thousands of traditional communities.

The problem with setting up SEZs at coastal areas is that the people in these areas not only practice farming but are also engaged in other occupations which thrive on the natural resources provided by the geo-biodiversity. It is very difficult, and in some cases impossible, to provide similar conditions and livelihoods to the people displaced by big projects like SEZs. For example, fertile and productive estuary like the one at Aghanashini, Tadri cannot be created elsewhere. Similarly, salt pans for the production of quality salt in sufficient quantities and in specific period of time cannot be found in the entire coastal areas. Displacing people with ideal salt pans will not only affect their livelihoods but also affect the production and supply of salt. Similar is the case with fishing grounds. Forcing thousands of people to move away from the rich fishing grounds having abundant potential for regular catch of the desired species of fish may seriously disturb the balance of supply of seafood in the coastal areas and even beyond.

It is, therefore, necessary that before notifying an SEZ in the coastal area, its overall impact on the people who are likely to be displaced is carefully considered. If the necessary geographical situations are not available in the nearby area where the displaced people can be rehabilitated, it is better to shift the venue of the proposed SEZ itself.

Environmental Concerns

Our SEZ policy is modeled on China, but we are not prepared to learn from the Chinese experience. After growing at a high rate of around 20 per cent for the last fifteen years or so, the Shenzhen SEZ is now dealing a deadly blow to the environment in the surrounding areas. There is a big haze of smoke over the entire horizon. If we do not want our cities to be under such holocaust we will have to consider the environmental problems before setting up the SEZs, particularly near the cities.

It won't be an exaggeration to call our SEZ policy anti-environment. The SEZs have been made free from the environmental laws and are exempted from public hearing under Environment Impact Assessment notification. They are also permitted to have "non-polluting facilities" like golf courses, desalination plants, hotels, and non-polluting services like Information Technology in the Coastal Regulation Zone. All the environmental clearance powers, particularly the clearances required from the State Pollution Control Board are vested in the hands of the respective Development Commissioner, appointed for the administrative supervision, and to solve the problems for the SEZs.

Reliance Industries' proposed multi-product SEZ at Gurgaon is adjacent to the Sultanpur National Bird Park, one of India's

10 most important bird sanctuaries. It will violate the norm that no industry should be allowed within 8-10 km radius of a sanctuary. This SEZ will greatly disturb the birds. The flights of migratory birds will be blocked, the natural habitat of the birds maybe destroyed within a few years due to effluents, drainage from the SEZ and other industrial activity.

Many areas demarcated for the setting up of SEZs in the coastal areas are fragile ecosystems whose dynamic ecological nature and productivity are yet to be fully studied and protected. The importance of coasts was legally established when CRZ notification was drawn up under the Environment Protection Act, 1986. It lays down norms for safeguarding the sensitive coastal ecology in recognition of the fact that these areas provide livelihood base for thousands of traditional communities. Unfortunately, however, the CRZ notification was amended in 2002 to allow for the setting up of SEZs, defying the very spirit of the law. Many environmentalists and social activist groups including the National Fishworkers Forum (NFF) and the Bombay Environmental Action Group (BEAG) expressed concern over the move but the authorities paid no attention to it. The State-level policy documents on SEZ emphasize on "more efficient use of local resources" but it is likely to end up harming the natural ecosystems. The investors are being promised several support facilities such as transport and communication including roads, ports, airstrips and other provisions like health care, education, entertainment, shopping, etc. It is illegal to permit tourism, beautification, hotels and ports upto 12 nautical miles (22 km) in the sea. But some quarters apprehend that there is a conspiracy to dilute CRZ in order to regularise past violations and invite megatrawlers of transnational companies.

Setting up an SEZ at Tadri in Uttara Kannada, Karnataka has been severely criticized by the local people for its negative environmental impacts. The place had, in fact, a ship-breaking unit in early 1990s, which was shut down under public pressure on the grounds of ecological damage. Now, clearing an SEZ proposal at Tadri is reflective of the fact that the people are more concerned about the problems of environment and ecology than the Government.

Another important issue relating to environmental protection is that of impact assessment procedures. It is apprehended that only some of the units proposed in the SEZs may come within the ambit of Schedule-1 of the Environment Impact Assessment (EIA) notification, 1994. Only those projects which come under Schedule-1 have to comply with the conditions of organising a public hearing and allowing local people to voice their objections and give suggestions about the project. The projects not falling in this schedule are assessed by the State Government, and the clearance processes do not mandate a public hearing.

The industrial units set up in the coastal areas are likely to bring incalculable harm to the delicate ecosystem and environment of these areas. Such harm is often irreversible. The effluents, chemical wastes and drainage water ultimately flow into the sea. This toxified water kills aquatic animals in large number. The fishing grounds are wiped out in the nearby area. Even the salt produced in such areas contains harmful toxins. The fish and prawns caught from the nearby areas and consumed cause various kinds of disorders and deformities. Environmental protection in the coastal areas assumes greater importance due to the fact that the nearby sea is a perpetual source of food. Polluting it would affect the quantity and quality of seafood that we get from it regularly. There is a need to bring a legislation whereby all the SEZs and other industrial units are brought under the purview of Schedule-1 of the EIA notification so that the clearance is given only after considering all the issues relating to likely impact on the environment, and remedial action, wherever required is taken, and if need be the setting up of the unit stopped or shifted to some other place where the damage is negligible.

The Ministry of Commerce has given no break-up of the types of land that are being acquired to set up SEZs. Many of these lands, apart from agricultural and wastelands are forest lands with some form of vegetation on them, in most cases trees, scrubs and dense vegetation. Many pastoral communities entirely depend on this vegetation for their livelihoods that include collecting herbs, honey, resins, wood, and livestock rearing, etc. If these forests are cleared, not only these communities will be driven to hunger but also many natural habitats will be destroyed. In Maharashtra, three big SEZs are coming up in the Konkan district which contains parts of the ecologically sensitive Western Ghats. These SEZs will adversely impact the ecosystems and hence, the flora and fauna of the region.

Eminent journalist Kuldip Nayar has pointed out the fact that India's green cover has come down from 15 per cent to 6.5 per cent during the last 50 years. "As the land in cities becomes scarce, a forest, a park or for that matter, any green patch is blotted out to make room for concrete contraptions. The Government itself is a party to the changing complexion of India through steel and cement"[6], he says.

The environmental losses that the country would incur for all the forest and coastal land lost due to setting up of SEZs cannot be calculated in terms of money. The damage to ecosystems, natural habitats, biotic and abiotic atmosphere will be huge. Respiratory problems and other disorders due to acute air and water pollution particularly in the areas nearby industrial units in SEZ shall worsen. Global warming with all its adverse manifestations will become more threatening. At present India is favourably placed in carbon trading as per the norms of Kyoto Protocol but may lose its advantageous position if large amount of greenhouse gases are released into the atmosphere due to burning of coal and petroleum for industrial processes. It is therefore time that we should have a relook at this frenzied development and consider all its fallouts before giving it a green signal.

Other Problems Related to SEZs

Adverse Effect on Existing Schemes: It has been argued that setting up of SEZs will make the fate and future of existing Export Processing Zones, Export Oriented Units Scheme, Export Intensive Area Sub Plan, and Infrastructure Development Scheme aimed at developing 93 'no-industry districts', etc. uncertain. Once the SEZs are established, all these schemes will lose their attraction. What is even more disturbing is the fact that the fairly successful experiment of setting up Software Technology Parks (STPs) will suffer a major setback. The IT Ministry apprehends that many of the 6,500 companies located in the 47 STPs would prefer to shift to the new IT SEZs, rendering the STPs unviable. The companies located in the STPs have made huge investments in importing software (slated at Rs. 1,00,000 crore per annum). The exports from these Parks are expected to increase at a healthy rate. The National Association for Software Service Companies (NASSCOM) has demanded that all the 47 STPs be given SEZ status, but the Commerce and Industry Ministry has refused to allow the same. It is being felt that NASSCOM's proposal should have been placed before the Empowered Group of Ministers (EGOM) as there was a strong case for extending SEZ status to the STPs.

Scarce Resources: The problem of use of scarce resources like water may also crop up. Dr. Mukund Ghare, Director of an organisation for sustainable land and water management, says:

> When there is a crying need to distribute the scarce water equitably between urban and rural sectors and between the rich and the poor, there is an apprehension as to how much water the SEZ will use? Who will own the water? How it will be used, when there is no environmental law applicable to the SEZ? This is nothing but an attempt to privatise water.[7]

In the Pen taluk of Raigarh district, the farmers have been fighting for water from the Hetawane dam. There are 52 villages in the command area of the Hetawane project, proposed in 1980 to irrigate about 5,750 hectares of land and provide drinking water to Pen and Navi Mumbai. Now a huge area of the land is being given to Reliance Industries in violation of the law that says that once the land falls in the command area of an irrigation project, it cannot be used for any other purpose. The other problem is that if 5000 acres of land is given to Reliance Industries to set up the proposed SEZ at Pen, which covers 86 per cent of the total command area of the project, who will supply drinking water to Navi Mumbai and the remaining part of Pen? The project is in progress since 1983 and over Rs. 220 crore have already been spent on it. All this effort and money will go waste if the command area is acquired for the proposed SEZ.

The farmers in this part of the Raigad district have plans to develop the area for growing sugar beet, a five-month crop, if they get irrigation. If the Government sets up a processing factory, sugar can be produced. They can also grow *basmati* rice if sufficient water is made available from the project. The farmers have suggested that setting up a special agricultural zone in the area shall be more useful than the SEZ.

Tax Exemptions: It has also been pointed out that the tax exemptions being offered by the Government may be challenged in the World Trade Organisation (WTO) in the same vein as we have objected to the advanced countries like America's giving subsidies to their farmers. We have to be careful about our policies so that they do not attract retaliatory measures from the importing countries.

Even otherwise, the large-scale tax and tariff exemptions have been severely criticized by the experts. It has been felt that the Indian Government, desperate to create jobs in globally competitive, export-oriented factories, is giving up its taxation powers, which may be hard to reclaim. Moreover, the key to SEZ success does not lie in just handing out the incentives. Giving huge tax exemptions does not necessarily mean greater investment flows. But it will surely hurt the economy. The Finance Minister has suggested that since there was no obligation on SEZs to export if they do not import any capital goods or raw materials, tax breaks should be withdrawn to the units which do not export. However, the Commerce Ministry has turned down this suggestion saying that it will send wrong signals. Thus, the whole policy of tax and tariff exemptions needs to be reviewed.

Foreign Capital: The Special Economic Zones will thrive on attracting and utilising foreign capital. The Government has planned to create around 300 Special Economic Zones, and achieve full capital account convertibility (CAC) over a period of five years. The economists have warned that in an economy where other factors of production—land and labour—are not fully mobile and tradable, it is extremely risky to remove restrictions on capital flows. The CAC may result in capital flight. The speculative investors who are in search of quick profits can cause serious disruptions in an economy. Just imagine what will happen if the foreign investors withdraw their money quickly from the SEZs, capital markets and other industrial units. The whole economic scenario will go topsy turvy. The SEZ policy has been designed to attract huge amounts of foreign direct investment, which means more exposure of the Indian economy to the external forces. IMF economist Raghuram Rajan argues that "in the long run, capital account opening is unlikely to help poor countries grow by providing resources.... Foreign capital is no panacea for capital poor countries."[8] Even China, a much stronger economy than India has fiercely resisted CAC.

Labour Laws: The Special Economic Zones have been made free from labour laws. Perhaps the appeal of the SEZs lies in the fact that the units would be freed from the outdated, pernicious rules including India's labour laws. The States had even been given the option to repeal chapter V-B of the Industrial Disputes Act, 1947 which stipulates that companies employing more than 100 workers must obtain Government approval before firing people or closing down. Needless to say, this permission is never granted. The opinion is divided on the issue. In the absence of softening of labour laws, the employers are reluctant to hire workers because they won't be able to dismiss if there is a sudden slump in demand for their products. As a matter of fact India is competing for foreign direct investment inflow on the strength of progressive policies. States like Maharashtra and Andhra Pradesh have already relaxed rules on employing contract workers, the latter State has already declared strikes in the export-oriented units illegal.

There is, however, a great resentment among the workers. Apprehending that the labour laws would be diluted within the SEZs, the Centre of Indian Trade Unions (CITU) has reminded the United Progressive Alliance Government of the National Common Minimum Programme commitment to protect labour rights in the industrial manufacturing regions.

In this regard, it is pertinent to note that the policy of hire and fire will attract stiff opposition from workers and their organisations. Although China has been following this policy with a fair degree of success, the socio-economic scenario in India is different. China has a surplus labour available at cheap rates. Its economy has shown a perceptible tilt towards opening up and capitalism after the 1980s but still remains a country with communist roots. If the labour in China is fired by an employer, they have the means of subsistence with help from the State which follows socialist policies regarding workers. In India's case there is no such help and the fired labour immediately face starvation. Even the much hyped National Rural Employment Guarantee Scheme provides employment only to one person in a family and that too for only 100 days in a year. Moreover, the scheme is operational in only 330 districts of the country. The protection of labour is thus necessary to avoid social tension.

Further, India is a country with wide socio-economic disparities. We need policies and laws which might remove these disparities instead of perpetuating them. What India needs is a balanced development and in a manner which reduces the inequalities of income and wealth between people as stipulated in the Directive Principles of State Policy. The Government must not therefore repeal any clauses from our labour laws which provide protection and job security to the labour.

Another drawback in changing the labour law to empower the employers to retrench the workers will bring a sense of insecurity among the labours. They may not want to work with such companies from the outset and may seek employment at some other place where there is job security.

Employment: According to the Commerce Ministry, the SEZs shall create employment for hundreds and thousands of people. However, serious doubts have been raised over this claim. Since the SEZ units shall work with latest machinery and technology, they may not actually generate much employment. They will hire only people with technological skills who have the ability to get employment anyway. Their numbers may not be as large as anticipated by the Ministry. Moreover the number of people—farmers and others—who are displaced due to setting up of the proposed projects may actually be more than the employment created by the SEZs. Since most of these displaced people are illiterate and unskilled, they may not find employment elsewhere easily. As such, there may not be any advantage of setting up of SEZs so far as the issue of employment is concerned.

Cultural Loss: Smitu Kothari, a socialist, has drawn attention to the cultural loss due to displacement of people. He says that the tribals constitute 7.5 per cent of India's total population. Nearly 50 per cent of them have been displaced since independence due to one project or the other. Such forced dislocation is eroding India's cultural pluralism, wiping out some valuable beliefs that serve as a storehouse of knowledge and memory. Many communities have been displaced a second time and are gathering pieces of their lives.

Some of the displaced communities are craftsmen and artisans. They may not get the necessary raw material and conditions to continue their craft. The village or settlement from which these communities move away becomes bereft of specific culture, traditions and craft.

Political Opportunism: The SEZs are supposed to be the engines of economic growth but as things are, they are being used as political opportunism. In West Bengal for example the dissident group led by Mamata Banerjee of CPI (M)—has severely criticized the State's policy of industrialisation through SEZs at Singur and Nandigram. The purpose seemed to instigate the farmers and workers against the ruling CPM led by Chief Minister Buddhadeb Bhattacharya and get political mileage. There was a showdown between police and the farmers at Nandigram, the resultant firing took the life of many innocent farmers. The State Government was forced to change the policy and the political stature of Mamata Banerjee was enhanced which she may encash in some subsequent election. It is interesting to note that the CPI(M) had given its crucial support in passing the SEZ legislation in May 2005. The party had voted for the package in both Lok Sabha and Rajya Sabha. It has been stated that the CPI(M)'s role in the SEZ policy is similar to that in other social issues—to act as a political safety valve for protests and popular opposition—while providing the Congress-led Government with crucial parliamentary support to remain in the hunt for some ministership.

Corrupt politicians and bureaucrats have made SEZ policy 'a land grab movement'. There have been several instances where land has been acquired by the politicians at cheap rates in connivance with Government officials. Now the State Governments have been barred from acquiring land. The developers will have to buy the land at the proposed sites of SEZs directly from the landowners. Real estate agents have mushroomed around SEZ areas to act as brokers and strike rich bargains. The interference of politicians in these land deals is still not ruled out.

Decentralisation of Power: The major reason for SEZ success in China is decentralisation of power. Provincial and local authorities have been made partners and stakeholders by delegating to them the power to approve foreign investment. The SEZ authorities in China can approve foreign investment proposals up to US$30 million.

In India, on the other hand, only the State Governments are allowed to set up SEZs, and the powers for foreign investment approvals are vested with the Development Commissioners who are the representatives of the Central Government. Such anomalies need to be removed for the smooth functioning of the SEZs.

Changes in the SEZ Policy

The Empowered Group of Ministers, headed by the External Affairs Minister Pranab Mukherjee, met in the first week of April 2007 to consider a whole gamut of charges—from putting a cap on the area of an SEZ to restricting the scope of diversion of land for non-core activities. The Group brought some major changes in the SEZ policy which are discussed below:

The Group fixed the upper limit on multi-product SEZs at 5,000 hectares and raised the minimum share of the processing area within the Zones from 35 per cent to 50 per cent. It also gave State Governments the discretionary power to reduce the size of SEZ in their jurisdiction.

The decision of putting an upper limit on the SEZs will affect four SEZs—two of Mukesh Ambani's Reliance Industries, and one each of realtors DLF and Omaxe. Besides, increasing the processing area shall force the companies to revise their projects entirely. The norm may upset the plans of multi-product Zone developers who not only have to create space for more offices and industrial units, but may also be forced to cut down on plan to build hotels, schools, roads, power units, sewage treatment plants, hospitals and other facilities. Of the 162 Zones which have already got first stage clearance from the government, 56 are multi-product Zones which will have to rework their strategy. The Government also intends to review the list of permissible activities that qualify for non-processing work.

Given the uncertainty that had developed over the tax-exempt enclaves after the Nandigram bloodbath which threatened to reduce the very concept of SEZs to a political slur, these changes should please those who were against jettisoning the policy. As a matter of fact, the Empowered Group of Ministers turned down another demand of the critics—that of restricting tax exemptions. Even the 5,000 hectare ceiling may appear a satisfactory outcome for the developers considering the fact that the Commerce Ministry seemed resigned to accept a 2000-hectare ceiling to save the concept amidst many controversies.

The Commerce Ministry, the prime mover of the SEZ policy, however, managed to ward off pressure to fix a cap on the number of Zones that may come up in the country. The Government had earlier formally approved 234 SEZs. Of these, 63 had been notified when the row over land acquisition compelled the Government to take a fresh look at the issue. Now the EGOM has allowed the Ministry to notify 83 projects for which land has been acquired. The list of Zones which are likely to be notified as soon as the Board of Approvals meets, includes some big names like Infosys Technologies, Wockhardt Pharma and Ascendas. The IT major Infosys will have a double bonanza as its proposed SEZs at Mysore and Pune are expected to be notified and become operational soon. Singapore's Ascendas is waiting for clearance from the Government to start work at Hyderabad and bring sizeable FDI into India. With the lifting of the freeze on SEZs, more companies under Singapore Government are expected to enter India with plans to set up multi-product Zones in Tamil Nadu where land has already been identified.

As per the new norms brought by EGOM, the State Governments cannot acquire land for setting up Special Economic Zones, the developers will have to do it on their own. However, to ensure that the existing projects do not get hit, the ministerial panel has decided to fix February 10, 2006 as the cut-off date, and any proposal where the State has gone in for compulsory land acquisition after that date will not be cleared by the Board of Approvals. This clause is also expected to be built into the Comprehensive Land Acquisition Act. The decision is clearly intended to rebut the allegations that the Government is aiding speculation on real estate lobbies. But the Left Parties are not going to be pleased with developers being given the right to acquire land while the States will be playing second fiddle. According to a CPM leader, "Land acquisition cannot be left to the mercy of developers."[9] The CPI central secretariat expressed the opinion that the EGOM should have waited for the report from the parliamentary standing committee instead of making such changes. It expressed a shock over clearing the passage of approval of 83 SEZs at one go and fixing the upper limit of 5,000 hectares. The CPI has stated that this is an open declaration of acquiring huge tracts of agricultural land despite all earlier pretensions that the Government will exercise caution and look at the issue afresh. The party further said that the Government has carried on as before and yielded supinely to the demands of the land grabbing entrepreneurs.

The EGOM has also made it mandatory that at least one person from the family of those displaced shall be given the job in the SEZ set up on their land. Though this is a welcome step and shall prevent starvation in the displaced families, yet it is doubtful whether it would be possible. The SEZs will need highly skilled, qualified and trained staff. The farmers and people of other communities likely to be displaced are illiterate and untrained for any of the jobs in an SEZ except as casual labour. This norm, therefore, may prove to be impracticable in most of the SEZs. The CPI was not happy with the promise of job for one member of each displaced family and felt that it makes a mockery of the rehabilitation process.

The EGOM has tried to address the problems of land acquisition, land use and rehabilitation while remaining firm on tax exemptions. This combination of firmness and flexibility will help take the SEZ process forward. The most significant change brought by the EGOM is the insistence that the SEZ developers, rather than the State will acquire the land. This would shield landowners from the State's unique power under the Land Acquisition Act to alienate an individual's property rights. It is for the first time in India's history that the exercise of 'the principle of eminent domain' as mentioned in the National Rehabilitation Policy has been officially questioned. The new norm would place sellers and buyers on an equal footing. The acquisition of land by the State under the 'eminent domain' would have forced the farmers to sell their land at the last recorded prices in the Government records and would have created an army of losers. With the new caveats in place the Government seems to recognize the necessity of reconciling entrepreneurial interest with the public good.

Increasing the size of the SEZ area for core activities from 35 per cent of the total area of 50 per cent also seems to be a step in the right direction in terms of efficient land use. However, the rule should have allowed for green cover for the cause of environment. The move to put a cap on the maximum size of the SEZ to 5,000 hectares may reduce the magnitude of displacement and dilute the issues related with land acquisition particularly when the State has been barred from acquiring land. But the move has run into trouble with the affected companies threatening to sue the Government for breach of contract. Major SEZ players, who were planning to work on an area in excess of the new cap, argue that their plans have been disturbed by the new development. Some quarters feel that the Government should have shown some flexibility. Instead of announcing a blanket cap on SEZ area, it should have laid down conditions—legal, social, environmental, etc.—under which the size of an SEZ could be limited.

Conclusion

The Special Economic Zones are a highly visible component of the former Chinese premier Deng Xiaoping's modernisation programme. Overwhelmed by the success of China's SEZs, India's policymakers have reposed much faith in the experiment not only for export growth but also to boost Foreign Direct Investment, which has become imperative as the domestic investments have remained subdued due to slow rate of capital formation. The setting up of SEZs will also promote value-addition to exports, generate employment and mobilize foreign exchange. The SEZs have been established in many countries as testing grounds for implementation of liberal market economy principles. They are viewed as instruments to enhance the acceptability and credibility of transformation policies to attract foreign investment generally, and for opening up of the economy in the globalised world.

The success of China's SEZs has been brought about by a number of factors such as unique location, large size, investment, friendly attitudes, incentive packages, liberal custom procedures, flexible labour laws, strong domestic market, etc. The key question is: Can India replicate China's immensely successful SEZ model? The incentives offered to the Indian SEZs are in no way less than those in China. From tax holidays and duty-free imports to freedom from Custom procedures, the facilities for Indian SEZs match those in China. Hence, theoretically at least, India's SEZs should be no less attractive to foreign investors than China's SEZs.

However, there is no consensus within the nation, whether within the Central Government or in the public at large, which includes economic experts and social activists on the utility of the market economics to promote Chinese system, values and beliefs. There was an intense ideological criticism within China too, against the SEZ model of growth. It was only Deng Xiaoping's towering personality, his private and public support for the SEZs which leant credibility to reform efforts and stifled the voice of the dissenters. The party hardliners in the Indian Government—both at the Centre as well as the State—are vehemently opposing the setting up of SEZs as they feel that there is no pressing need to do so and that too by offering all kinds of sops and incentives. The inter-ministerial differences, doubtful nature of potential benefits, open opposition by farmers likely to be displaced—which has resulted in incidents of violence and death due to police firing at some proposed sites of SEZs—have led many people to believe that this policy should be abandoned.

However, considering the enormous success of China's SEZs, and given the fact that both India and China have a similar socio-economic set-up and are evenly matched in human capital and other resources, the SEZ model of development is likely to lead to higher growth in India too. Doing away with such a policy would, therefore, be a retrogressive step. The scope of SEZs is wide and their linkages with the domestic economy stronger. SEZs provide supportive infrastructure such as housing, roads, ports, airports, telecommunication and power supply, and as a result, have a wider industrial base. Notwithstanding the aforesaid affinities between India and China, the fundamental objectives for setting up SEZs and their role in the economy are different in the two countries. We need to make the required structural changes to make this policy successful. Moreover, our delicate social structure and our responsibility as the biggest democracy in the world require that our policymakers should appropriately sequence the nation's priorities to sustain the popular support for reforms and reconcile the conflicting interests and beliefs.

NOTES

1. Jake Skeers, "India's Policy on Special Economic Zones Under Fire" World Socialist web site: News & Analysis.
2. I. McKenney (1993), "An Assessment of China's Special Economic Zones". *Executive Research Project*, the Industrial College of Armed Forces, National Defence University, Washington DC, USA.
3. Saikat Neogi, "Pay Market Price for Farmland" in *Hindustan Times*, New Delhi, March 6, 2007.
4. *Ibid.*
5. Manju Menon (2006), "Resettlement and Rehabilitation" in *Advocacy Internet*, Vol. VIII, No. 3. www.infochangeindia.org.
6. Kuldip Nayar, "Manic Development-Government Harsh on the Poor, not Poverty." *Ibid.* www.tribuneindia.com
7. Mukund Ghare, Director AFARM, Pune—an organisation for suitable land and water management. Quoted in Editorial *Advocacy Internet*, Vol. VIII, No. 3.
8. Raghuram Rajan—Chief Economist IMF. Quoted in Praful Bidwai "A Very Special Land Scam Afoot at Furious Pace", *Advocacy Internet* Vol. VIII, No. 3.
9. "Denying State Role in SEZ Land Buy Irks CPM" *The Times of India,* New Delhi, April 6, 2006.

2

The Role of Special Economic Zones in Regional and National Development

Ramakrishna Nallathiga

Introduction

Special Economic Zones (SEZs) are insulated export areas that offer benefits such as duty concessions to industrial units, so that the industrial exports can be given a boost and higher growth rates can be attained; they are analogous to the concept of Free Trade Zones (FTZs) but extend beyond that. They are coupled with several advantages like boost to productivity of capital, labour and innovation, enhanced technology deployment and better management practices in the industries. This, in turn, will provide long-term and short-term impetus to the growth of industrial manufacturing sector, and transform it into the one better oriented towards attaining the levels of global competitiveness. Often, the SEZs are created as tax havens in over-regulated economies so that the general taxes do not eat away profits, and manufacturers will have the flexibility to use their entire gamut of resources, i.e. capital, labour, infrastructure and technology, in a much more efficient manner. However, the concept of SEZs goes much beyond mere facilitating exports generation; they are integrated townships with well-laid infrastructure and services without any encumbrances for trade. Also, the value addition ladder can be very high in the SEZs to provide world-class facilities that exert a strong pull on domestic Capital and Foreign Direct Investment (FDIs)

The SEZs are subsequent to the similar industrial zoning attempts in the past with the Export Processing Zones (EPZs), which were essentially industrial clusters or industrial complexes with basic infrastructure but are devoid of any planning done for human inhabitations (*The Hindu*, 2001). The SEZs are large industrial EPZs that have been modeled on the line of townships wherein all the activities, including residential, commercial and infrastructure services, are planned alongwith the industrial settlements. The idea is to make them self-sustaining autonomous industrial enclaves with stronger economic base, and in such manner that all inhabitants, apart from industry owners, can reap the benefits. Whereas EPZs achieved moderate success worldwide in giving boost to manufacturing exports, the Chinese experiment with SEZs proved to be far more successful and has provided greater dividends to the country's exports, inflow of foreign investments, economic development and employment generation.

The economic benefits of SEZs are well documented across the world; their success in the Chinese context, however, drew much of the attention. India has also embarked on the creation of SEZs as the drivers of industrial production and export trade. India embarked on the Special Economic Zone (SEZ) development policy in the year 2002, when the Union Ministry of Industries announced it in its EXIM policy. The Indian model of development of SEZs drew much upon the experiment, experience and success of the Chinese model of SEZs. This is because both the countries have had a similar socio-economic development background in the past 25 years or so. Whereas India worked on a mixed economy model and then balanced economic development model, China embarked on creating growth centres that became nodes of manufacturing, exports and foreign trade. Although first mover advantage prevails and increases the scope for success in China, it is interesting to compare both these countries in economic parameters, which is attempted in Table 2.1 below:

The statistics not only reflect the large differences in economic development in spite of a similar demographic size, but also they imply the potential for India to achieve it by shifting its policies towards more foreign and domestic investments, better operational environment for industries and deploying new power structures with emphasis on improved economic powers to local Government in decision-making. India has liberalized its economy

Table 2.1: India and China: Comparison in terms of Economic Parameters

Economic Parameters	Unit	China	India
GDP Growth	10 yr CAGR	10.3	6.0
GNP per capita	PPP US$	4180	2471
Population	Mn	1275	1033
GNP in PPP	US$ bn	5329	2553
Exports	$ bn	287	43
Share of Exports in World Exports	Per cent	5	0.8
Imports	$ bn	248	50
Foreign Direct Investments (FDI)	$ bn	43	2.5
Forex Reserves	$ bn	250	75

Source: Bhinge and Pauly (2003)

in the early 1990s, which paid good dividends, which was evident from a consistently good growth rate of 7-10% shown by manufacturing sector (ADB, 2002), however, it is yet to reform the regulatory environment and power-sharing institutions. Evidently, the Indian model for proposed SEZ development appears to rely on power sharing between Union and the local Governments in a different way—the State and local Governments take the initiative for developing SEZs, while the Central Government will take crucial policy decisions and will hold the responsibility of joint administration in the special purpose vehicle (SPV) launched for this purpose. In China, the SEZ development is at the initiative of Central Government, but once it has been formed the management and administration powers are completely vested to the local authorities.

International Experience of the SEZs

India has only recently embarked on the SEZ experiment through its EXIM policy. However, the experience of economic zones is not new to countries across the world. In fact, the formation of EPZs, which was precursor to SEZs, was widely prevalent across the world, particularly in the Europe. The agglomeration effect of industrial settlements and the benefits to technological growth and innovation are well documented in the industrial economic literature (e.g. Philip 2000, Ferguson and Ferguson 1994). However, SEZs go beyond the concepts of industrial concentrations as they have a mix of both industrial and human settlements and have much wider flows of goods and services within the enclave as well as their transfer with domestic economy, besides exports to other nations. Conceptually, they are similar to Free Trade Zones (FTZs), which also offer similar incentives and benefits of trade and commerce within the regions, but they are also different from them in the sense that they normally involve laying down of huge infrastructure and developing integrated townships comprising both industrial settlements and human habitations. Undoubtedly, it is this infrastructure that gets created from the SEZs which would offer much longer benefits to the nation and the region, giving boost to their development. As an example, the contribution of the Chinese SEZs to regional trade shown in Table 2.2 illustrates the benefits associated with SEZs.

Table 2.2: Select Chinese SEZs' Trade with Hong Kong, 1990 and 1994

	1990				1994			
SEZ	Exports ($ mn)	Share (Per cent)	Imports ($ mn)	Share (Per cent)	Exports ($ mn)	Share (Per cent)	Imports ($ mn)	Share (Per cent)
Shantou	2,549	85.1	1,614	65.2	4,605	25.1	2,019	12.1
Zhuhai	170	57.5	820	90.9	1,094	84.3	2,326	78.3
Shenzhen	360	73.6	135	84.3	1,057	71.1	746	68.0

Source: Almanac of China's Foreign Relations and Trade

Several countries have used the concepts surrounding economic zoning, i.e. EPZ, FTZ and SEZ, for giving a boost to their manufacturing exports and attracting foreign direct investments (FDI) into their nations. A detailed discussion on the experience of the economic zones in various countries is discussed in Siddiqui (2002). Realizing the fact that the SEZs would contribute in several ways to the regional and national economic development, many regions in Asia began to experiment with them. But, each of them had a different focus, a different set of objectives, and had experienced different levels of success. For example, the Chinese model of SEZs placed heavy focus on raising FDI; SAIF focused on ready-to-do business facilities; and Poland had the primary objective of employment generation (A summary of salient features of SEZs in these countries is provided in Table 2.3). While all of them are important in SEZ development, it is the relative preference given to each of them that determines the outcomes. This makes it very difficult to assess the success of SEZs across the world. Yet, one can make a comparison of the countries in terms of the key characteristics of each Zone against set features, which is summarized below:

(a) The objectives of all these Zones are intertwined with current development priorities and objectives of the respective country, e.g. Gulf Zone focusing on deepening of economy, China focusing on FDI inflows and Poland focusing on employment growth;
(b) All these Zones are advantageously located or they are benefited from the strategic locational advantage, e.g. nearness to ports;
(c) Most of the Zones are large in size with the areas ranging from 60-300 sq km. The large size appears to be quite critical for a variety of reasons—economies of scale, achieving diverse activity mix, social infrastructure and attractiveness to private investors;
(d) The targeted activities in the Zone are activities like high-tech, R&D, trading and light manufacturing, all of which are semi-skilled to skilled jobs;
(e) Most of them offer some kind of incentive, be it tax concession or cheap infrastructure, which is essential for attracting foreign investors;
(f) The critical universal selling point (USP) of these Zones is the excellent physical and social infrastructure offered. Some of them, like SAIF Zone, go beyond this by providing industrial/service infrastructure as an integrated component.

Chinese Experience of SEZs

The Chinese experiment with the SEZs is by far the most successful example of the SEZs worldwide. The conduct and continuation of SEZ experiment were largely due to the strong political will expressed by its Premier Mr. Deng Xiaoping on one hand and due to the responsibility delegated to local provincial authorities on the other. The primary objectives of the Chinese

Table 2.3: Salient Features of the SEZ Development in Various Countries

Focus area	Shenzhen, China	Jebel Ali, Dubai	SAIF Zone, Sharjah	Poland
Location	Guangdong province, opposite to Hong Kong	35 km away from Dubai city	Near Sharjah International Airport and 120 km away from Khortakkam sea port	Several Zones in the country
Area (sq km)	327	100	60	27 (of all)
Economic activity focus	• Production of hi-tech products • Real estate, finance and telecommunications • R&D/Hi-tech	• Trading • Light manufacturing • Metals • Chemicals • Rubber • Beverages • Paper	• Trading • Light/medium manufacturing • Assembling, packaging	• Employment-oriented units • Semi-conductors • Telecom • Automobiles
Fiscal status	• 50% deduction in income for first 5 years • Reduced interest rate loans, water/ electricity charges	• No corporate tax • No income tax • No other duties	• No import/export duties • No corporate/ personal taxes • Low electricity/water rates	• No tax for first 10 years • 50% tax for next 10 years • Tax exemptions on profits • Property tax and stamp duty exemptions
Physical development planning	• Good social and physical infrastructure and no natural boundaries • Special industrial parks developed inside Shenzhen such as Longgang industrial area	• Furnished offices and light industry structures • Long lease for 30 years • Developed land sites and storage facilities at concessional rates	• Plots of different sizes • Pre-built warehouses and office spaces • On-site staff accommodations	• Choice of different plot sizes • Within bonded area all physical infrastructure available
Policy framework	• FDI • High technology infusion	• Strengthen Dubai's entrepotential status • Diversify, deepen economy	• Competing with Jebel Ali • Diversifying economy	• FDI • Employment • Economic growth

Source: CIDCO (2003b)

SEZ development were to (McKenney 1993): (i) develop coastal area of China through experimental, controlled enclaves; (ii) attract and exploit foreign investment to modernize China; and (iii) provide a window to the outside world in technology, knowledge and management.

The first four SEZs were set up in 1978 in Shenzhen, Zhuhai, Xiamen and Shantou, all of them located along Southeastern coastline, in close proximity to trading and financial centres of Hong Kong, Macao and Taiwan. The last one was set up in Hainan in 1988. The SEZs began to show significant progress only by mid-1980s, with the Shenzhen SEZ in Guangdong leading over others, i.e. its share of foreign investments increased from 10% in 1980 to about 50% in mid-1980s (*ibid*). By the end of 1980s the four SEZs had attracted $4.1 billion foreign investments and exported $10 billion worth of products. This has further raised FDI $50 billion FDI in 2000 and took away 25% of inflows (*ibid*). Table 2.4 summarizes the export performance of the Chinese SEZs in the year 2001.

Table 2.4: Exports of SEZs in China

SEZ-China	Exports ($ mn)
Xiamen	5,068.5
Shenzhen	17,813.2
Zhuhai	3,197.9
Shantou	1,054.7
Nanhai	798.0
Total	27,932.3

Source: Majumdar (2003)

The role played by SEZs in China's economic growth is evident from the growth rates of its economy after 1980; it grew at a rate of 10.9% since then primarily because of the performance of the SEZs. The GDP per capita grew from Y 455 in 1980 to Y 4754 in 1995 (McKenney 1993). Consistent with it, the growth of the FDI between 1990 and 1995 itself has been quite large; from about 1.7% share in the global FDI, its share reached 11.9% of total capital flow by 1995 (*ibid*), as a result of which China attained a trade surplus of 6%. The significance of growth of FDI will be more obvious when one looks at the share of FDI in the country's GDP, which increased from 0.9% in 1984 to 16.1% in 1996, which is quite substantial (*ibid*). Similarly, the share of FDI in exports has increased from 1.1% in 1985 to 20.4% in 1992 and 40.7% in 1996 (*ibid*). Even in terms of employment, the contribution of SEZs had been remarkable. Around 5.4 million people were employed by foreign investment enterprises; this is around 2.7% of total employment in 1996 and much higher than mere 0.05% in 1985 or 0.39% in 1990 (*ibid*).

The following are some of the important factors of success of Chinese experience with SEZs (*ibid*):

- Relaxation of import duties coupled with no export duties, low uniform indirect taxes, numerous special tax holidays and favourable regulatory environment have been a major catalyst for the growth of industrial production and exports from the SEZs in China;
- The flexible labour laws, productivity linked wages, technological innovations and a steady infusion of global best management practices brought by the MNCs contributed to enhanced labour productivity, improved quality of goods and reduction of costs;
- The SEZ creation was also accompanied by laying down of extensive infrastructure—transportation, telecommunications, power supply and water supply, which helped the private foreign players to deploy their investments in the creation of manufacturing units and concentrate on enhancing their production;
- As all the above factors helped to reduce the factor input costs of production, the SEZs, with the favourable regulatory policies and tax treatment, have become cradles of manufacturing; the excellent infrastructure provided right kind of impetus to large manufacturers to exploit the scale economies of production;
- Manufacturers in the SEZs have attained better output cost efficiency due to the favourable tax and duty regime, which would have kept the Chinese prices

30% of those in India, for comparison (CII-McKinsey, in Binge and Pauly 2003);

- All of the SEZs were strategically located close to the boundary of Hong Kong, a commercial and financial hub. This resulted in large amount of foreign investment inflows from the nearby region into China. Almost 60% of the FDI inflows come from Hong Kong. In fact, some of the SEZs like Guangdong have been able to attract almost 25% of China's FDI (Majumdar 2003);
- Delegation of powers to local authorities in decision-making might have also mattered in the flexibility to the manufacturers and the unrestrictive labour laws have helped the firms to plan their operations much more efficiently while increasing employee turnover (*The Hindu*, 2001);
- The size of the SEZs also mattered in their success. Unlike their precedents the EPZs, which spread over a few hectares or tens of hectares, they were created over a large area of thousands of hectares. On an average, each SEZ was spread over 1000 hectares (*The Hindu*, 2001);

However, the Chinese experiment with SEZs is not devoid of the problems; many a time they are either not fully understood or underplayed. McKenney (1993) performed an assessment of Chinese experience with SEZs and drew the following critical observations on their performance:

- As the economic reforms in China did not happen alongwith the emergence of SEZs, they were in an insulated condition without the major structural reforms, particularly pricing and financial system, which affected their performance later, especially by raising the costs of doing business;
- The laying down of infrastructure and construction of large buildings, bridges and roads by the Government has increased manifold due to industrial expansion, which was to be done by the Government

and financed through public borrowings, resulting in high indebtness of the central and provincial Governments;

- The SEZs also have shown trade deficit, which was as high as 20% of the China's trade deficit. The main reason was the infrastructure-laying, equipment and their spares were mostly imported, which resulted in the rise of production costs above the value of exports;
- The geographic concentration of the foreign direct investment was also a matter of concern. Almost 70% of it came from Hong Kong and Taiwan (to the tune of $15.4 billion during 1979-89) alongwith the high immigrant worker population (2 million), which was a matter of concern from the security and national interests. China essentially depended on both these countries for investment, management expertise and knowledge about financial and international markets;
- It has to be remembered that the SEZs relied heavily on low wage rates, low real estate costs and low overhead expenses rather than technological progress/ transfer. The envisaged technology transfer did not take place to the level it was expected. Moreover, their management lacked the three main ingredients necessary for promoting technological advance: (a) strategic vision and strong enterprising spirit; (b) courage to take risks and be a pioneer; (c) high level of scientific culture and strong aptitude for management;
- The problems of corruption began to grow as early as mid-1980s. Although SEZs were free enclaves, they were still subject the policies and politics of Central Government by means of controls over exports/ imports, foreign currency availability;
- Further, an important shortcoming was the lack of outward look to the world. Being insulated from the rest of the world, the organization and functioning of Chinese people was highly influenced by the prevailing

communist ideologies, and the result was a lack of gel between the necessary outlook/orientation and prevalent ideologies that were inward, insular and communist;

- There are serious deficiencies in China's financial, banking, foreign exchange, accounting and tax collection systems which prevent the Government from maintaining stable economic conditions through the appropriate use of a variety of economic tools. The expansion of SEZ concept throughout China without implementing appropriate measures to control inflation and to ensure equitable tax policies might invite social and economic chaos;
- An important factor in the success of China's SEZs, in spite of the resisting factors like political system, culture and ideologies, was the leadership and strong pursuit of the policies of Deng Xiaoping. The future of SEZs depends critically on the support of political leadership, which may take a turn in case of its changes and any public disruptions. The maintenance of social order and political drive and overcoming the deficiencies poses greater challenge to the Government in future.

SEZ Experiment in India

Evolution of SEZs in India

India had experimented with the policy of Export Processing Zones (EPZs) in the past; EPZs were established in those areas that have either a strategic advantage or have already clustered with concentration and specialization. However, much of the focus of the EPZs was on better organization of exports and insulating them from domestic consumption. As this led to the license raj, this model was unsuccessful in tapping the investment and technology inflows, and began to offer secured advantages to those favoured by the EPZ authorities and benefit the authorities themselves. Moreover, EPZs were not well integrated with the domestic areas in terms of their structure and functional linkages.

Under the new industrial policy announced in 2002 and the export-import policy announced thereafter, SEZs have been sought to be created in several parts of the country for promoting industrial production and export growth. Indian SEZ policy delegated the authority of creation of the SEZs to State Governments. Some State Governments, particularly those having the coast and port infrastructure, have first approached the Union Government. The first SEZ creation proposal came from Gujarat State to set up SEZ in Kandla. Subsequently, the proposals came from the States of Maharashtra (SEEPZ SEZ), Kerala (Cochin SEZ), Tamil Nadu (Chennai SEZ), West Bengal (Falta SEZ), Uttar Pradesh (Noida SEZ), Gujarat (Surat) and Andhra Pradesh (Vishakhapatnam). Subsequently, some of the existing EPZs, i.e. SEEPZ, Mundra EPZ and Poorva EPZ have also sought the SEZ status. Table 2.5 gives the list of SEZs approved and under establishment in India.

Table 2.5: Special Economic Zones Approved and Under Establishment in India

Greater Noida SEZ (U.P.)	Salt Lake SEZ (West Bengal)
Vishakhapatanam SEZ (Andhra Pradesh)	Indore Special Economic Zone (Madhya Pradesh)
Kakinada SEZ (Andhra Pradesh)	Moradabad Special Economic Zone (Uttar Pradesh)
Paradeep SEZ (Orissa)	Sitapura SEZ Jaipur (Rajasthan)
Gopalpur SEZ (Orissa)	Bornada SEZ Jodhpur (Rajasthan)
Kulpi SEZ (West Bengal)	Maha Mumbai SEZ (Maharashtra)
Vallarpadam/Puthvypeen SEZ (Kerala)	Positra SEZ (Gujarat)
Baikampady SEZ (Karnataka)	Nanguneri SEZ (Tamil Nadu)
Dahej SEZ (Gujarat)	Hassan SEZ (Karnataka)
Ennore SEZ (Tamil Nadu)	Navi Mumbai SEZ (Maharashtra)
Mundra SEZ (Gujarat)	Bhadohi SEZ (Uttar Pradesh)
Ranchi SEZ (Jharkhand)	Kanpur SEZ (Uttar Pradesh)
Calcutta Leather Complex SEZ (West Bengal)	Mahindra City SEZ (Tamil Nadu)

Source: <http://sezindia.nic.in/sez.asp>

Features of Indian SEZ Experiment

Although modeled on the success of Chinese experiment, the development of SEZs in India has different objective and has different socio-economic, political and policy conditions in place. By comparison, Indian experiment with SEZs appears to be mature, given the results of tried and tested SEZ model in several countries, particularly in China. Some of the salient features of Indian SEZ experiment are the following:

- India stands out as a country that has already adopted economic reforms and steadily stood by them over the past. There should be no policy, political and idealogical problems in the adoption of SEZs, which were faced by the Chinese and East European countries. Moreover, India has always had an excellent relation with the countries in South-East Asia, South Asia, Middle East and Africa and these countries stand out as the major potential target areas of its exports (CIDCO, 2003a).
- The SEZ experiment, in fact, gels well with the economic reform programme, and serves as a good succession after the required economic conditions are well laid. There will not be any conflict due to inertia in the system; rather, it is conducive for investments into and exports from the country. India has progressively opened up the economy and began to integrate itself into global economy much faster than in the past. Mumbai is the regional financial and trade capital that has the market conditions similar to those found in modern cities.
- The market processes are not new to India and there exists a vast amount of English-speaking population with professional, technical and managerial skills to understand the market dynamics and move strategically in achieving success. Cities like Mumbai, in particular, have a large populace with diverse education and skills to offer to several kinds of professions. Most of these skills are available at relatively low wages.
- India also has a diverse mix of activities and a wide range of industries, which give it an edge in the expansion process. There is an abundant supply of all kinds of labour at a reasonable price, well below international prices, which can provide inputs to

production of goods. In the year 2001, the exports rose to $44 billion and the FDI inflows rose to $2.3 billion (CIDCO, 2003a). India has been enjoying a good amount of forex reserves and a moderate rate of inflation.

- India has a long coast which is also a host to several important cities, some of which have a long history of trade and commerce as well as exports. The coast and hinterland can be used effectively to overcome the costs of doing business by exploring better transportation routes. It is also closely linked to the regional centres of South Asia like Colombo, Mauritius, Karachi and Dhaka, and it can find in these countries, apart from those in the Arabian Gulf, good avenues for its exports. Even China's South Coast SEZs formed such growth triangle with Hong Kong and Taiwan, which resulted in greater boost to the economy of the entire region.
- Indian SEZ experiment is also complemented by the industrial policies encouraging the formation of regional export clusters and industrial growth triangles or quadrilaterals that are based on the growth poles. This regional concentration will greatly facilitate the functioning of SEZs and promote competitive advantage in the products as well as prices (Anon 2004). The stronger link with Domestic Tariff Area (DTA) renders the SEZs with better outlook in terms of reaching the consumer preferences and their changes.

Performance of Indian SEZs

The performance of Indian SEZs, however, has not been overwhelming (Majumdar, 2003). Whereas five SEZs of China produced exports worth $18 billion in the year 2001, eight SEZs in India attained only $2 billion; their share in the national exports was low at 4.4% as compared to 19.5% in the case of China (*ibid*). Table 2.6 gives the exports figures of various SEZs in India. Indian SEZ performance is somewhat insulated from the economic and political risks and the strong financial institutions. They would perform well with better institutional environment for laying down infrastructure. The setting up of Offshore Banking Units (OBUs) in the SEZs, as announced in the policy, will have a definite positive impact on the financial performance of the SEZs. Some of the critical factors for enhancing the performance of the SEZs are discussed in the following section. Besides these factors setting into motion, the returns from the SEZs might be reaped only in the long run, after a decade or so. The short run performance of SEZs has always not been impressive even in the Chinese case; it proved to be not recovering the costs, which gives a message that India has to wait for a reasonably good amount of time for achieving results and should not expect immediate results. A cost-benefit analysis of the Chinese SEZs is provided in the Annexure for illustration.

Table 2.6: Exports of SEZs in India

SEZ-India	Exports ($ mn)
Cochin	51.4
Falta	194.3
Kandla	100.1
Chennai	160.4
Noida	205.3
SEEPZ	1,099.4
Surat	65.6
Vishakhapatnam	52.8
Total	1,929.3

Source: Majumdar (2003).

Some Critical Issues of SEZ Development

In the development and successful operation of an SEZ, the following are some of the factors that assume critical importance in the various stages. Apart from these factors, a favourable regulatory and operational environment is necessary, towards the creation of which reforms are required to be undertaken.

Labour Issues

Labour is one of the most important factors of industrial production, particularly when the land is a fixed factor and financial capital depends on investment decisions made by potential investors. The labour is perhaps the only value-adding flexible element in the production processes in SEZ. In an SEZ, it is expected that the businesses would operate in a hassle-free environment without any imposition of major restrictions. But, on the contrary, most of the Government labour laws form a major hurdle to free conduct of business, e.g. Industrial Disputes Act (IDA) mandates that any labour force streamlining by the companies with more than 100 employees requires approval from Government (Majumdar, 2003). In particular, the importance of restrictiveness of labour laws will be felt more by those production processes which would implement technologies like e-commerce, improved production processes, e.g. JIT manufacturing, and optimizing supply and distribution networks. At least, labour laws do not give adequate freedom to employers to recruit, retain and retrench the labour to the business needs. The inability to retain and retrench the labour restricts the operation of businesses, particularly when he is bound to retrenching the labour when it is not required due to down run of business (*The Hindu,* 2001). The SEZ development essentially is an export-led industrial development; protectionist trends maybe tempting politically but will distract investments. The firms coming up in SEZ will rather work on the principle of incentives for employees for better output and flexible but unrestricted working hours so that the market demands are met.

Factors Attracting Highly Educated High Skilled Population

Attracting highly educated and high skilled population is an important factor of the success of modern high-tech industries in the SEZs. Unlike the skilled and semi-skilled workers, the knowledge workers of modern era are not attracted of wages alone. Besides better wages, they certainly would like to ensure that they enjoy a better quality of life, which includes all comforts, facilities and services. The major factors that form a good pull on such educated and skilled populace are:

- Easy availability or surplus of jobs, i.e. unsaturated labour markets;
- Better physical infrastructure, i.e. roads, railways, water supply and sewerage;

- Good social infrastructure, i.e. parks, playgrounds, clubs and educational facilities;
- Availability of and easy access to entertainment centres, communication channels, recreation facilities, medical facilities and learning centres;
- Access or connectivity to transport modes and the speed of transport;
- Good reliable power supply;
- Less amount of pollution and low crime rate;
- Reasonable tax rates such that they are not high to usurp the gains and not low enough that result in poor and inefficient public goods and services;
- Budgeting of city finances, particularly public spending on infrastructure.

Good Transportation Network and Logistical Hubs

Good transportation network alongwith major nodes or hubs which handle the majority of incoming and outgoing traffic—either goods or people—is an important requirement in the development of a parcel of land as well as formation of land value. The impact of logistical hubs—particularly, air transport—has been observed to be very high on the high-tech, modern and high value sectors because of these sectors' time-critical operations. Most of the businesses and companies that would come up in the SEZ are going to be of this type, i.e. time critical, high-tech and high value industries generating products that will reach destinations across the world while avoiding all risks of delays.

In fact, rapid advances in information technology, high speed transmission and communication have helped production processes become faster, flexible and just-in-time on one hand and necessitated regulating supply chain, distribution network and inventories on the other. As a result, products and services are virtually available at the doorsteps of consumers with almost 40% of value of world trade going by air now. (Cambridge Systematics, 2003). In the US, nearly two-thirds of all US air cargo is transported via 24-48 hour door-to-door express shipments (*ibid*). Airport access is becoming powerful attraction to a wide range of high-end services like consulting, advertising, legal services, data processing, accounting and auditing. It is estimated that knowledge/technology workers travel by air anywhere between 60–400% more frequently than those in general work force (*ibid*).

The presence of hub airports results in clustering of time-sensitive goods facilities around airports which stimulates further expansion of air cargo, less than load trucking, freight forwarding, third-party providers along major activities leading into and out of gateway airports (*ibid*). The impact of hub airports on employment growth in high-tech fields is very high. For example, it was found in a survey of Metropolitan Statistical Areas (MSA) in the USA that the presence of a hub airport in an MSA increased the number of high-tech jobs by over 12,000 and covered 64% of high-tech job growth (*ibid*).

Size of the SEZs

One of the important factors of the SEZs is their size. Normally, they are spread over an area of more than 1000 hectares. Some of the Chinese SEZs like Shenzhen are spread over 5000 hectares. Even though a figure of 1000 hectares was kept as a norm for development of SEZs in the initial EXIM policy, this was diluted when the existing EPZs were converted into SEZs. SEEPZ SEZ, for example, is spread over an area of 93 acres; likewise, several EPZs and several other SEZs promoted in the private sector are spread over less than 200 acres (or, 80 hectares) (Majumdar 2003). The disregard for the size might affect long-term performance and success of Indian SEZs, turning them into another cluster of industrial complexes. The smaller size will throw the SEZs into the same problems as some of the existing EPZs, like SEEPZ, Mumbai, face now. The scope for expansion will be very less, and the functional obsolescence of space will render the existing space not suitable for the target industries. Smaller size of SEZ will also pose the difficulties in providing internal connectivity and external connectivity, which might lead to congestion and inefficiency on those corridors. Moreover, smaller size means many of the States jumping on the bandwagon, which might affect the overall performance of the SEZs and their success.

Institutional and Governance Reforms

Indian SEZ experiment, however, is not rid of certain basic difficulties that lie in the institutions and the governance of current system. The SEZ management is delegated to the Development Commissioner appointed by the Union Government, and the participation of local as well as State Government is marginal. This is almost opposite of the Chinese experiment, and the lack of participation of these constituents of Government can potentially result in conflicts that might impact on their long term success. Decentralisation and delegation of powers to local and State Governments and ensuring their participation in the management of the entities are essential actions needed for long-term success, which needs some reforms in public institutions.

Although the policies of industrial and commerce ministries are quite encouraging, policy reforms are expected on the fronts of finance, trade and infrastructure. Financial reforms include liberalizing the norms for setting up the financial institutions, like OBUs, in the SEZs, and perhaps different operational rules in the transactions in foreign exchanges. The trade policy also requires liberalization in the list of goods and products covered under exports with concessions or promotion and in the quotas system of providing export licenses. Too much of the regulation in the trade and commerce sector needs to be curbed somehow in order to promote the cause of SEZs.

Among the major areas of reform, spatial planning assumes major importance. Spatial planning in India is still largely governed by the norms and guidelines of urban planning, which are archaic and outdated. The regional planning system is largely strategic in nature and does not guide much of the operational aspects. Although industrial areas do prepare their own plans, they are purely based on the commercial outlook of a developer. Special Economic Zones require different sets of guiding rules and planning methods for laying down world class infrastructure and establishing industries migrating from other world. We need to make use of industrial zoning experiences in the USA for strategic planning purposes and develop principles for industrial estate construction on the lines of modern industrial estates or industrial parks. These will render the SEZs much more attractive in terms of the provision of better fixed inputs to industrial production.

Case Study: The role of Navi Mumbai SEZ in Regional Economic Development

Introduction

The City and Industrial Development Corporation (CIDCO) proposed to develop an SEZ in Navi Mumbai in association with a private partner spreading over a large area of 4377 hectares, at a cost of Rs 2,216 crores. It prepared a draft development plan for the Navi Mumbai Special Economic Zone (NMSEZ) as per the guidelines of new EXIM Policy 2002 of Government of India. The development plan not only envisaged the master plan for phase-wise growth but also it identified the key industrial sectors into which the investments would be coming forth in the NMSEZ. The Navi Mumbai SEZ is aimed at creating a world-class SEZ that offers all benefits, advantages and privileges of any other SEZ. The need for such an SEZ is much stronger in the State and the region, when they began to show signs of decline in the industrial progress. With the State's GDP growth rate is lower than India's growth rate, the contribution of this State to the overall economy is on the decline. It is the creation of conducive environment for the growth of industries and increase in trade and commerce that can lead to improving its status and benefit the people. SEZs not only can become drivers of industrial progress but also contribute to the economic development of the entire Mumbai Metropolitan Region, and in turn, that of the Maharashtra State.

Incidentally, it is observed that both the Maharashtra State as well as Mumbai have been experiencing a downfall in the economic growth in recent past. Even though Maharashtra's GSDP grew in absolute terms, i.e. GSDP at constant prices has risen from Rs 155,875 crores in 2001-02 to Rs. 166,516 crores in 2002-03, the GSDP growth rate fell from 6.8 % in 2001-02 to 4% in 2002-03 (GoM, 2002). The State's ten-year average growth rate of 5% is well below India's growth rate of 8%. In order to attain a higher growth rate of 8-10% which it achieved in the past, it has to increase its share of investments coming from abroad as well as within India. The fluctuating economic growth is often attributed to bad monsoon rainfall as agriculture is still a major contributor to the economy. However, a disturbing feature is that the share of private sector investment is on the decline from a 70% in the past to 45% in 2000, while, at the same time, the Government's share in projects has increased from 22% to 36% during this period (*ibid*). The main problem is with the lack of growth in predominant growth centres like Mumbai and Nasik. These trends can be reversed only if the growth boosting SEZs are set up and impetus is given to manufacturing.

At the same time, Mumbai's economic growth rate slipped down to 2.5% over last five years (*ibid*). In its report, McKinsey & Co. has clearly outlined the need for enhancing the economic growth of Mumbai in order to bring it back to growth path and reduce all other problems relating to underdevelopment, e.g. unemployment, poor housing and poor infrastructure (Bombay First—McKinsey 2003). Mumbai has been experiencing a decline of industrial development as well as the commercial growth because of a variety of reasons. Wrong choice of policies like industrial decongestion policies in the 1980s, overregulation of land and its development, poor fiscal and administrative governance have left infrastructure in a crippling state, resulted in high cost of space for doing business as well as for living, which, in turn, led to the proliferation of slums (Nallathiga 2003a). McKinsey report identified facilitating the hinterland of New Mumbai through creation of SEZ as an important lever of achieving industrial growth, which can provide impetus to a whole range of economic activities (Bombay First—McKinsey 2003). SEZ is a right means for achieving this goal by facilitating the industrial investments flowing into the region.

By this way, for the State of Maharashtra as well as to the Mumbai Metropolitan Region, establishing an SEZ is an opportunity to boost their economic development led by industrial growth.

The Navi Mumbai SEZ

The Government of Maharashtra proposes to develop parts of Navi Mumbai as a Special Economic Zone (SEZ) with the active pursuance, support and follow-up of the CIDCO. Navi Mumbai has long been viewed as a strategic location for shifting the majority of the trade, commerce, industry and domestic activities so that the island city would be freed from the huge demand for space for various commercial activities, and also remain centre of the core value-adding services like finance, banking and insurance. CIDCO has long before recognized the importance of Navi Mumbai to this region and embarked on building a township for residential, commercial and recreational activities; it has already developed a good infrastructure across the region. However, the lack of integration of these activities with industrial activities is attributed as a limiting factor of overall development; also, it has been negatively affecting the shifting of population and businesses into this region.

Essentially, manufacturing and modern industrial sectors were not given much importance in the planning, and incentives were lacking. The now proposed NMSEZ attempts to build this gap in the development of the region by making it an integrated township through the rapid industrial development and expansion of trade activities. The region has an adjoining Jawaharlal Nehru port, which handles the largest amount of cargo in the country. Navi Mumbai is well connected through railways and roadways to the rest of the State, country and Mumbai city. The proposed international airport in its region will give it a big advantage for the promotion of industrial trade and commerce, particularly exports. The incentives offered to the investors in the SEZ for setting up units and making exports will definitely attract the investors from India as well as the world. Initially, NMSEZ was the only SEZ proposed in the region. However, with the attractiveness of the region, the Maharashtra State Government would like to propose development of another SEZ, known as Maha Mumbai SEZ, which is very close to NMSEZ. Both of them will definitely give a boost to development of Navi Mumbai.

Advantages of Navi Mumbai SEZ

Apart from the major advantages and features of India Inc. (already discussed in the previous section), there are a few more advantages of Navi Mumbai SEZ concept. Besides the strengths of the region mentioned above, it has the potential to become a good regional hub of industries, more so when there already exists a large financial and trade hub in Mumbai. The coastal city of Navi Mumbai is ideally suited for all kinds of industrial expansion and also quite important in the formation of regional urban growth triangle with the cities of Pune and Nasik. The formation of urban growth triangle has the basic objective of creating conducive environment for the functioning of industries through synergisation of various factors in the region formed by urban growth poles of Mumbai, Pune and Nasik. China's growth triangle formed with Hong Kong, Taiwan and South Coastal SEZs, which resulted in greater boost to the economy of entire region, serves as a good illustration of strength of such concepts.

Moreover, the creation of SEZs and the formation of Urban Growth Triangle can complement each other, as the former involves creation of large physical infrastructure and support services which when coupled with the latter providing a host of changes in the legislative and operational environment to create favourable conditions for trade and commerce will result in increased volumes of business. Both also have the commonality of promoting clustering of industrial units through promotion of specialised theme parks like technology and industrial parks. There is a definitely good amount of overlap between the goals or objectives of both the proposals in the case of Mumbai Metropolitan Region (MMR), which is the reason why it is perhaps better suited for development of the region.

Socio-Economic Benefits of NMSEZ

The SEZs contribute to regional and national economy, as already discussed. Among several other benefits that the proposed investments into export-oriented industries coming into the SEZ will bring in, it is the quantum of investments coming in that assumes importance, which will result in generation of employment, demand for large industrial machinery, creation and utilization of transportation systems and logistical infrastructure. These are very long-term benefits that the region will receive. As a result of the demand for these activities, additional indirect benefits spill over to other nearby regions, e.g. Pune and Nasik, as well as far off regions. It is these indirect benefits to the regional economy which might be large and can spill over to several other sectors through multiplier effect on them. Thus, it will kickstart the overall economic growth process and improve employment options.

The NMSEZ will give a big boost to the country's net exports and the volume of industrial output, trade and commerce, for the purpose of which several privileges, concessions and exemptions are given to the entrepreneurs so that they can concentrate on core business. The economic development benefits arising from the SEZs are much beyond these structural changes alone. These include, for example, higher than the average growth rates, inter and intra regional trade, trade links to global economy, diversified industrial base and improved infrastructure. One of the important benefits is the employment generation that shall take place through the industrial activities themselves, which is known as direct employment, while the support services, trade and commerce also create secondary (even tertiary) employment benefit, which is known as indirect employment. However, the attractiveness of the Zone to the investors also lies in the way the Master Plan for creating integrated township is developed.

The creation of SEZ will lead to the inflow of substantial investments and an accompanied increase in industrial output as well as employment. The following are some of the major benefits of the NMSEZ.

- Firstly, it will give a boost to industrial development in the Navi Mumbai region, and a spillover of the benefits to other areas of the MMR. As the MMR has already been experiencing an industrial decline in the Thane-Belapur-Taloj-Ambernath areas due to economic slowdown, these areas will find a renewal of development due to demand for input materials from Domestic Tariff Area (DTA). The surpluses and idle capacities in capital (e.g. large physical infrastructure in Navi Mumbai and financial infrastructure in Mumbai), labour (particularly, those displaced due to industrial closures) could be put to use, while technology/know-how (good number of educational institutes exist in Navi Mumbai and Mumbai) will benefit from using the industry to sell their education/knowledge products as well as provide student placements.

- Secondly, the emergence of SEZ will lead to generation of a large amount of employment opportunities, both direct and indirect as well as induced employment, through forward and backward linkages of the industrial development in the region. The direct and indirect employment generation benefits have been estimated as almost 1.5 million by 2014 (TECS, 2002). The TECS study estimated that the IT and support services would generate about 69,000 jobs, pharmaceutical sector about 24,000, electronics and telecom equipment about 15,000 jobs. The overall employment potential for direct technical staff, workers and services works out to 225,000 (*ibid*). Similarly, employment on account of utilities and infrastructure services works out to another 198,500. In the first phase of the SEZ development, i.e. during 2003-04 to 20007-08, the employment generation in the form of direct, indirect and support services can be as high as 595,000. In the very long run, i.e. by 2015, it is estimated that the employment potential can be as high as 1,785,000 (Nallathiga 2003b).
- Thirdly, the upcoming of SEZ will bring in foreign capital, knowledge, technology, management skills and will develop good interface with the state-of-the-art production systems in the world. The well-built world class infrastructure will be a permanent benefit that can service the industries and population for a significant time. As this region is already a host to world-class educational facilities, the development of SEZ emerges as an important means for deploying highly skilled knowledge workers and managerial staff. The promotion of SEZ will also provide long-term solution to accommodating the rapid population growth of Mumbai city.

REFERENCES

ADB (2002). "India—Economic Trends and Prospects in Developing Asia: South Asia", *Asian Development Outlook 2002*, Chapter II, pp. 1-81, Asian Development Bank (ADB), Manila, <http://www.adb.org>

Anon (2004). "Economic Growth Clusters: A Strategy for Integrated Development", *Bombay Chamber Bulletin*, Vol. IV, No. 3, March, Bombay Chamber of Commerce and Industry, Mumbai, India.

Balchin, P.N., Isaac, D. and J. Chen (eds.) (2000). *Urban Economics: A Global Experience*, Palgrave Books, UK.

Bhinge, R. and B. Pauly (2003). "Indian Manufacturing: A New Dawn?," TSMG Article, Tata Strategic Management Group, Pune, India.

Bombay First—McKinsey (2003): *Vision Mumbai: Transforming Mumbai into a World-Class City*, A Report prepared by McKinsey & Co. in association with Bombay First, Mumbai, India.

Cambridge Systematics (2003). *Macroeconomic Impacts of the Florida Department of Transportation Work Program*, Report prepared by Cambridge Systematics Inc. in association with Glaze Associates Inc., USA.

CIDCO (2003a). "Navi Mumbai Special Economic Zone", Brochure of the proposed NMSEZ for inviting Expressions of Interest, City and Industrial Development Corporation (CIDCO), Navi Mumbai, India.

CIDCO (2003b). "Navi Mumbai Special Economic Zone", Information Memorandum of the proposed NMSEZ for inviting Expressions of Interest, City and Industrial Development Corporation (CIDCO), Navi Mumbai, India.

Ferguson, P.R. and G.J. Ferguson (1994). *Industrial Economics: Issues and Perspectives*, Macmillan Press Ltd., London, UK.

GoM (2002). *Economic Survey of Maharashtra*, Government of Maharashtra, Mumbai, India.

Majumdar, S. (2003). "SEZs: Go the Chinese Way", *The Business Line*, May 7, The Hindu Group of Publications, Mumbai, USA.

McKenney, I. (1993). "An Assessment of China's Special Economic Zones", *Executive Research Project,* The Industrial College of Armed Forces, National Defence University, Washington DC, India.

Nallathiga, R. (2003a). "The Impacts of Density Regulation on Land and Housing Markets: A Case Study of Mumbai", Paper presented in the 47th IFHP World Congress held at Vienna on October 8-11.

Nallathiga, R. (2003b). "Estimating the Direct and Indirect Employment Generation Potential due to the Economic Activities in the Navi Mumbai SEZ", Unpublished Discussion Paper.

Philip, C. (2000). "Evolutionary Processes and Regional Practices", *The Associational Economy: Firms, Regions and Innovation*, Oxford University Press, Oxford, UK.

Siddiqui, J.A. (2002). "Economic Zoning: Strategy for Development", <http://www.rediff.com>

TECS (2002). *Techno-economic Feasibility Report of the Navi Mumbai SEZ*, Tata Economic Consultancy Services, Mumbai, India.

The Hindu (2001). "SEZs: how well they perform?', *The Hindu* http://www.hinduonnet.com/2001/08/16/stories/06160001.htm

ANNEXURE

COST-BENEFIT ANALYSIS OF CHINA'S SEZS

As Chinese Government embarked on setting up SEZs as test-beds for development policies and bases for foreign investments, it made huge investments in developing them, particularly in the construction of buildings and laying down the infrastructure. Even though these investments are a specific policy outcome, their economic justification can be sought under Cost-Benefit Analysis (CBA) of the SEZs. Here, this analysis is applied to the one of the foremost and leading SEZs—Shenzhen. The CBA exercise carried out by Balchin et al. (2000) uses the concept of public investments as social costs and project benefits as social benefits, while making use of shadow prices which reflect the actual scarcity of resources rather than do market prices. One major assumption is that as most of the units in SEZs (70%) were Joint Ventures (JVs), all the firms are treated as if they were JVs.

Economic Features of Shenzhen

Shenzhen SEZ of 327.5 sq km area is located in close proximity to Hong Kong, which was set up with substantial investments of over US$8 billion in a remote coast with the objectives same as those mentioned earlier. Since its establishment, the Shenzhen SEZ became the fastest growing economy in the country, with an average annual growth rate of its GDP around 20% and industrial output 50%. With more than 80% of the products being exported, the Zone's exports contributed to 15% of the country's total exports by the end of 1993. The real estate development and service sector received more than 50% total FDI in the Zone and has contributed most to the foreign exchange earnings.

Cost-Benefit Analysis of Infrastructure Investment

The benefits to the Zone include: foreign exchange earnings, employment opportunities, technology transfer, tax revenues and insurance premiums, and Chinese partners' share of the net profits of the JVs. The costs to the Zone include: construction expenditure, administrative expenditure, and electricity and water subsidy borne by Chinese Government. Now the details and methods of estimation are laid down below.

The net gain from the foreign exchange earnings (in terms of market exchange rates, rather than administrative exchange rates) in 1988 amounted to $26 million. The employment benefits are the net gains from employing the labour in SEZs as compared to other parts of country, which was as high as 56% of the wage bill. The net gains from technology transfer are the net of wage differential between foreign and domestic manager and the costs of training, which was as high as $7.2 million in 1988. The tax revenue benefits to the Zone were almost 10% of the profits due to preferential treatment, but which constituted $55 million in 1988. The net profit share to China as a share in the JV was their profit share minus opportunity costs of the inputs, which was $1.32 million.

Now the major cost of construction for infrastructure laying was country's contribution towards this, which amounted to $92.8 million in 1988. The administrative cost of the personnel was another $4.1 million. As electricity and water are supplied at cheaper rate, however, as the shadow/adjusted rates are used in the net profits, the subsidy element was not accounted for. The discounting rate appropriate to Chinese market conditions was 7.5%.

Conclusion

Incidentally, the benefit-cost ratio was negative until 1986, i.e. the net benefits were less than the net costs. However, these were only in the short run. If one extrapolates the benefit stream and costs stream into the next 18 years and assesses the benefit-cost ratio, the investments show a net present value of $59 million and an internal rate of return of 10.7% is obtained. This implies that the investment in SEZs is justifiable given the positive net benefits. Moreover in the case of large projects like SEZ development, the benefits, particularly those arising from infrastructure, can only be reaped in the long run, and hence, despite short run losses (as evident from negative benefit-cost ratio from 1980 to 1986) the long-term gains can offset the costs to result in net positive benefits and good rate of return.

Special Economic Zones: Lessons from China*

3

Bhaskar Goswami

China's record economic growth rate fuelled by the Special Economic Zones (SEZs) is often advocated as the reason for India to adopt this approach. Since the 1980s, China implemented a series of measures and policies with the sole purpose of achieving rapid economic growth. As evidence over the years has shown, this single-minded pursuit of growth has lowered the efficiency and effectiveness of economic policies, besides incurring huge resource and environmental costs. The Chinese experience offers a valuable lesson for India.

Cost of Export-driven Growth

China has to feed 22 per cent of the world's population on only 7 per cent of land. In July 2005, China's countryside had over 26.1 million people living in absolute poverty and was home to 18 per cent of the world's poor, according to Chinese Minister Li Xuju, quoted in the *People's Daily*. Every year, an additional 10 million people have to be fed. Despite this daunting target, between 1996-2005, "development" caused diversion of more than 21 per cent of arable land to non-agricultural uses, chiefly highways, industries and SEZs. Per capita land holding now stands at a meagre 0.094 hectares. In just thirteen years, between 1992 and 2005, twenty million farmers were laid off agriculture due to land acquisition.

* This Article was first published in *India Together* (www.indiatogether.org) and is republished here with permission.

As more arable land is taken over for urbanization and industrialisation, issues related to changes in land use have become a major source of dispute between the public and the Government. Protests against land acquisition and deprivation have become a common feature of rural life in China, especially in the provinces of Guangdong (south), Sichuan, Hebei (north), and Henan province. Guangdong has been worst affected. Social instability has become an issue of concern. In 2004, the Government admitted to 74,000 riots in the countryside, a seven-fold jump in ten years. Whereas a few years ago, excessive and arbitrary taxation was the peasants' foremost complaint, resentment over the loss of farmland, corruption, worsening pollution and arbitrary evictions by property developers are the main reasons for farmers' unrest now.

While rural China is up in arms against acquisition of land, SEZs like Shenzhen in Guangdong showcasing the economic miracle of China, are beset with problems. After growing at a phenomenal rate of around 28 per cent for the last 25 years, Shenzhen is now paying a huge cost in terms of environment destruction, soaring crime rate and exploitation of its working class, mainly migrants. Foreign investors were lured to Shenzhen by cheap land, compliant labour laws and lax or ineffective environmental rules. In 2006, the United Nations Environment Programme designated Shenzhen as a 'global environmental hotspot', meaning a region that had suffered rapid environmental destruction.

There's more. According to Howard French, the *New York Times* Bureau Chief, most of the year, the Shenzhen sky is thick with choking smoke, while the crime rate is almost nine-fold higher than in Shanghai. The working class earns US$80 every month in the sweatshops and the turnover rate is 10 per cent—many turn to prostitution after being laid off. Further, real-estate sharks have stockpiled houses which have caused prices to spiral and have created a new generation of people French called "mortgage slaves" in an article in the *International Herald Tribune* on 17 December 2006.

The mindless pursuit of growth following the mode of high input, high consumption and low output has seriously impacted the environment. In 2004, China consumed 4.3 times as much coal and electricity as the United States and 11.5 times as much as Japan, according to the *The Taipei Times*. Some 20 per cent of the population lives in severely polluted areas (*Science in Society*) and 70 per cent of the rivers and lakes are in a grim shape (*People's Daily*). Around 60 per cent of companies that have set up industries in the country violate emission rules. According to the World Bank, environmental problems are the cause of some 300,000 people dying each year. The Chinese Government has admitted that pollution costs the country a staggering $200 billion a year—about 10 per cent of its GDP.

While export-driven policy for economic growth has helped China touch record growth figures, the income gap is widening and rapidly approaching the levels of some Latin American countries. Going by a recent report by the Chinese Academy of Social Sciences, China's Gini coefficient—a measure of income distribution where zero means perfect equality and 1 is maximum inequality—touched 0.496 in the year 2006. In comparison, income inequality figures are 0.33 in India, 0.41 in the US and 0.54 in Brazil. Further, the rural-urban income divide is staggering—annual income of city dwellers in China is around US$1,000 which is more than three times that of their rural counterparts.

It is in this backdrop that India's SEZ thrust must be seen. Following China, India is replicating a similar model where vast tracts of agricultural land are being acquired for creating SEZs and other industries. The September 2005 notification on Environment Impact Assessment is lax for industrial estates, including SEZs, and apprehensions of dirty industries coming up in these Zones are quite real. Further, with drastic changes in labour laws favouring industry being considered, the plight of workers in these SEZs will be similar to those in China. Such a mode of development is environmentally unsustainable and socially undesirable.

Further, it is now widely acknowledged that China's exports have also been boosted by its undervalued currency, something which Ben Bernanke, Chairman of the US Federal Reserve, terms as an "effective subsidy". This is a luxury that Indian exporters do not enjoy. The argument for setting up SEZs to emulate China's export-led growth is therefore questionable.

Is Export-Driven Growth Through SEZs Desirable for India?

There is no doubt that exports play a significant role in boosting GDP. However, in the case of a country with a sizeable domestic market, the choice lies with the producer to either export or supply to the domestic market. Ila Patnaik of the National Institute for Public Finance and Policy wrote in the *The Indian Express* in December 2006 that household consumption in India at 68 per cent of the GDP is much higher than that of China at 38 per cent, Europe at 58 per cent and Japan at 55 per cent. This is an important source of strength for the domestic manufacturing industry of India.

Given the high level of consumption of Indian households, it is quite possible that this rush is fuelled not by the desire to export out of the country but by the possibility of exporting from SEZs into the Domestic Tariff Area (DTA). The SEZ Act is also designed to facilitate this. Any unit within the SEZ can export to the DTA, after paying the prevailing duty, as long as it is a net foreign exchange earner for three years. It is therefore a win-win situation for these units.

The sops in an SEZ will reduce the cost of capital while labour reforms will ensure trouble-free operations. Further, given the considerable international pressure to reduce industrial tariffs, SEZs will be able to export to the DTA at highly competitive prices. This does not augur well for units outside the SEZs who will now face unfair competition. As cheaper imports have already played havoc with the livelihoods of artisan sector of the economy, cheaper imports into DTA from SEZs will also adversely affect the domestic industry. No wonder many of them now want to migrate into SEZs.

In a country with 65 per cent of the population depending on agriculture as a means of livelihood, industry ought to be complementary to agriculture. Through SEZs however, industry is being promoted at the cost of agriculture. Valuable resources spent to create SEZs will be at the cost of building better infrastructure for the rest of the country, something that will affect both the domestic industry as well as agriculture.

Other Lessons India Could Learn from China: Welfare

While the Chinese experience with export-driven economic growth definitely offers many sobering lessons, there are many other areas where India can learn from China. China has initiated a series of measures to arrest social tensions and rising inequality in rural areas. In April 2004, the State Council, China's cabinet, halted the ratification of farmland for other uses and started to rectify the national land market. The Minister of Agriculture, Du Quinglin, promised "not to reduce acreage of basic farmland, change its purpose or downgrade its quality".

China also abolished agricultural tax in 2006 and increased subsidy for food grain production by 10 per cent. To boost rural income, the selling price of grain was increased by 60 per cent in 2005. In 2004, out of a total 900 million farmers in China, 600 million received US$1.5 billion (Rs. 6,630 crores approximately) as direct subsidies. Nearly 52 million of the Chinese farmers have joined in the rural old-age insurance system and 2.2 million received pensions in 2005. More than 80 million farmers had participated in the rural cooperative medical service system by the end of 2004, and 12.57 million rural needy people had drawn allowances guaranteeing the minimum living standard by the end of 2005.

India, on the other hand, either does not have any of these safety nets or is in the process of dismantling the few that exist. There is much to learn as well as unlearn from the Chinese experience. Until that is done, millions of poor across the country will be made to pay an even higher price than the Chinese did for following this flawed approach.

Development through Displacement: A Study of Singur, West Bengal

4

Suhita Mazumdar

Introduction

The "irresponsible design"[1] of the Indian government to carry on with development projects has resulted in displacement of large numbers of people. Over the years, issues and concerns are raised for minimizing the effects of displacement and making rehabilitation a part of the overall development process. The colonial law ensures smooth transfer of lands of people to the government. But there is no provision in law to ensure an equally smooth rehabilitation of people who give away their lands to the government. The government has time and again failed to guarantee proper rehabilitation and resettlement package for the poor. The drive for industrial development, construction of mega projects over fertile agricultural land and displacement of large number of people and so on, raises serious ethical questions on the credibility of the government. We are living in a democracy and "democracy requires a conscience." But these unethical policies of the government with regards to developmental projects will soon transform democracy into "democrazy."

The nature of displacement is varied. Before I move on to analyze the nature of displacement that takes place as a result of mega developmental projects, it becomes necessary to discuss various forms of displacement arising as a result of man-made or natural disasters.[2]

1. Voluntary Migrants: People who migrate away from their home voluntarily in search of employment or better prospects are known as voluntary migrants. Usually in such cases the issue of resettlement and rehabilitation does not arise, as migration is voluntary.

2. Refugees: People who are forced to move out of their habitat because of wars and civil unrest are known as refugees. Usually in war time, the immigration and emigration of refugees from one country to the other is high. None of the concerned states takes up the responsibility for refugees as a result of which resettlement and rehabilitation of refugees does not occur.

3. Disaster Refugees: Natural or human made disasters which force people to leave their homes or lands produce disaster refugees. The Union Carbide disaster in Bhopal, the earthquake in Gujarat and the Tsunami disaster forced many people to leave their households. Assistance is in the form of immediate relief and compensation but there is no provision for permanent rehabilitation of disaster refugees.

4. Process Displaced Persons: Due to changes in the economy of an area many people lose out on their livelihood. Deforestation has resulted in loss of livelihood for millions of the tribal population. The government hardly takes note of such displacees and neither are they provided any compensation or resettlement.

5. Displaced Persons (DP's/ PAP's): "Persons deprived of their livelihood after their lands and other assets are acquired for development projects are known as displaced persons and PAP's (project affected persons)."[3] Displaced persons are those who are only displaced and PAP's are people whose livelihood is alienated from them though they may remain where they are. It is for these types of displaced persons for whom usually Resettlement and Rehabilitation is hereafter worked. If relief and rehabilitation can be properly and successfully planned for those people, then such a plan can also be used for rehabilitating other categories of displaced people.[4] The research will only confine itself to people who are displaced by mega developmental projects. It is important here to note that unlike other forms of displacement, displacements as a result of mega projects are carried out by agents of development, i.e. the state. The state generally takes no responsibility of rehabilitating people who have voluntarily migrated either for better opportunities or were forced to migrate as a result of process change and war time crises. Only disaster refugees find some kind of assistance in the form of cash compensation but no effort is made towards rehabilitating them. Project induced displacement calls for resettlement and rehabilitation of refugees as the state forcibly evicts them from their current physical location. Till late 1970's and early 1980's, cash compensation was regarded as the best remedy but pressure from World Bank to meet certain human rights standards forced the agents of development to come up with a flurry of draft rehabilitation polices until a weaker version of it was announced in February 2004.

It was very necessary for us to categorize the nature and form of displacement. When we talk about DID we need to expand our horizon beyond that of a dam or a project? Firstly[5], development induced displacement (DID) is not only about dams and projects. The existing image of DID in policy circles includes large infrastructural undertakings, airports and roads. Secondly, a shift from project-to-policy induced displacement makes it necessary to "include displacement caused by private as well as public policy."[6] The liberalization of the Indian economy has over the years embraced policies that rely heavily on the benefits accrued from private investments. And thirdly, displacement of people and sometimes even of the whole community need not be direct always. We need to draw a line between direct and indirect forms of displacement. In most of the cases, the worst form of displacement is carried out by the state to evict people. Ironically, the agents of development are the ones who are responsible for the forceful displacement of outsees. In this context, we really need to understand as to what is development in the actual sense of the term. Since displacement has become a foreseeable consequence of development, we need to analyze the term in brief before we move on to analyze displacement as perceived by law and displacement problems outside the parameters of law. Development is not only about growth. Development means changes—changes in the social, economic and political spheres that are beneficial to most of the people in the society rather than a few. Any mega project constructed in the name of development will result in displacement and impoverishment of people, people who do not actually participate or benefit in this development process.

At the macro-economic level, there is development as the land occupied is infinitesimal compared to the total agricultural land, like for instance the one acquired in Singur in West Bengal. The acquisition of the land in Singur by the Tatas will not affect the overall agricultural production in any plausible way. The problem lies at the microeconomic level. People are displaced, they lose their livelihood and land and there have been instances of human rights violations whenever there is government takeover of lands either for public or private companies. The land that is acquired results in both direct and indirect displacement. The coercive power of the state is used to directly evacuate the people from the land that is to be acquired and Singur is a glaring example of it. There are landless agricultural laborers, local traders and also sharecroppers who derive economic benefits from the agricultural land indirectly. Not only they lose out on their source of livelihood but cannot expect any kind of solid compensation from the government. Protest from displacees, non-governmental organizations, social activists and opposition parties and so on are mainly focused on rights of the displaced people, their loss of livelihood and the way they are to be compensated by the government.

Displacement: An Inevitable Consequence of Development

Most mega projects have "irresponsible designs,"[7] that focus more on profit making motives rather than minimizing the effects of overall displacement problems. Till date, we have no strong national policies that focus effectively on the rehabilitation and resettlement problems. Developmental projects should find successful methods to avoid any and all kinds of displacement. Development cannot be carried out by impeding the developmental opportunities of the displaced people and sometimes even of the entire community. In his book, Michael Cernea[8] argued: "...rather than impoverishing outsees in order to meet development needs of others, the benefits of development must be available more evenly throughout both communities."[9] That is why the resettlement and rehabilitation of displaced people is considered to be so important in the construction of mega projects. Mega projects, constructed in the name of development, cannot create job opportunities for all displaced people. Cash compensation is restricted to only those people who have legal rights over the land. The Land Acquisition Act of 1894 applies to only those households who have legal rights over the land. For people who have "disputed legal rights"[10] over the land or no legal rights at all cannot receive any kind of compensation as mentioned under the law. In order to simplify things, Sobhita Jain and Madhu Bala[11] categorized six types of households who are affected by mega projects and have disputed or no legal rights over the land that is being acquired by the government. The households are classified as:

(1) households possessing land with legal rights
(2) households possessing land with disputed legal rights
(3) households possessing land without legal rights
(4) tenant households
(5) landless households
(6) households with land not submerged.[12]

The LAA, 1894 only covers first category of households. The Act is more or less silent on households who fall in the other categories. Agricultural laborers, artisans, local traders and sharecroppers and so on cannot perceive any such advantage. It becomes extremely difficult for agricultural laborers and artisans to sustain themselves as they lose their occupational base and are forced to seek work somewhere else that is extremely difficult to come by. Vulnerable social groups especially children, women and economically disadvantaged people suffer more than others as a result of displacement. The problems faced by them are varied and therefore cannot be roofed under one solution. Agricultural laborers, artisans, vulnerable groups and socially and economically deprived people and so on have different needs and problems. They require special attention which our representatives forget and also a strategic plan that will minimize their relative insolvency and also "lessen their dependency, subordination and vulnerability of exploitation."[13] Rather than eliminating them from the whole development process, it is very necessary that the reigning government should give them an opportunity to voice their opinions. Most of the time the consent for land acquisitions is based on coercion. An ideal situation will be one where voluntary acquisitions are based on the consent of the DP's. Displacement will inevitably cease to be a major economic or human issue-an ideal situation that can never be real. If acquisitions are voluntary then human rights violations, environmental concerns and other community related concerns can be dealt with efficiently without weakening the ties of the people to their culture, community and, above all, to their land. All these are ideal setups to minimize displacement problems. But in reality, mega projects like car factories, housing and infrastructure, all require adjacent lands that are not readily available if some villagers refuse to sell them. That is why the government exercises its exclusive domain—the land acquisition laws that outrightly violated the property rights of the people in the name of "public purpose." Acquisitions have never been ethical because displacement has never been minimized in an ethical way. Developmental efforts that involve displacement will be continuously subjected to ethical criticism unless we have a responsible design for developmental projects. If ethical concerns are raised then the need of the hour is to follow the *pari passu* principle whereby the project can be allowed to proceed if and only if rehabilitation of the one being displaced is completed.

Industrial Development in West Bengal[14]

Before we move on to analyze the whole development versus displacement problem in West Bengal, we should understand the current industrial output of the state. We condition ourselves to think that development means industrialization. It cannot be denied that industrial development is indeed one of the major factors for the economic transformation of a particular state or a nation at large, but economic growth is not determined by industrialization alone. India is a glaring example of the fact that industrial development does not determine the economic growth of a country. India's GDP growth rate[15] did not change significantly even though there was an economic boom over the last few years. West Bengal which was once at the level of "industrial primacy"[16] is now becoming a fading memory. The huge industrial investments that are taking place in West Bengal, and also in other states especially Gujarat, Maharashtra and Tamil Nadu are raising serious concerns on the credibility of the CPM led government in West Bengal and what it has done to the overall development of the state. Eminent personalities like V.S. Naipaul even went to the extent of pronouncing that "Bengal was the economic and intellectual leader till it discovered Marxism."[17] But when we look at facts, the story is something different than what Naipaul observed. It is true that West Bengal follows Marxism but whether it committed suicide like "poor Russia in 1917" by following the tenets of Marxism is yet to be proved. It must be remembered that we need to move beyond "poetic licenses" to understand the reality and the reality lies in facts. In 1993-94 West Bengal was only next to Karnataka and had a growth rate of about 7.2%. The per capita income was also far better than that of other states. When compared to the nationwide per capita growth rate of 4.3%, West Bengal fared much better and attained an average per capita growth rate of 5.5%.[18] Since 1991, the population[19] in West Bengal grew at an alarming rate of about 18%. The irrepressible and unabated migration from Bangladesh contributed significantly to the staggering rise of population in the region. There can be many reasons for the incredible rise of population in the state. But, it cannot be denied that if the migration problem had been tackled efficiently the per capita income of the state would have been much higher. Every year there are innumerable immigrants coming from neighboring states of Bihar and Orissa to West Bengal in search of better economic prospects. Poor immigration records do not highlight the exact percentage of immigrants from neighboring countries like Nepal and Bangladesh. The continuous flow of migrants from neighboring states and countries has had a greater impact on the economy as well as the on the population density of the state. Today, West Bengal ranks highest among all states in terms of population density per square kilometer.[20]

Rural West Bengal does not have an impressive picture to present. It ranks third from the bottom and only 28.1% of its land is under agricultural cultivation. Punjab and Haryana have a fairly high percentage of agricultural land and are continuously benefiting from the centrally financed irrigation and centrally subsidized procurement. If West Bengal had benefited equally from this centrally financed irrigation and subsidized procurements[21], its economic performance would have been much better and of a higher order. Majority population in West Bengal derives their livelihood from agriculture. If a fertile agricultural land, like the one in Singur, is acquired then within a few years time, the agricultural output from the state will be negligible. Buddhadeb Bhattacharya defends his measures of acquisition of fertile land as an unavoidable event. He argues, "If we do not do so, it will reverse the progress. While the national average of fallow land is 17%, it is only 1% in Bengal. While 24% of the state's territory covers urban and industrial areas, forests comprise 13% of the land mass. Thus, the state is left with no option but to use some parts of the remaining 62%

Table 4.1: Land Availability and Usage, 2001-02

States	Total Area (Lakh Ha.)	Total Agri Area (Lakh Ha.)	Agri Area as % of Total Area	Irrigated Area (Lakh Ha.)	Irrigated Area as % of total Agri Area
Andhra Pradesh	275.45	70.00	25.41	39.45	56.36
Assam	78.44	28.00	35.70	5.72	20.43
Bihar	173.80	71.00	40.86	36. 42	51.30
Gujarat	196.24	35.00	17.84	30.42	86.91
Haryana	44.21	43.00	97.26	27.93	65.00
Karnataka	191.79	72.00	41.92	23.63	32.82
Kerala	38.86	–	–	3.50	–
Madhya Pradesh	443.44	112.00	25.26	63.04	56.29
West Bengal	88.75	68.00	76.61	19.11	28.10
Orissa	155.71	54.00	35.00	20.90	38.70
Punjab	50.36	42.88	85.15	38.47	89.72
Rajasthan	342.24	127.00	37.10	54.21	42.68
Tamil Nadu	130.06	38.00	29.21	29.45	77.50
Uttar Pradesh	294.42	200.00	68.00	120.12	60.06
Maharashtra	307.71	128.00	41.60	25.67	20.06
India	3287.26	1219.00	37.08	–	–

* The data on total area of Bihar, Madhya Pradesh and Uttar Pradesh includes areas of Jharkhand, Chhattisgarh and Uttaranchal respectively.

Source: Directorate of Economics & Statistics, Ministry of Agriculture, 2002.

agricultural lands for industrialization." It is true that West Bengal has to move ahead with industrialization but not at the cost of fertile agricultural lands. As per the Directorate of Economics and Statistics Report of 2001-02, the total percentage of agricultural land in West Bengal is 76.61% out of which only 28.1% is under irrigation and the land in Singur comes under that 28.1%. If CPM government has to "strike a balance between food production and industrial growth," it should reconsider its decision of acquiring fertile lands for mega projects twice. If you give away your fertile agricultural lands, which have the potential for higher agricultural output in future, you cannot expect to strike an effective balance between food production and industrial growth. Economic growth of a region can only be ensured when you think of an all-round development.

What made the CPM government, which once considered itself "as the main architect of land reforms," to go for rapid industrialization? It is not the question as to which government is in power. We need to look as to how West Bengal fared, in comparison to other states, in terms of industrialization. From 1984 to 2001, industrial capital investment in West Bengal had increased only fourfold. In other parts of India it grew by more than seven times. The percentage of the number of industries that came up during that period was almost static. Approximately, 722 industries came up during a span of 17 years in west Bengal, whereas it grew from almost 97,000 to almost 131,000 for India.[22]

The picture of the overall industrial development in the state is not so pleasant. The "slackening pace of industrialization, flight of capital and prolonged industrial unrest have taken their toll,"[23] in the state. The high handedness on the part of CPI (M) has invited intense criticism from opposition parties, social activists, non-governmental organizations and other people's organizations. The government has been frightfully non-transparent right from the acquisition process to the announcement of compensation package and other financial considerations for the displacees. The government is thus facing the wrath for aggravating the uncomfortable relationship between industry and agriculture.

It cannot be denied that communists have played a very strong role in the industrial decline of the state. During CII[24] gathering Buddhadeb Bhattacharya was very honest in admitting that they have committed mistakes and have played a very irresponsible role in carrying out the acquisition process. Today, the word "gherao" which means surrounding the management has found place in the English dictionary. Trade unions having affiliations to different political parties in West Bengal resorted to "gherao" or similar methods to put forward their demands. Using the "gherao" method, the trade unions in West Bengal became more comfortable with state ownership and the benefits accrued from it, like, for instance, assured salaries and assured pay increases, annual bonuses and full tenures without any relation to corporate wealth. Whenever an industry was rendered sick the state government used to take over to protect the jobs. These sick industries did not contribute much to the economic growth of the state and the result was inevitably slackening pace of industrialization in West Bengal. The overall sickness rate of industries in the state was 4.14% while for the rest of India it was only 2.54%.[25] Industrial decline impacted heavily on West Bengal's economy. There was an overall decline in the share of agriculture in India. West Bengal was no exception. Agricultural production declined from 33.43% in 1993-94 to 27.36% in 2001-02.[26] Moreover, the share of manufacturing sector in the state declined from 23.02% in 1993-94 to 21.68% in 2001-02.[27] Fortunately, the share of service sector in the state was higher and grew by almost 7.81% during the period 1984-2001.[28] Many critics argued that West Bengal was rapidly moving towards post-industrialization without even becoming industrialized. The power sector had a relatively bad performance like other sectors. Though per capita consumption of electricity increased in the state, electrification in villages lagged far behind. Electrification of villages for the rest of India was 86.65%, while in West Bengal it was 78.17%. However, in spite of having such a dismal industrial growth over the years, the percentage of people below poverty line decreased from 60.52% in 1977 to 27.02% in 1999-2000.[29] It was the same party in power that brought about such a change. Industrial expansion has been undoubtedly depressing over the last few years in West Bengal, but at the same time we need to seriously think whether CPM government in the state is pro-people or anti-people in the light of past and present day changes.

The obvious fact is that the rapid pace of industrialization will displace thousands and thousands of people if rehabilitation and resettlement process continues to be a big failure. The problem of displacement will worsen as industrialization deepens. Though Singur is not a proposed site for SEZ[30], the question of land acquisition for economic purposes fits in well. If we go by the recent numbers, "around 263 companies have received formal approvals to set up SEZs, and another 169 had been granted in-principle clearance by the government."[31] Whether it is SEZ[32] or formal land acquisition by the government for "public purpose," one thing is for sure that in future a large number of people will continue to be displaced as it happened in Kalinagar in Orissa and Singur in West Bengal. Singur has really sent an alarm to all political and non-political organizations throughout India that the time has come where we chalk out a pro-people rehabilitation and resettlement program based on justice and equity.

Singur is not an SEZ. It is only the logic of land acquisition that applies perfectly to Singur as well as to the politics of SEZ. The first thing that is noticeable about Singur is that it is not more than forty-five kilometers[33] away from Kolkata. Any industrial house that plans to set up its unit will definitely take into consideration the distance factor from mainland Kolkata. Singur was the ideal location for Tata Motors. The problem was that Tata acquired one of the most fertile lands in West Bengal. Almost 30% of the land is highly fertile in Singur and cropped more than once. The Left government, which has governed West Bengal for more than thirty years contradicts its own demand that an "outcropped land must not be procured for industrial projects."[34]

According to various experts, Singur offers a diversity of vocation for people who are associated with this agricultural area for generations. The land owning farmers, share croppers, small traders, agricultural laborers, landless migrants, resident laborers and so on, are dependent on the fertile lands of Singur.

Inter-state migration was never a big problem in India. People from neighboring states relocated themselves in or near Kolkata for better job opportunities not only in the agricultural sector but also in private enterprises that were established by "taking over the land for non-agricultural purposes."[35] Over the years, no such major protests took place because such changes in the economy of West Bengal were acceptable to the people inspite of the inequality and social and economic compulsions it created. Economic transformation that was taking place at a snail's pace was acceptable as it was manageable for most.

When Buddhadeb Bhattacharya went on to portray himself as an agent of change and hurried on with the industrialization process, it shocked many including the die-hard supporters of CPM (Communist Party of India). The immediate response from supporters, critics, non-governmental organizations and several other pro-people organizations was, "how could a party committed to the poor and marginalized, ...a party that initiated Operation "Bargha", that so fundamentally empowered the rural poor, now turn against the very poor peasants, who have voted for it year after year?"[36] Now see the other side of the picture—the election scenario in West Bengal. Buddhadeb Bhattacharya promised a change that got him three-fourths of the majority. His campaign agenda promised a "new industrial policy" for West Bengal. Within one year, the changes are quite apparent. But, he did not study the implications well. And the result was massive protest against the Left Government for uprooting the lives of many agricultural farmers in Singur and moving on with the "Tata Motors" project which does not fit into the category of what actually defines a "public purpose."

Because of police resistance in the area the actual number of displacees is not known. The government of West Bengal came out with a report in which identified the number of households that are to be compensated, i.e. the reported number of displacees. According to the records, 9389 persons have been identified for compensation which means that they fall in the first category, as mentioned above. Persons having disputed or no legal rights such as agricultural laborers, sharecroppers and small traders are automatically eliminated from the compensation package offered by the government. If anyone wants to read a summary of the Land Acquisition Act, 1894, then a momentary look at the West Bengal report on Singur is a must.

The real picture is obviously different from what the government report says. But to make things clearer and to highlight the discrepancy arising as a result of displacement and inadequate rehabilitation policy, we need to analyze the report in detail as well as the micro-economic problems arising as a result of acquisition of the agricultural land in Singur. Right after the state assembly elections in 2006, Ratan Tata and representatives of the Tata Company met the Chief Minister and struck a deal that was meant to push forward the new industrial policy as promised by Buddhadeb Bhattacharya, the reigning Chief Minister of West Bengal. What was in the deal was not made public till the Tatas chose Singur. The Tatas asked for 1000 acres of land. There were five or six sites offered to the Tatas including some in the backward districts. The Tatas chose Singur situated in the Hooghly district of West Bengal. The formal acquisition of land as on 31st December, 2006 stands somewhat like this—997.11 acres of land were acquired which included five mouzas.[37]

Table[38] 4.2: Details of Land Acquired in Singur

Total land acquired 997.11 acre

Mouzas involved 5

Land Details:

Name of Mouza	Total area of The Mouza (in acres)	Land acquired in the Mouzas (in acres)
Gopalnagar	1656.55	399.98
Beraberi	1043.82	327.21
Khaserbheri	229.62	180.59
Bajemelia	355.13	47.77
Singherbheri	310.75	41.56
Total	3595.87	997.11

As per the report, the acquisition of land had taken place with "due process of law." Under Section 4 of LAA, 1894, the government of West Bengal published a notification that the land in Singur can be required in the foreseeable future for a "public purpose" or for a company. "Desperate to bring in investments in West Bengal," the government gave in to the demands of the Tatas and on 30th August a notification was published thereby declaring that the land in question will be required for "public purpose." On the whole, the entire acquisition with 'due process of law" advanced in the following manner:

1. Issue of notification under Section 6 of Land Acquisition Act—30th August & 1st September 2006.
2. Declaration of Award under section 11 of the Land Acquisition Act—23rd & 25th September, 2006.
3. Payment of compensation in accordance with the Award—From 25th September 2006 onwards and is still continuing.[39]

All the important provisions of the Act, Sections 4, 5A, 6, 9, 11, 16[40], were taken into consideration while moving on with the acquisition process. Any objections[41] filed by the "persons interested" have to be decided by the government and the decision of the government on these objections is final. "The state government, vide Govt. Order No. 1703-LA-3M-07/06 Dated 6th June, 2006,"[42] made provision for consent award under section 11(2) and also set the form in which the consents are to be made. The government also agreed to pay an "additional payment of up to 10% of the assessment of compensation made by the Collector to the consenting awardees." Each and every section of the Act that eased the acquisition process was followed very carefully. The compensation award is not viable for change even if the "person interested" does not accept the compensation after the declaration of Collector's Award.

The Collector's Award for the entire 997.11 acres was declared on 23rd and 25th September 2006. After the declaration of the award, the Collector took possession of the land in Singur and on the same day handed all the official documents on land acquisition to WBDIC. The day-4th of October was important for Singur as 997.11 acres of land was acquired to promote industrial development of West Bengal. It was vested into the hands of the government free from all impediments. On

17th November, 2006, WBIDC acquired the record-of-rights for the acquired lands. Everything went in accordance with procedure laid down under section 50 of the West Bengal Land Reforms Act, 1955. Under Section 4(C) of the Act of 1955, the "conversion of the land from agriculture to factory was done on 21st November, 2006."[43] The "permissive possession" to the Tatas to carry on with the preliminary works was given on 27th December, 2006.

As per the terms and conditions of LAA, 1894, certain procedures should be taken into consideration while deciding on the compensation amount payable to the landowners, namely,

- Basic price.
- Solatium@30% of the basic price.
- Interest@12% per annum for the period between the date of notification under Section 4 and the date of declaration of award.
- Crop compensation, etc. as assessed by the Collector as laid down in Section 23 of the Act.[44]

The state government also agreed to pay an additional 10% compensation to the landowners. For single cropped land (Sali land) the compensation amount was Rs. 8.70 lakh[45] per acre and for double cropped land (Suna land) it is Rs. 12.76 lakh per acre. In all, Rs. 119 crores is the total compensation amount that has to be paid to the landowners and as per government reports only Rs. 83 crores have been disbursed.[46] A total of 9839 people have been identified, on whose name the cheques are to be issued. Rs. 36 crores need to be disbursed and around 2400 people are yet to receive the compensation amount. The area of land in respect to which payment has been made is 658 acres.

Everything looks good on the report. But the displacement scenario is not so good in Singur. The broader issue is of development versus displacement and Singur is at the epitome of this debate. What constitutes development is still not clear. On one side, the Tata project is promising so many things that will, according to chief minister Buddhadeb Bhattacharya, "...change the face of not only Singur, but also of the whole of West Bengal."[47] It is a "precious project" because the Tatas are planning to launch the cheapest and the most fuel efficient car that will cost around one lakh. As far as employment is concerned, the factory will "generate employment to 2000 people directly and 10,000 people indirectly."[48] The Tata Motors factory will cover around 700 acres of land and the remaining land will be for ancillary units. Moreover, the project will also lead to the establishments of second-tier units in the small and medium enterprises sector (SME). SMEs are generally known to be the largest providers of employment and are usually run by local entrepreneurs employing the local workforce. The establishments of SMEs will serve a dual purpose for the government. It will fulfill the prime motive of industrialization of West Bengal and secondly, it will generate employment opportunities as a result of rapid industrialization. On the whole, "the small car project will be the flywheel that will set in motion the other wheels of industrial progress in the state."[49] But, once again, industrialization is only one component of development. It is indisputable that if West Bengal has to catch up with other states it has to go for rapid industrialization. But, certainly not at the cost of agricultural land and people who have been dependent on it for generations. When we talk about development, especially in this matter, we have to balance both the sectors (industry and agriculture) very well to ensure all are benefiting from this developmental process.

Displacement Scenario in Singur[50]

As mentioned earlier, the displacement problem is predominantly microeconomic. The problem is about people who are losing out on their lands and also on their livelihood, leave alone other problems. Agriculture has and still continues to be the bread and soul for tillers of the soil, especially sharecroppers, landless agricultural workers, small traders and owner cultivators and so on. When government knew that the proposed land in Singur has the potential to reap good production in the coming years, irrespective of being a Sali and Suna land, why did it then compromise with the interests of the farmers?

The government dealt with the entire land acquisition process very high-handedly. As mentioned earlier, the problem is hardly macroeconomic as the land under question is minuscule when compared to the total cultivated land in the state. According to Abhirup Sarkar[51], its appropriation by the Tatas cannot affect aggregate food output. The problem is entirely microeconomic that concerns the livelihood problems of the cultivators, sharecroppers, landless farmers and so on. For decades, their "economic existence has depended on those tiny plots in Singur." Acquisition of land will not only mean displacement of a large proportion of people but it will also be depriving them of their only source of livelihood, i.e. agriculture.

Not many were willing to sell their lands to the government. It is a case of consent through coercion. The result was quite apparent. Local farmers comprising mostly of women stood against the concerned authorities and decided to drive away the authorities. In a clash between tillers of the soil and government authorities, many were injured and a few were even killed. The worst case of human rights violations happened in this development versus displacement debate. A sixteen year old was raped and burnt alive in Singur as she stood up against the forced acquisition by the government.[52]

In one of the studies[53] where around 400 households were interviewed, the numbers of unwilling sellers were 315. Nearly 261.50 acres of land fell under the proposed Tata project out of which only 24.36 acres of land was sold willingly to the government. Going by the number, it is very clear that the consent which the government mentioned in the report is through coercion. This report by Sanhati Udyog[54] was very important as it defeated the repeated claims of the government that the land was given up voluntarily "in lieu of the compensatory cheques."[55] The report also highlights as to who are actually displaced, i.e. the numbers who can never find a place in the compensation packages offered by the government. Landholdings in Singur are not very large. Only few of the landowners possess more than 0.66 acres of land. Majority of them are poor or subsistence farmers. As far as bargadars are concerned, there are more than 1200 unregistered bargadars and 607 registered ones.[56] The migrant labor force who arrive daily from Bardhaman, Bankura and Hooghly districts to earn their livelihood from agricultural activities are the worst affected. Around 800 seasonal laborers coming from economically backward sections of Jharkhand work in the fields of Hooghly for six-eight months and eke out a hand to mouth existence. Apart from migrant workers, there are also several permanent migrant families who have settled in Singur for more than two to three decades.

Since the basic issue is one of displacement, it becomes mandatory to include the non-farming households in Singur who derive their income from farming-related occupations. There are around 450-500 cycle cart drivers who "transport crops and agricultural inputs to and from the fields, nearly 200 households are engaged in animal husbandry and over 150 households are vegetable vendors in Howrah, Sealdah, Chucura and the two local markets." The reason why people do not part with the land thus becomes obvious. The first and the most basic question is "what will they eat? For generations these people have relied on agriculture or related activities. The number of dependents on a small amount of land possessed by each household is considerably large. The cash compensation, no matter how big the amount, will not last long enough to cater to the livelihood needs of the displacees. It may be very easy for the pro-SEZ political leaders to suggest that the displacees can earn by working as domestic help in some officer's quarters. No self-respecting farmer, irrespective of his or her economic status, will voluntarily and contentedly accept such jobs in lieu of tilling their ancestral lands?[57] Whose development are we talking about? "Does the economy and politics of development need put a price of the self respect of these farmers and their families?"[58] For generations they have been cultivating land and any alternative occupations other than agriculture is beyond their imagination.

The worst affected will be the peasant women and children, many of whom have no legal rights over the land. Their skill and knowledge are centered on agricultural production. Agriculture is one sector where participation of women in the production process is the most. Singur is just one of the many occurrences where the vulnerability of the woman will be exposed to a greater extent as they will "lose their access to food producing resources such as land and this could result in hunger and starvation."[59] As the history of displacement studies indicate, children inevitably remain the "weakest section of the society"[60] and are the first to "bear the brunt of economic diseases."[61] None of the two reports bother to take into consideration that in this whole quest for industrial development they are sacrificing two secondary schools and thirteen primary schools in Singur. The schools in Singur will be demolished (or have been demolished as Singur stands isolated and cut off from the rest of the world although the media is not barred from going there) soon to give way to this new Tata Motors factory.

Several rounds of fact-finding missions were carried out by local, national and international teams. There was one unanimous observation—no matter what their economic status is, the majority of people are not ready to give up the lands that have sustained them for so long. "Despite the rising input costs, Singur farmers still want to stick to farming."[62] The government has withdrawn the provision of seeds and fertilizers at subsidized rates to the farmers. Considerable damages have been done to the two deep tube wells in the area surveyed by Sanhati Udyog. Inspite of all these restrictions, the farmers are expecting to make a "big profit from potato cultivation."

Conclusion

It is very difficult at this stage to state the exact number of people who are displaced and face the threat of permanent eviction. If we have to summarize in detail the economics and politics of displacement scenario in Singur it would stand as given below.

In a desperate attempt to bring investments into West Bengal, the state government gave in to the demands made by Tata and offered them the most fertile tracts which are just 45-60 km from Kolkata. The acquired land will cost the government around 140 crores. Compare it with the price that the Tata's will be offering—20 crores, and that also after a period of five years.[63] The biggest irony is that never has a car factory occupied such large acres of land.[64] In addition to this, the Tatas also demanded a compensation for giving up the "16 per cent excise duty exemption offered by Uttarakhand for locating the car factory."[65]

The car factory proposes to directly generate 2000 jobs and 8000 indirect ones. But according to noted economist Amit Bhaduri,[66] the Tata car factory will only generate about 300 direct jobs and 1000 indirect ones. Only time will tell what is in store for West Bengal.

The acquisition process has really put the government in big trouble. As mentioned earlier, the Tata Motors factory that is coming up in Singur is not an SEZ. It is part of the natural process of development and industrialization that requires land. Right from the beginning there were numerous discrepancies when the government went on to acquire the land in Singur under Land Acquisition Act, 1894. Since early 2006, there were constant demands to make the land deals between the Tatas and the West Bengal government more transparent as it was about to decide the fate of the people in Singur. Critics argue that the deal is a clear violation of RTI (Right to Information) Act, 2005. Even after the resistance, the state government did not negotiate well with the people to chalk out an alternative rehabilitation plan. The result was more than obvious. People of Singur formed a local organization to resist the acquisition of agricultural land-the Krishi Zameen Raksha Committee.[67] No detailed information on the project had been disclosed for long, even though it was acquired in the name of "public purpose." According to a survey[68], almost 45-50% of landholders have not accepted the notices, nor given their consent on transfer of land to the government. The survey also stated that publication of notification u/s 4 of the Act was not proper nor was any public hearing held.[69] The compensation package has always been a bone of contention in any mega project undertaken by the government. Compensation is only in the form of cash as there is no proper state rehabilitation policy in West Bengal. Almost all fact-finding studies have found the compensation package as inadequate as it is based on the "notional value of the market." The land record reports have not been updated regularly "creating complication in land acquisition process and stalling payment of compensation."[70] Though the compensation award is far better than other projects (6 lakhs to 12 lakhs per acre), it is much lower than the present market rate of Singur, which is around

12-24 lakhs per acre.[71] Above all, the land is agricultural and not a wasteland where an industry should come up. Less than 60 acres out of the 997.11 acres of land acquired is wasteland. The survey outrightly challenges the false claim of the government that most of the land in Singur is a wasteland.

There can be no difference of opinion when we talk about the slackening pace of industrialization in West Bengal. There is a need for development of industries in West Bengal. The Tata project is bringing in industrial development—development which has stirred up a controversy. This development has both positive and negative consequences; the latter can be termed as the "cost of development." On the positive side, we have a project that will, in the words of Ravi Kant, managing director of Tata Motors, give a kickstart to the re-industrialization process of West Bengal.[72] For the first time, the Tatas are planning to "roll out cars that will cost around one lakh."[73] It will generate direct employment to about 2000 people and 10,000 indirect jobs. In a nutshell, the project will, in the words of Buddhadeb Bhattacharya, change the face of not just Singur, but also the whole of West Bengal. The costs of this development (negative consequences) are enormous. More than 10,000 families who live on this 997.11 acres of land, "are living under the threat of imminent eviction and their livelihood is endangered." A fertile agricultural land has been taken up that had the potential to produce more than two-three crops a year and was the main source of livelihood for thousands of families, irrespective of them having a legal share on the land. Women and children remain the most vulnerable groups and this is evident by the fact that the ongoing protest in Singur saw maximum participation from women and school children. This acquisition witnesses all sorts of mishaps which could have been avoided—gross human rights violations where a 16 year old was raped and burnt alive, mass arrests of people in Singur and fact-finding teams, massive "bandhs" all over the city that disrupted civic life and presence of rapid action force to curb people's resistance to acquisition and so on. This form of "arrested" development really questions the proponents of development to redefine as to what constitutes actual "development" because, as witnessed over the years, whenever there is displacement the notion of development has been challenged.

And finally, we need to recapitulate the role of our political leaders and mass leaders who are epitomized as torchbearers of democracy. For Buddhadeb Bhattacharya it has become a prestige issue. His reaction was simple. If Lenin can face grave attacks when he was "leading Soviet Russia on the road of socialism," why not him? He made it clear that there would be no looking back as the project "involves the very future of the state."[74] Buddhadeb Bhattacharya has taken over the duty of a reformer/ agent of change. He has everything—the vote of the people, a strong party organization, and a mandate that can really turn West Bengal into a star state. If he really wants to maintain CPI (M)'s image as a pro-people organization he needs to create a whole new language of economic reforms that does not sideline the poor.

What is happening right now in Singur is more or less a "wrestling match between the party in government and the parties in opposition." Mamata Banerjee suddenly became the leader of the people in Singur and then one fine day she disappeared. The craziest electoral party politics is played here. Democracy was just reduced to a protest that involved bloodshed and mass arrests. She belongs to a party which has involved itself in similar practices, i.e. violations of people's rights in brutal ways.[75] If it addresses Singur, it has to take into consideration the right of the people that has continuously been violated over the years across all states in India, especially where BJP government is in power. What Mamata Banerjee has in hand, is the support of the people, especially the poor. Rather than refusing the invitation of the Chief Minister for open talks, she and her party cadres should enter into a healthy political discourse to draft a solid rehabilitation plan or even propose the setting up of a rehabilitation team of experts who can minimize the displacement problem in the coming years. This is very important as Singur is just a part of the "larger plan of the state government to acquire 43,775 acres of land (mostly agricultural) for industrial purposes in the state."[76] Moreover, the rehabilitation of the

Table 4.3: Project Land Requirement in West Bengal

Proposed Project	Location	Requirement (in acres)
Chemical Hub	Haldia	25,000
Eastern Express(Barasat to Raychak)	North and South 24 Parganas	600
Setting up industrial units by WBIDC	Various places	850
Garment Park	Sankrail, Howrah	1,325
Shifting District HQ of 24 Parganas SEZ	Baruipur Kulpi	3,000 3,000
Integrated Industrial Development Center	Uluberia, Howrah	2,000
Industrial Estate	Kharagpur	750
Modern Township	Dankuni	5,000
SEZ	Howrah	2,000
Tata Car Project	Singur	1,000
Knowledge City, Health Park, Biotech Park	Near Kolkata Airport	850
Cement Factory	Sagardighi, Murshidabad	150
Telcon's Payloader Plant	Kharagpur	250
TOTAL		**43,775**

Source: ET, The Telegraph

displaced people has not been very impressive. During 1947-2000, 47 lakhs acres of land were acquired for developmental projects in West Bengal. It affected around 70 lakh people out of which "thirty-six lakh were displaced (DP) and 34 lakh were deprived of their livelihood without being physically relocated (project affected people, or PAP)[77] Displacement is a persistent problem irrespective of the government in power. The need for a wholesome political discourse thus necessitates the plan for a strong rehabilitation program/team.

The "political double talk"[78] is amazingly manifested in West Bengal. One of the eminent leaders of BJP compares Singur and Nandigram massacres with Jallianwala Bagh tragedy, conveniently putting aside Gujarat riots. Congress has a remarkably short memory about the Sikh massacre of 1984.

Each and every party has involved themselves in a series of human rights violations. Irrespective of the party in power, such cases of forced evictions are bound to occur when the state gives in to the demand of large corporations in order to promote industrial development. The call for open talks by Buddhadeb Bhattacharya to opposition parties as well as to people's organizations can have two repercussions. First, taking into consideration the ineffectuality of open talks, it will be nothing more than a "wrestling match" between conflicting interests, or second, we can have two solutions, i.e. minimizing displacement through a strong rehabilitation policy and a pro-poor economic reform that gives way to the industrial growth of a region without obstructing the growth and development of the people.

NOTES

1. Sobhita Jain, Madhu Bala (2006). *The Economics and Politics of Resettlement in India*. Pearson Longman. p. 101.
2. Twisha Adhikary (2005). "Resettlement and Rehabilitation Strategy for Displacement Caused due to Mining." National Seminar on Policies, Statutes and Legislations in Mines, Postale. The following categorization has been taken from this paper. For further reference please refer to page 6 of this article.
3. Twisha Adhikary. Op. cit. 2005. People who have not been physically dislocated as a result of acquisition fall into this category. The livelihood and impoverishment risks that they undergo as a result of acquisition qualify them for rehabilitation.
4. Twisha Adhikary. Op. cit. p. 3.
5. A detailed analysis on development induced displacement is provided by Sobhita Jain and Madhu Bala in their book, *The Economics and Politics of Resettlement in India*. Please refer to Chapter 4 of this book as most of the articulation on development versus displacement is based on the arguments provided by contributing authors.
6. Sobhita Jain and Madhu Bala. Op. cit. p. 100.
7. Sobhita Jain and Madhu Bala. Op. cit. p. 101.
8. Michael M. Cernea. 1990. *Poverty Risks from Population Displacement in Water Resources Development: Policy and Operational Issues*. DDP 335, Harvard University: Cambridge.
9. *Ibid.*
10. Sobhita Jain and Madhu Bala. Op. cit. p. 82.
11. *Ibid.*

12. Note: This categorization is done by Sobhita Jain and Madhu Bala. The categorization deals with only first four classifications of households. For further details please refer Sobhita Jain and Madhu Bala (2006). *The Economics and Politics of Resettlement in India.* Pearson Longman. pp. 82-85.
13. Sobhita Jain and Madhu Bala (2006). Op. cit. p. 101.
14. The analysis is based on a paper series written by Mohan Guruswamy and others who have worked extensively on the economic growth of West Bengal during the CPM era. I have basically taken inputs from Mohan Guruswamy's paper on "Industrial Decline in West Bengal," and "Economic Growth and Development in West Bengal: Reality versus Perception." A few data has been collected from these two paper series.
15. Mohan Guruswamy (2005). *Industrial Decline in West Bengal.* http://www.cpasind.com/articles/mg-05-03-17-industrial-decline-west-bengal.html. 17-03-2005.
16. *Ibid.*
17. *Ibid.*
18. See data (1980-2003).
19. The population of West Bengal as of March 1, 2001 stood at 80,221,171. The population rose at an alarming rate of 17.84% when compared to the last consensus. The population density per square kilometer is 904 in the state—the highest amongst all Indian states. For more information on population of West Bengal visit Census of India, 2001, http://www.censusindia.net/profiles/wbe.html
20. See data (1999-2000). Migration from other countries to West Bengal is not known. Till date, we only have records of inter-state migration, i.e. people moving to other states within the territory of India.
21. Under the land procurement scheme, the Government of India announced a minimum support price for rabi and kharif crops. Wheat, paddy and rice come under this minimum support price scheme and only fair average quality (FAQ) food grains are procured by the Food Corporation of India under the directions laid down by the government of India. There are special purchase centres allotted by the state government that facilitate "the purpose of food grains from the farmers in such a manner that farmers need not to cover more than 10 km." In case the farmers get a higher price from their produce they are free to sell it to independent traders or grain dealers. The percentage of levy to be charged is decided by the state government in consultation with Ministry of CA, F&D before the commencement of the marketing season. As mentioned, Punjab and Haryana are the highest beneficiaries of the land procurement scheme

and the percentage of levy charges is 7.5%. Uttar Pradesh and Uttarakhand have followed the decentralized land procurement system whereby the state controls the purchase, storage and distribution of food grains. The main idea behind this scheme is to release the stored food grains during times of shortage and urgency. Generally, the FCI moves food grains from surplus states like Punjab, Haryana and Uttar Pradesh and so on to deficit states. West Bengal is not covered under the land procurement scheme.

22. Mohan Guruswamy, Kamal Sharma, Jeeven Prakash Mohanty. *Economic Growth and Development in West Bengal: Reality versus Perception*. Centre for Policy Alternatives.
23. Mohan Guruswamy. Op. cit. 2005.
24. Confederation of Indian Industry.
25. Mohan Guruswamy. Op. cit. 17-03-2005.
26. *Ibid.*
27. *Ibid.*
28. *Ibid.*
29. Mohan Guruswamy. Op. cit. 17-03-2005. The state-wise poverty projection for the year 2006-07 is provided.
30. SEZ or Special Economic Zone was first introduced on 1st April 2000. With the liberalization of the Indian economy, SEZs were formally approved to provide a "hassle-free environment for exports." SEZs primarily focused on manufacturing of goods and rendering of services. The production units in the SEZs have to be a net foreign earners and are not subjected to "any pre-determined value addition or minimum export performance requirements." Payment of full Custom Duty and import policy in force becomes mandatory for the production units in the Zone. The April 2000 policy allows for the establishment of SEZ in the public, private, joint sector or by the state governments themselves. The policy also envisioned that certain Export Processing Zones would also be converted into SEZs. The SEZ Act, 2005 was first announced in 2005 but has been put on hold because of the controversies it attracted. The controversy over SEZ has once again questioned the "flawed nature of Indian Democracy" where the government announced policies without taking into consideration their future implications. At macroeconomical level, everything looks good with the SEZ coming into force in India. At microeconomical level, there is hardly any policy. The present break in proceedings is mainly due to the absence of a just National Rehabilitation Policy that will look into the resettlement and livelihood concerns of displacees to ensure all round development.

31. M. Ramanathan Anand, S. Kalyana and Sunitha Natti. *The Business of SEZs.* Business World, 13th November 2006.
32. To know more about SEZ, see the SEZ Act, 2005. [http://www.sezindia.nic.in/SEZ%20Act,%202005.pdf]
33. The actual distance is not known. The distance factor varied in different individual reports. However, from mainland Kolkata, Singur will not be more than 45-60 kilometers.
34. Mahasweta Devi, Malay Sengupta, Dipankar Chakraborti and Medha Patkar. *The Public Hearing and Further Investigation on the Struggle by the People of Singur.* http://aidindia.org/main/content/view/348/74/. 08-12-2006.
35. *Ibid.*
36. Sagarika Ghose. *A Reformer of the Poor.* http://www.ibnlive.com/blogs/sagarikaghose/223/33706/a-reformer-for-the-poor.html#. 16-05-2006.
37. Mouza is a revenue unit for a village.
38. West Bengal Industrial Development Corporation (2006). "Status Report on Singur—as on 31st December, 2006" and "Status Report on Land Acquisition in Singur, District Hooghly." http://www.wbidc.comFinalReportSingur 31Dec.pdf. 21-02-2007.
39. West Bengal Industrial Development Corporation (2006). Op. cit. 21-12-2006.
40. For further reference see The Land Acquisition Act, 1894.
41. Section 5A of LAA, 1894.
42. West Bengal Industrial Development Corporation (2006). Op. cit. 21-12-2006.
43. *Ibid.*
44. For further reference see the West Bengal Industrial Development Corporation (2006) Report.
45. Normally, the compensation amount for single cropped land would have been Rs. 6.02 lakh per acre and for double cropped land Rs. 8.80 lakh per acre.
46. 31st December, 2006.
47. Shurid Shankar Chattopadhay. *Starting Trouble.* Controversy, Frontline, Volume 23, Issue 25, December 16-29, 2006.
48. Chattopadhay, Shurid Sekhar. Op. cit. December 16-29, 2006.
49. *Ibid.*
50. Most of the analysis is based on fact-finding studies conducted by different organizations. I have taken recourse to the one conducted by ISI in the month of December-January, Sanhati Udyog, West

Bengal and Action Forum, New Delhi. Because of restricted entry in Singur, the number of recent displacees not known. The intensity of displacement is still not clear. The figures provided by these fact-finding studies are all approximations which may or may not correspond to the actual number of displacees.

51. Abhirup Sarkar is Professor of Economics, Indian Statistical Institute, Kolkata. His studies include one on the problems of the potato farmers in West Bengal. In an interview with D.Murali and Gautam Ghosh from *Business Line*, *The Hindu*, he quoted the above statement.

52. Tapasi Malik was a sixteen year old girl and the only daughter of a sharecropper in Singur. A few policemen who were on post in Singur and CPM party cadres have been blamed for this brutal rape and murder of Tapasi Malik on 18th December, 2006. Investigations are still on.

53. Sukhendi Bhattacharya, Amitdyuti Kumar, Pradip Banerjee and Others. "*Singur* 'People's Survey.' Facts From the Field." Sanhati Udyog.

54. Sanhati Udyog is coming up with a comprehensive report on the displacement scenario in Singur on 19th March 2007.

55. Till 4th December, the consent status as per the WBIDC report stood as 632 acres for pre-award consent and 332 acres for post-award consent. The total consent was for 952 acres out of the total 997.11 acres of land acquired.

56. The number of registered and unregistered bargadars again stands in sharp contrast to the first status report on Singur published by the WBIDC. The total number of recorded bargadars according to the Collector was 237. Based on a local enquiry, the total number of unrecorded bargadars is about 170.

57. Avik Sarkar and Biplab Kumar Kisku. *Special Economic Zones*. Working Paper Series. PGDM, PGP II, IIM Calcutta. Batch 2007

58. *Ibid.*

59. D.P. Lahiri and Arpita Ghosh (2006). "Our Land Their Development. A Report of the International Fact Finding Mission on the Forced Eviction of the Farming Communities in the State of West Bengal in India." People's Coalition on Food Sovereignty (PCFS) and Pesticide Action Network Asia and the Pacific (PANAP).

60. *Ibid.*

61. *Ibid.*

62. Sukhendi Bhattacharya and Amitdyuti Kumar, Pradip Banerjee and Others. Op. cit.

63. Praful Bidwai. "From Singur to Nandigram and Beyond: Development as Dispossession." *Kashmir Times*. http://prafulbidwai.net/. 29-01-2007
64. The Tata Motors factory in Pune that is considered to be one of the giant car factories, occupies 188 acres of land that includes housing for its employees.
65. Praful Bidwai. Op. cit.
66. Amit Bhaduri and Medha Patkar. "Industrialisation: Which way now?" *Ekak Matra,* May Issue (Vol. 7 No. 6), Krishi Bonam Shilpo?
67. Delhi Solidarity Group. "Explaining Ground Realities in Singur; State Violence on Protesting Local Peasants." Report based on inputs from fact finding reports from various networks and recent articles in the Seminar and other journals on the Singur case (Courtesy: M.V. Bijulal, ISI, Delhi).
68. Mahasweta Devi, Malay Sengupta, Dipankar Chakraborti and Medha Patkar. Op. cit. December 8, 2006.
69. *Ibid.*
70. *Ibid.*
71. *Ibid.*
72. Shurid Sekhar Chattopadhay. Op. cit. December 16-29, 2006.
73. *Ibid.*
74. Shurid Shankar Chattopadhay. Op. cit. December 16-29, 2006.
75. Bijulal, M.V. (2006). "Background Note on Singur." http://mail.sarai.net/pipermail/urbanstudygroup/2006-December/001176.html. Urban Study. 8-12-2006.
76. D.P. Lahiri and Arpita Ghosh. Op. cit. October 2006.
77. Walter Fernandes. "Not a People's State." http://timesofindia.indiatimes.com/OPINION/Editorial/LEADER ARTICLE Not a Peoples State/articleshow/792598.cmsLEADER
78. Amit Bhaduri and Medha Patkar. Op. cit.

Special Economic Zones Scheme

5

Scheme	1.	This may be called the Special Economic Zones Scheme.
Definitions	2.	For the purposes of Special Economic Zone Scheme, unless the context otherwise requires, the following words and expressions shall have the meanings attached to them as given in the Policy.
Status of SEZs	3.1	Special Economic Zone (SEZ) is a specifically delineated duty-free enclave and shall be deemed to be foreign territory for the purposes of trade operations and duties and tariffs.
	3.2	Goods and services going into the SEZ area from DTA shall be treated as exports and goods and services coming from the SEZ area into DTA shall be treated as if these are being imported.
	3.3	The Special Economic Zones may have areas, demarcated as:

(a) Processing areas for setting up of units for production of goods and rendering of services; and

		(b) non-processing areas, if any.
Setting up of SEZ in Private/Joint/State Sector	4.1	A SEZ may be set up in the public, private or joint sector or by State Government. Guidelines for setting up of Special Economic Zones in the public/ private/ joint Sector or by the State Government is given in Appendix-14-II.N.
	4.2	Project proposal for setting up of SEZ, recommended by the concerned State Government, shall be considered by the Board of Approval in the Department of Commerce as given in Appendix 14-ID.
	4.3	On approval of the proposal, a Letter of Permission shall be issued to the developer for development, operation and maintenance of SEZ as given in Appendix-14-II.O. Format of Letter of Permission for developers engaged in operation and maintenance of SEZ is given in Appendix 14-II.P.
Registration of Developer	5.1	The developer shall obtain RCMC from the concerned Development Commissioner of SEZ.
Entitlements of SEZ Developer	5.2	For development, operation and maintenance of infrastructure facilities in SEZs, the developer shall be eligible for the following entitlements: (a) Income tax exemption as per 80 IA of the Income Tax Act; (b) Import/procurement of goods without payment of Customs/ Excise duty;

(c) Exemption from Service Tax;

(d) Exemption from CST.

Zonal Development Board

6 The powers and functions of the Zonal Development Board notified by the Government (Appendix -14-II.Q) shall be as under:

(a) To approve import or domestic procurement of goods and services for development, operation and maintenance of infrastructure facilities in the Zone without payment of duty or tax;

(b) To monitor utilisation of materials imported/procured as per (a) above;

(c) To co-ordinate with other Government Departments and other agencies for the smooth implementation of the projects;

(d) Functions as may be delegated by the State Government or its agencies;

(e) Any other function as may be notified by the Central Government.

Eligibility of SEZ units

7.1 SEZ units may be set up for manufacture of goods and rendering of services.

Application/Approval and Renewal of Approval

7.2 For setting up a unit in SEZ, three copies of the application in the form given in Appendix-14-IA may be submitted to the Development Commissioner (DC) of the SEZ concerned.

7.3 Applications for setting up a unit in SEZ other than proposals for setting up of unit in the services sector (except software and IT-enabled services, trading or any other service activity as may be delegated by the BOA), shall be approved or rejected by the Units Approval Committee within 15 days as per the procedure indicated in Appendix 14-IB. In other cases, approval may be granted by the Development Commissioner after clearance by the Board of Approvals. Sector specific conditions relating to the approval are given in Appendix14-IC.

7.4 Proposals for setting up units in SEZ requiring Industrial License may be granted approval by the Development Commissioner after clearance of the proposal by the SEZ Board of Approval and Department of Industrial Policy and Promotion within 45 days on merits.

7.5 Letter of Permission (LOP)/Letter of Intent (LOI) issued to SEZ units as per standard format indicated at Appendix-14-IE shall be valid for a period of 3 years for commencement of production. The LOP/LOI shall be valid for a period of five years from the date of commencement of production and would be construed as a license for all purposes. On completion of 5 years' operation, the approval may be renewed by the Development Commissioner concerned for a period of 5 years at a time on receipt of application for renewal from the unit.

7.6 Each LOP/LOI shall have separate earmarked premises and shall specify the items of manufacture/ service activity, annual capacity, projected annual export for the first five years in dollar terms, Net Foreign Exchange Earnings (NFE), limitations, if any, regarding sale of finished goods, by-products and rejects in the DTA and such other matter as may be necessary and also impose such conditions as may be required.

7.7 In case of any change in approved activity or undertaking any new activity by SEZ units, the Development Commissioner shall issue amended LOP within six days on receiving intimation from the unit.

Legal Undertaking

8. The unit shall execute a legal undertaking with the Development Commissioner concerned in the form given in Appendix 14-IF.

Export

9.1 SEZ units may export goods and services including agro-products, partly processed goods, sub-assemblies and components except prohibited items of exports in ITC (HS). The units may also export by-products, rejects, waste scrap arising out of the production process. Export of Special Chemicals, Organisms, Materials, Equipment and Technologies (SCOMET) shall be subject to fulfillment of the conditions indicated in the ITC (HS).

9.2 SEZ units, other than trading/ service unit, may also export to Russian Federation in Indian Rupees against repayment of State Credit/Escrow Rupee Account of the buyer, subject to RBI clearance, if any.

9.3 At the time of export of jewellery, the shipping bill and the invoice presented to the Customs authorities shall contain the description of the items, its weight, purity of gold/ silver/platinum, type of gem & jewellery stone (diamond, ruby, sapphire, cubic zircon, etc.) used for studding and studding weight in carats, FOB price rate of the jewellery item, quantity in pieces and total value.

9.4 The SEZ unit may export jewellery on the basis of a notional rate certificate to be issued by the nominated agency. This rate will be based on the prevailing Gold/ USD rate and the USD/INR rate in the notional rate certificate. The certificate issued by the nominated agency should not be older than 3 working days of the date of shipment.

9.5 The exporter shall have the flexibility to fix the price and repay the gold loan within 180 days from the date of export. The price shall be communicated to the nominated agencies who will issue a certificate showing the final confirmation of the rate to the bank negotiating the document, to ensure that export proceeds are realized at this rate.

9.6 Software units may undertake exports using data communication links or in the form of physical exports (which may be through courier service also), including export of professional services.

Import/domestic procurement

10.1 SEZ unit may import/procure from the DTA without payment of duty, all types of goods and services, including capital goods, whether new or second-hand, required by it for its activities or in connection therewith, provided they are not prohibited items of imports in the ITC(HS). However, any permission required for import under any other law shall be applicable. Goods shall include raw material for making capital goods for use within the unit. The units shall also be permitted to import goods required for the approved activity, including capital goods, free of cost or on loan from clients.

10.2 In case of doubt as to whether the item is required by the unit for its activities or in connection therewith, the decision of the concerned Development Commissioner shall be final.

10.3 The import shall be subject to the following conditions:

(a) The goods shall be imported into the premises of the unit;

(b) The procedure as prescribed under Customs/ Excise rules for SEZ will be followed and general bond executed with Customs/Excise authority;

(c) Goods already imported/ shipped/ arrived before the issue of Letter of Permission (LOP)/Letter of Intent (LOI) are also eligible for duty-free clearance under the SEZ Scheme provided Customs duty has not been paid and the goods have not been cleared from Customs.

10.4 SEZ units may procure goods required by it without payment of duty, from bonded warehouses in the DTA set up under the Policy and/or under Section 65 of the Customs Act from International Exhibitions held in India.

10.5 SEZ units, may import/procure from DTA, without payment of duty, all types of goods for creating a central facility for use by units in SEZ. The Central facility for software development can also be accessed by units in the DTA for export of software.

10.6 Gem and jewellery units may also source gold/ silver/ platinum through the nominated agencies.

10.7 SEZ units obtaining gold/silver/platinum from the nominated agencies on loan basis shall export gold/silver/platinum jewellery within 120 days from the date of release. This shall not, however, apply to the outright purchase of precious metal from the nominated agencies.

10.8 SEZ units may import/procure goods and services from DTA without payment of duty for setting up, operation and maintenance of units in the Zone.

10.9 Goods, except capital goods and sapres, shall be utilized within the approval period of 5 years.

Leasing of Capital Goods

11.1 SEZ unit may, on the basis of a firm contract between the parties, source the capital goods from a domestic/foreign leasing company. In such a case the SEZ unit and the domestic/ foreign leasing company shall jointly file the documents to enable import/procurement of the capital goods without payment of duty.

11.2 Capital goods procured from indigenous sources on the basis of lease agreement between the leasing company and the SEZ unit will be eligible for Central Excise exemption .

11.3 The value of imported capital goods financed through leasing companies or obtained free of cost and/or loan basis shall also be taken into account for the purpose of calculation of Net Foreign Exchange Earning (NFE).

Net Foreign Exchange Earnings (NFE)

12.1 SEZ unit shall be a positive Net Foreign Exchange Earner. Net Foreign Exchange Earnings (NFE) shall be calculated cumulatively for a period of five years from the commencement of production according to the following formula:

Positive NFE = A – B >0

Where:

A is the FOB value of exports by the SEZ unit; and

B is the sum total of the CIF value of all imported inputs and the CIF value of all imported capital goods, and the value of all payments made in foreign exchange by way of commission, royalty, fees, dividends, interest on external borrowings during the first five year period or any other charges. "Inputs" mean raw materials, intermediates, components, consumables, parts and packing materials.

12.2 If any goods are obtained from another SEZ/EOU/ EHTP/ STP unit or bonded warehouses or procured from an international exhibitions held in India or precious metals procured from nominated agencies the value of such goods shall be included under B.

12.3 If any capital goods imported duty-free or leased from a leasing company, received free of cost and/ or on loan basis or transfer, the CIF value of the capital goods shall be included pro-rata, under B for the period it remains with the unit.

12.4 For annual calculation of NFE, the value of imported capital goods and lump sum payment of foreign technical know-how fee shall be amortized as under;

1st –10th Year: 10% each year

Maintenance of Accounts

13.1 SEZ unit shall maintain proper account, and shall submit quarterly and annual report as prescribed in annexures to Appendix-14-IF to the Development Commissioner/ Customs.

13.2 The unit shall be able to account for the entire quantity of each category of homogeneous goods imported/procured duty-free, by way of exports, sales/supplies in DTA or transfer to other SEZ/EOU/ EHTP/STP units and balance in stock. However, at no point of time the units shall be required to co-relate every import consignment with its exports, transfer to other SEZ/ EOU/ EHTP/STP units, sales in the DTA and balance in stock. Any matter for clarification as to whether goods are homogenous or not shall be decided by the Unit Approval Committee.

Monitoring of Performance

14.1 The performance of SEZ units shall be monitored by the Unit Approval Committee as per the guidelines given in Appendix-14-IG.

14.2 Failure to ensure positive NFE or to abide by any of the terms and conditions of the LOP/LUT shall render the unit liable to penal action under the provisions of the Foreign Trade (Development & Regulation) Act, 1992 and the Rules and Orders made thereunder without prejudice to action under any other law/rules and cancellation or revocation of LOP.

DTA Sale and Supplies

15.1 SEZ unit may sell goods, including by-products, and services in DTA in accordance with the import policy in force, on payment of applicable duties.

15.2 DTA sale by service/trading unit shall be subject to achievement of positive NFE cumulatively. Similarly for units undertaking manufacturing and services/ trading activities against a single LOP, DTA sale shall be subject to achievement of NFE cumulatively.

15.3 Scrap/waste/remnants arising out of production process or in connection therewith may be sold in the DTA on payment of applicable duty.

15.4 Scrap/dust/sweeping of gold/silver/ platinum may be sent to the Government of India Mint/Private Mint from the SEZ units and returned to them in standard bars in accordance with the procedure prescribed by the Customs authorities or may be permitted to be sold in the DTA on payment of applicable Customs duty, on the basis of gold/silver/platinum content, as may be notified by Customs authorities.

DTA Supplies to count towards NFE

16.1 The following supplies effected from DTA to SEZ units will be counted for the purpose of fulfillment of positive NFE:

(a) Supplies effected in DTA in terms of Chapter 8 of the Policy;

(b) Supplies made to bonded warehouses set up under the Policy and/or under Section 65 of the Customs Act;

(c) Supplies against special entitlements of duty-free import of goods;

(d) Supplies of goods and services to such organizations which are entitled for duty-free import of such items in terms of general exemption notification issued by the Ministry of Finance;

(e) Supply of services (by services units) relating to exports paid for in free foreign exchange or for such services rendered in Indian Rupees which are otherwise considered as having been paid for in free foreign exchange by RBI;

(f) Supplies of Information Technology Agreement (ITA-1) items and notified zero duty telecom/electronic items indicated in the Appendix C.

Supplies to other EOU/STP/EHTP/ SEZ units

16.2 Supplies to other EOU/SEZ/ EHTP/ STP units shall also be counted towards NFE, provided that such goods are permissible for procurement by units.

Entitlement for Supplies from the DTA

17.1 DTA supplier to SEZ shall be entitled for:

(a) Drawback
or
DEPB in lieu of Drawback;

(b) Discharge of export performance, if any.

17.2 Notwithstanding the above, SEZ units/SEZ developer shall, on production of a suitable disclaimer from the DTA supplier, be eligible for obtaining the entitlements specified above.

17.3 SEZ units shall be entitled for:

(a) Exemption from Central Sales Tax;

(b) Exemption from payment of Central Excise Duty on all goods eligible for procurement as per paragraph 8.1.

(c) Reimbursement of Central Excise Duty, if any, paid on bulk tea procured by SEZ units so long as levy on bulk tea in this regard is in force.

(d) Reimbursement of Duty paid on fuels or any other goods

procured from DTA as per the rate of Drawback notified by the Directorate General of Foreign Trade from the date of such notification.

17.4 Supplier of precious and semi-precious stones, synthetic stones and processed pearls from Domestic Tariff Area to the units situated in SEZ shall be eligible for grant of Replenishment Licenses at the rates and for the items mentioned in of the *Handbook* (Vol. I).

17.5 The procedure for submission of application for grant of Replenishment License for cut and polished diamonds, precious and semi-precious stones, synthetic stones and processed pearls shall be as contained in the Policy. However, the application shall be made to the Development Commissioner of the SEZ concerned. Such supplies to SEZ are not treated as exports for the purpose of any of the export benefits.

17.6 The entitlements under paragraphs 17.2 and 17.4 (a) and (b) above shall be available provided the goods supplied are manufactured in India.

Export through Status holder

18. SEZ unit may also export goods manufactured or software developed by it, through a merchant exporter/ status holder recognized under this Policy or any other EOU/

SEZ/ EHTP/STP unit subject to following conditions:

(a) The goods/software shall be produced/developed in the SEZ unit concerned.

(b) The level of NFE or any other conditions relating to the imports and exports as prescribed shall continue to be discharged by the SEZ unit concerned.

(c) The export orders so procured shall be executed within the parameters of SEZ Scheme and the goods shall be directly transferred from the SEZ unit to the port of shipment.

(d) Fulfillment of positive NFE by SEZ unit in regard to such exports shall be reckoned on the basis of the price at which the goods and services are supplied by SEZ units to the status holder/merchant exporter or other EOU/ EPZ/ SEZ/ EHTP/ STP unit.

(e) All export entitlements, including recognition as status holder would accrue to the exporter in whose name foreign exchange earnings are realized. However, such export shall be counted towards fulfillment of obligation under SEZ Scheme only.

Inter-unit Transfer

19.1 SEZ units may transfer manufactured goods, including partly processed/semi-finished goods and services from one SEZ unit to another SEZ/EOU/ EHTP/ STP unit.

19.2 Goods imported/procured by an SEZ unit may be transferred or given on loan to another unit within the same SEZ which shall be duly accounted for, but not counted towards discharge of export performance.

19.3 Capital goods imported/procured may be transferred or given on loan to another SEZ/EOU/ EHTP/ STP unit with prior permission of the Development Commissioner and Customs authorities.

19.4 Transfer of goods as per paragraphs 19.1 and 19.2 within the same SEZ shall not require any permission but the units shall maintain proper accounts of the transaction.

Other Entitlements

20.1 Units set up in SEZs established by the Government will be charged rent for lease of industrial plots and standard design factory buildings/ sheds as per rates fixed from time to time.

20.2 Exemption from Service Tax.

20.3 Exemption from Income Tax as per the provisions of the Income Tax Act.

20.4 FOB Value of export of an SEZ unit can be clubbed with FOB value of export of its parent company in the DTA, or vice versa, for the purpose of according Export House, Trading House, Star Trading House or Super Star Trading House status;

20.5 Foreign Equity up to 100% is permissible for all manufacturing activities under automatic route except for the following:

(a) arms and ammunition, explosives and allied items of defence equipment, defence aircraft and warships;

(b) atomic substances;

(c) narcotics and psychotropic substances and hazardous chemicals;

(d) distillation and brewing of alcoholic drinks; and

(e) cigarettes/cigars and manufactured tobacco substitutes.

20.6 Sectoral norms as notified by the Government shall apply to foreign investment in services and trading activities.

20.7 SEZ units may retain 100% of their export proceeds in their EEFC account.

20.8 Export value of goods, software and services by SEZ units may be realized and repatriated to India within 12 months from the date of export or within the time extended by Reserve Bank of India.

20.9 Software units may, in addition, also be allowed to use the computer system for training purpose (including commercial training) subject to the condition that no computer terminal shall be installed outside the Zone premises for the purpose.

20.10 Procurement of raw materials and export of finished products shall be exempt from Central levies.

20.11 Exemption from Industrial Licensing for manufacture of items reserved for SSI sector.

20.12 State Trading Enterprises Policy shall not apply to SEZ manufacturing units. Export of iron ore shall, however, be subject to the decision of the Government from time to time. Requirements of other conditions like minimum export price/export in consumer pack as per Exim Policy shall apply in case the raw materials are indigenous and exported without further processing/manufacturing by the SEZ unit. Export of textile items shall be covered by bilateral agreements, if any. Wood based units shall comply with the direction of Hon'ble Supreme Court contained in its order dated 12.12.1996 in Writ (civil) No, 202 of 1995—T.N. Godavarman Thirrumulppad v/s Union of India and others with WP(Civil) No. 171 of 1996 in regard to use of timber/ other wood.

20.13 SEZ unit may install one fax machine at a place of its choice, outside the Zone, subject to intimation of its location to the concerned Customs/Central Excise authorities.

20.14 SEZ units may, temporarily take out of the Zone duty-free laptop computers and video projection systems for working upon by persons authorised by the unit.

20.15 SEZ units may install personal computers not exceeding two in number imported/ procured duty-free in the registered/administrative office subject to the guidelines issued by Department of Revenue in this behalf.

20.16 For IT and IT enabled services, persons authorized by the software units may access the facility installed in the SEZ unit through communication links.

Sub-Contracting

21.1 SEZ unit, including gem and jewellery units, may sub-contract a part of their production or production process through units in the DTA or through other SEZ/ EOU/EHTP/ STP units with the annual permission of Customs authorities. Sub-contracting of part of production process may also be permitted abroad with the approval of the Development Commissioner.

21.2 All units, including gem and jewellery, may sub-contract part of the production or production process through other units in the same SEZ without permission of Customs authorities subject to records being maintained by both the supplying and receiving units.

21.3 Sub-contracting by SEZ gems and jewellery units through units in other SEZ or EOUs or units in DTA shall be subject to following conditions:

(a) Goods, finished or semi-finished, including studded jewellery, taken outside the zone for sub- contracting shall be brought back to the unit within 30 days;

(b) No cut and polished diamonds, precious and semi-precious stones (except precious/semi-precious stones having zero duty) shall be allowed to be taken outside the Zone for sub-contracting;

(c) Receive plain gold/silver/platinum jewellery from DTA/EOU/SEZ units in exchange of equivalent quantity of gold/silver/platinum, as the case may be, contained in the said jewellery;

(d) SEZ units shall be eligible for wastage as applicable for sub-contracting and against exchange;

(e) The DTA unit undertaking job work or supplying jewellery against exchange of gold/

silver/platinum shall not be entitled to export benefits.

21.4 Scrap/waste/remnants generated through job work may either be cleared from the job worker's premises on payment of applicable duty or destroyed in the presence of Customs/Excise authorities or returned to the unit. Destruction shall not apply to gold, silver, platinum, diamond, precious and semi-precious stones.

21.5 Export of finished goods from the job worker's premises may be permitted, provided such premises are registered with the Central Excise authorities. Where the job worker is SEZ/EOU/EHTP/STP unit, no such excise registration is required and export may be effected either from the job workers' premises or from the premises of the unit. Export of such products from the job worker's premises shall not be allowed through third parties as provided in the Policy.

21.6 SEZ units may, on the basis of annual permission from the Customs authorities, undertake job work for export, on behalf of DTA exporter, provided the finished goods are exported directly from SEZ units and export document shall jointly in the name of DTA/SEZ unit. For such exports, the DTA units will be entitled for refund of duty paid on the inputs by way of Brand Rate of Duty Drawback.

21.7 SEZ units may be permitted to remove moulds, jigs, tools, fixtures, tackles, instruments, hangers and patterns and drawings to the premises of sub-contractors subject to the conditions that these shall be brought back to the premises of the units on completion of the job work within a stipulated period. The raw materials may or may not be sent along with these goods.

21.8 In case of sub-contracting of production process abroad, the goods may be exported from the sub-contractor premises subject to the conditions that jobwork charges shall be declared in the export declaration forms, invoices, etc. and full repatriation of foreign exchange shall be ensured by the SEZ unit.

Contract Farming

21.9 SEZ units engaged in production/ processing of agriculture/ horticulture products, may on the basis of annual permission from the Customs authorities, take out inputs and equipments (specified at Appendix 14-IJ) to the DTA farm, subject to the following conditions:

(a) Supply of inputs by the SEZ to the contract farm(s) shall be subject to the input-output norms approved by the DGFT/BOA;

(b) There shall be contract farming agreement between the SEZ and the DTA farmer(s);

(c) The unit has been in existence for at least two years and engaged in export of agriculture/horticulture products; otherwise it shall furnish bank guarantee equivalent to the duty foregone on the capital goods/ inputs proposed to be taken out to the Deputy/Assistant Commissioner of Customs/ Central Excise till the unit completes two years.

Export through Exhibitions

22.1 SEZ units may export goods for holding/participating in exhibitions abroad with the permission of Development Commissioner subject to the following conditions:

(a) The unit shall produce to the Customs authorities the letter in original or its certified copy containing approval of the Development Commissioner. For gems and jewellery items, a self certified photograph of the products shall also be submitted;

(b) In case of re-import, such items on arrival shall be verified along with the export documents before clearance;

(c) Items not sold abroad shall be re-imported within 60 days of the close of the exhibition. However, in case the exporter is participating in more than one exhibition within 45 days of close of the first exhibition, then the 60 days shall be counted from the date of close of the last exhibition;

(d) In case of personal carriage of goods and for holding/participating in overseas exhibitions, the value of gems and jewellery shall not exceed US$2 million.

Personal carriage of gems and jewellery for Export Promotion tours

22.2 Personal carriage of gold/silver/platinum jewellery, cut and polished diamonds, precious, semi-precious stones, beads and articles as samples upto US$100,000 for export promotion tours and temporary display/sale abroad by SEZ units is also permitted with the approval of the Development Commissioner subject to the following conditions:

(a) SEZ units shall bring back the goods or repatriate the sale proceeds within 45 days from the date of departure through normal banking channel;

(b) The unit shall declare personal carriage of such goods to the Customs while leaving the country and obtain necessary endorsement.

Export through Showrooms Abroad/ Duty Free Shops

23.1 Export of goods is also permitted for display/sale in the permitted shops set up abroad or in the showrooms of their distributors/agents. The items not sold abroad within 180 days shall be re-imported within 45 days.

23.2 SEZ unit may set up showrooms/ retail outlets at the International Airports for sale of goods in accordance with the procedure laid down by the Customs authorities. The items remaining unsold after a period of 60 days shall be exported or returned to the respective SEZ units.

Personal carriage of Import/Export Parcels including through Foreign Bound Passengers

24.1 Import/ export through personal carriage of gems and jewellery items may be undertaken as per the procedure prescribed by Customs. The export proceeds shall, however, be realized through normal banking channel. Import/export through personal carriage for units, other than gems and jewellery units, shall be allowed provided the goods are not in commercial quantity.

24.2 For personal carriage of goods by foreign bound passengers, the following documents shall be submitted by SEZ units as proof of exports.

(a) Copy of the shipping bill filed by the SEZ units;

(b) A copy of the Currency Declaration Form filed by the Foreign buyer with the Customs at the time of his arrival; and

(c) Foreign Exchange Realisation/ Encashment Certificate from the Bank.

24.3 In addition to this, Personal Carriage by foreign bound passenger on Document Against Acceptance (DA)/Cash On Delivery (COD) basis is also allowed. The SEZ units will have to furnish the following documents as proof of export:

(a) Copy of Shipping Bill;

(b) Bank Certificate of Export and Realisation.

24.4 The procedure for personal carriage of import parcels will be the same as for import of goods by airfreight except that the parcels shall be brought to the Customs by the SEZ unit/ foreign national for examination and release. Instructions issued by the Customs authorities in this regard should be followed *mutatis mutandis*.

Export/Import by Post/Courier

25. Goods including free samples, may be exported/imported by airfreight or through Foreign Post Office or through courier, subject to the procedures prescribed by Customs.

Replacement/Repair of Goods

26.1 The general provisions of Policy relating to export of replacement/ repaired goods shall apply equally to SEZ units, save that, cases not covered by these provisions shall be considered on merits by the Development Commissioner.

26.2 The units may send capital goods abroad, for repair and return. Any foreign exchange payment for this purpose will also be allowed.

26.3 The goods sold in the DTA and found to be defective may be brought back for repair or replacement under intimation to Development Commissioner.

26.4 Goods or parts thereof, including gem stones and precious metal components for jewellery making, on being imported/ indigenously procured and found defective or otherwise unfit for use or which have been damaged or become defective after import/ procurement may be returned and replacement obtained or destroyed. In the event of replacement, the goods may be brought back from the foreign suppliers or their authorised agents in India or the indigenous suppliers. However, destruction shall not apply to precious and semi-precious stones and precious metals.

26.5 Goods may be transferred to DTA/ abroad for repair/ replacement, testing or calibration, quality testing and R&D purpose under intimation to Customs authorities and subject to maintenance of records.

26.6 SEZ units may transfer goods for quality testing/R&D purpose to any recognised laboratory/ institution, upto Rs 5 lakhs per annum without payment of duty, on giving suitable undertaking to the customs for return of the goods. However, if the goods have been consumed/ destroyed in the process of testing, etc. a certificate from the laboratory/institution to this effect shall be furnished to the Customs.

Samples

27.1 SEZ units may, on the basis of records maintained by them, and on prior intimation to Customs authority supply or sell samples in the DTA for display/market promotion on payment of applicable duties.

27.2 SEZ units may also remove samples to DTA without payment of duty under prior intimation to the Customs authorities subject to the condition that the goods shall be brought back within a stipulated period;

27.3 SEZ units may export free samples, without any limit, including samples made in wax moulds, silver mould and rubber moulds through all permissible mode of export including through couriers agencies/post.

Sale of unutilized material/destruction

28.1 In case an SEZ unit is unable, for valid reasons, to utilize the goods, and services, imported or procured from DTA, it may be transferred to other EOU/SEZ/EHTP/STP units or disposed off in the DTA on payment of applicable duties and submission of import license by DTA unit, wherever applicable or exported. Such transfer from SEZ unit to another SEZ/EOU/EHTP/STP unit would be treated as import for the receiving unit.

28.2 Capital goods and spares that have become obsolete/surplus may either be exported, transferred to another SEZ/EOU/EHTP/STP unit or disposed of in the DTA on payment of applicable duties. The benefit of depreciation, as applicable will be available in case of disposal in DTA.

28.3 SEZ unit may be allowed by Customs authorities concerned to donate imported/ indigenously procured (bought or taken on loan) computer and computer peripherals, including printer, plotter, scanner, monitor, key-board and storage units without payment of duty, two years after their import/procurement and use by the units, to recognized non-commercial educational institutions, registered charitable hospitals, public libraries, public funded research and development establishments, organisations of the Government of India or Government of a State or Union Territory as per Custom/ Central Excise notification issued in this regard.

28.4 No duty shall be payable in case capital goods, raw material, consumables, spares, goods manufactured, processed or packaged and scrap/waste/ remnants/rejects are destroyed within the Zone after intimation to the Custom authorities or destroyed outside the Zone with the permission of Custom authorities. Destruction as stated above shall not apply to gold, silver, platinum, diamond, precious and semi-precious stones.

Self-Certification

29. All activities of SEZ units within the Zone, unless otherwise specified, including export and re-import of goods shall be through self certification procedure.

Distinct Identity

30. If an industrial enterprise is operating both as a domestic unit as well as an SEZ unit, it shall have two distinct identities with separate accounts, including separate bank accounts. It is, however, not necessary for it to be a separate legal entity, but it should be possible to distinguish the imports and exports or supplies effected by the SEZ units from those made by the other units of the enterprise.

Powers of Units Approval Committee

31. The powers and functions of the Unit Approval Committee notified by the Government (Appendix-14-II.R) shall be as under:

(a) To consider the applications for setting up of units in SEZ other than proposals for setting up of unit in the services sector (except software and IT-enabled services, trading or any other service activity as may be delegated by the BOA) and items of manufacture requiring industrial license under the Industrial (Development & Regulation) Act, 1951 shall be considered by the BOA;

(b) To consider and permit conversion of EOU into SEZ unit;

(c) To monitor the performance of the Units;

(d) To supervise and monitor permission, clearances, licenses granted to the units and take appropriate action in accordance with law;

(e) To call for information required to monitor the performance of the unit under the permission, clearances, license granted to it;

(f) To perform any other function delegated by the Central Government or its agencies;

(g) To perform any other function as may be delegated by the State Government or its agencies;

(h) To grant all approvals and clearances for the establishment and operation of Units in the Special Economic Zone.

Management of SEZ	32.1	SEZ will be under the administrative control of the Development Commissioner.
Registration-cum-Membership Certificate	32.2	Registering authority for SEZ units, shall be the Development Commissioner of the SEZ concerned. A separate Registration-cum-Membership Certificate shall not be required in their cases as provided for in the Policy.

Powers of the Development Commissioner

32.3 Apart from the original power delegated elsewhere, the Development Commissioners of SEZ will exercise the following powers in respect of SEZ units. Jurisdiction of Development Commissioners is given in Appendix 14-IK.

Importer-Exporter Code No.

(a) Allot Importer-Exporter code number for SEZ units and SEZ developer;

(b) Approve all matters relating to post-approval operation of the unit including import/ procurement of additional capital goods, increase in value of capital goods on account of foreign exchange rate fluctuations, enhancement of production capacity, broad banding/ diversification, change in name of the company or the implementing agency and change from a company to another, provided the new implementing agency/ company undertakes to take over the assets and liabilities of the existing unit and merger of two or more SEZ units;

(c) Cancel LOP/ LOI/IL wherever warranted;

(d) Adjudication under Section 13, read with Section 11 of Foreign Trade (Development & Regulation) Act, 1992 in respect of SEZ units;

(e) Action under the Public Premises Eviction Act in case the rent on the plot/built up premises allotted to the units is in arrears or if the plot/shed is not utilised for the purpose for which the same has been allotted;

(f) Valuation of exports declared on SOFTEX form by the units located in Special Economic Zones;

(g) Issuing eligibility certificates for grant of employment visa to low level foreign technicians to be engaged by SEZ units;

(h) Issue of Green Card after execution of Legal Undertaking by the unit;

(i) Import of second-hand capital goods without age restrictions;

(j) Grant/renew Status Holder Certificate in respect of SEZ units provided it does not involve clubbing of FOB value of exports of its parent company in the DTA.

Exit from SEZ Scheme

33.1 SEZ unit may opt out of the scheme schemewith the approval of the Development Commissioner. Such exit from the scheme shall be subject to payment of applicable Customs and Excise duties on the imported and indigenous capital goods, raw materials, etc. and finished goods in stock. In case the unit has not achieved positive NFE, the exit shall be subject to penalty, that may be imposed by the adjudicating authority under Foreign Trade (Development and Regulation) Act, 1992.

33.2 Broad conditions governing exit of units from the SEZ scheme are indicated at Appendix-L.

33.3 In the event of a gem and jewellery unit ceasing its operation, gold and other precious metals, alloys, gem and other materials available for manufacture of jewellery, shall be handed over to an agency nominated by the Ministry of Commerce and Industry (Department of Commerce) at the price to be determined by that agency.

33.4 SEZ unit may also be permitted by the Development Commissioner, as one time option, to exit from SEZ scheme on payment of duty on capital goods under the prevailing EPCG Scheme, subject to the unit satisfying the eligibility criteria of that Scheme and standard conditions, as per paragraph above.

Depreciation norms for Capital Goods

33.5 The depreciation upto 100% is permissible for capital goods in 5 years in case of IT items, and 10 years in case of other items, or duty is to be worked out on transaction value, whichever is higher as per the norms notified by the Department of Revenue.

33.6 Depreciation for computers and computer peripherals for all SEZ units and for capitals goods of IT hardware/electronic units shall be as follows:

10 % for every quarter in the first year;

8 % for every quarter in the 2nd year;

7 % for every quarter in the 3rd year.

33.7 For capital goods, other than the above, the depreciation rate would be as follows:

4% for every quarter in the first year;

3% for every quarter in the second year;

2.5% for every quarter in the third year.

33.8 Clearance of capital goods imported as second-hand shall be allowed as per the Policy under EPCG Scheme. In respect of second-hand capital goods which are less than 10 years old on the date of import, clearance in the DTA may be allowed, on payment of applicable duties, after 2 years from the date of import. In addition, where the second hand capital goods are more than 10 years old, clearance in the DTA may be allowed only against an import license and payment of applicable duties.

Revival of Sick Units 34. Subject to a unit being declared sick by the appropriate authority, proposals for revival of the unit or its takeover may be considered by the Board of Approval as per guidelines in Appendix 14-IM.

APPENDIX-14-II.N

(GUIDELINES FOR SEZ DEVELOPERS)

(TO BE PUBLISHED IN PART II SECTION 3(ii) OF THE GAZETTE OF INDIA EXTRAORDINARY)

Ministry of Commerce & industry,
Department of Commerce,
EPZ Section

S.O No. In excise of the power conferred under Section 80 IA of the Income Tax Act, 1961, read with sub rule (2) of rule 18 C of the Income Tax Rules, 1962, the Central Government hereby makes the following scheme to develop, operate and maintain Special Economic Zones for the period beginning on the 1st day of April, 2001 for the Zones developed on or before 31.3.2006.

1. Objectives of the Scheme

(a) The scheme shall aim at development of integrated world class infrastructure for exports including carrying out manufacture of goods, rendering of services or in connection therewith and would include industrial, commercial and social infrastructure. Components of a Special Economic Zone shall include roads, airports, ports, transport system, generation and distribution of power, telecom, hospitals, hotels, educational institutions, leisure and entertainment units, residential/industrial/commercial complexes, water supply, sanitation and sewerage system and any other facility required for development of the Zone.

(b) Special Economic Zones may be developed and managed in the private sector or jointly by State

Government and a private agency or exclusively by the State Government or their agencies. In the case of privately developed Zones, the investors could be either Indian individuals, NRIs, Indian or foreign companies.

(c) New infrastructural development works such as construction of Standard Design Factory Building, etc. and operation and maintenance of infrastructure in the Zones may also be undertaken through private/joint/State sector in the Export Processing Zones converted into Special Economic Zones.

2. Criteria for approval

Proposals for setting up SEZ in the public/private/joint/State sector are required to meet the following conditions:

(i) Minimum size of the SEZ shall not be less than 1000 hectares. This would however, not apply to existing EPZs converting into SEZs as such or for notifying additional area as a part of such SEZ or to product specific SEZs or port/airport-based SEZs on a case-to-case basis.

(ii) The SEZ and units therein shall abide by local laws, rules, regulations or bye-laws in regard to area planning, sewerage disposal, pollution control and the like. They shall also comply with industrial and labour laws and such other laws/rules and regulations as may be locally applicable.

(iii) Such SEZ shall make adequate arrangements to fulfil all the requirements of the laws, rules and procedures applicable to such SEZ.

(iv) Only units approved under the SEZ Scheme would be permitted to be located in these SEZ. At least 25% area of the SEZ shall be used for developing industrial area for setting up of such units.

(v) The predominant objective of development of a SEZ would be to create infrastructure, which would facilitate setting up of industrial area for units therein as indicated in the para (iv) above.

3. Procedure for Approval

3.1 Applications (10 copies) indicating the name and address of the applicant, status of the promoter (whether individual/ private company/State Government/NRIs, etc.) along with a project report covering the following particulars shall be submitted to the Chief Secretary of the State:

(i) Location of the proposed Zone with details of existing and proposed infrastructure;

(ii) Area of the proposed SEZ and its aerial distance from the nearest Sea Port/Airport/Rail/Road head, etc.;

(iii) Financial details including investment proposed, mode of financing the project and viability of the project;

(iv) Details of foreign equity and repatriation of dividends, etc., if any;

(v) Whether the Zone will allow only certain specific industries or will be a multi-product Zone.

3.2 The State Government shall forward it along with their commitment to the following, to the Department of Commerce, Government of India:

(i) The area incorporated in the proposed Special Economic Zone is free from environmental prohibition;

(ii) Water, Electricity and other services would be provided as required;

(iii) Full exemption in electricity duty and tax on sale of electricity for self generated and purchased power;

(iv) To allow generation, transmission and distribution of power within SEZ;

(v) Exemption from State Sales Tax, octroi, mandi tax, turnover tax and taxes, duty, cess, levies on supply of goods from Domestic Tariff Area to SEZ units;

(vi) For units inside the Zone, the powers under the Industrial Disputes Act and other related Acts would be delegated to the Development Commissioner;

(vii) The Zone will be declared as a Public Utility Service under Industrial Disputes Act;

(viii) Single point clearances system would be provided to the units in the Zone under State Laws/Rules.

3.3 The Government may grant of in-principle approval to proposals for setting up of SEZs. The in-principle approval shall be valid for a period of 1 year. The validly period may be extended by the Department of Commerce on a case-to-case basis.

3.4 On acceptance of the proposal by the BOA, the Department of Commerce will issue a Letter of Permission to the applicant, hereafter referred to as "developer".

3.5 On acceptance of the proposal by the BOA, the Department of Commerce will issue a Letter of Permission to the applicant; hereafter referred to as "developer". The approval shall be valid for a period of 3 years within which time effective steps shall be taken by the developer to implement the project. The validly period may be extended by the Department of Commerce on a case-to-case basis. Provided that commercial, residential and recreational facilities shall be approved only if the applicant has at least 26% equity in such entities.

3.6 In case of converted EPZ into SEZ approval for development, operation and maintenance of requirements in infrastructure will have to be obtained from BOA on case to case basis. Para 3.5 shall *mutatis mutandis* apply to creation of new infrastructure in the converted SEZs.

4. General Conditions

(i) The undertaking applying for approval shall undertake to continue to operate under the SEZ Scheme during the period in which benefits under Section 80 IA of the Income Tax Act are to be availed.

(ii) The Central Government may withdraw the approval given to an undertaking for setting up of SEZ if the undertaking fails to comply with any of the conditions of approval.

5. Agreement with Central Government

The Letter of Permission issued by the Government of India (Department of Commerce) to the developer for setting up of Special Economic Zone shall be treated as 'Agreement' for availing exemption under Section 80-IA of the Income Tax Act.

New Delhi (D.K. Mittal)
Dated: 24.1.2002 Joint Secretary
No F. 2 (1)/3/2001-EPZ

APPENDIX-14-II.O

(FORMAT FOR LETTER OF PERMISSION FOR SEZ DEVELOPER)
Government of India
Ministry of Commerce & Industry
Department of Commerce
(EPZ Section)

To

Dated.............

Sir,

Subject: Proposal for setting up of Special Economic Zone at______________

1. The undersigned is directed to refer to your proposal for setting up of SEZ at _________ and to convey the approval of the Government of India to your proposal, the details of which are noted below:

(i) PROPOSAL: To set up a Special Economic Zone at————

(ii) PROMOTER:

(iii) PROJECT DETAILS:

2. General conditions:

(i) At least 25% (now 50%) of the SEZ's area shall be used for developing industrial area for setting up of units. Layout of the SEZ shall clearly delineate the industrial areas.

(ii) It would be the responsibility of the developer to obtain required approval from various statutory authorities under relevant statutes and regulation of the Government of India and the State Government.

(iii) Adequate provision for rehabilitation of the displaced persons will be made by the developer.

(iv) The State Government shall issue requisite notification giving effect to the policy announced by the State Government and shall enact a SEZ Act.

(v) The project shall be implemented and operated in terms of the parameters laid down by the Ministry of Commerce & Industry.

(vi) Units in SEZ shall be governed by the provisions of the SEZ Scheme in force and will abide by local laws, rules, regulations or bye-laws in regards to area planning, sewerage disposal, pollution control, labour laws and the like as may be locally applicable.

(vii) The funds required for the project will be fully raised by the developer. The external borrowing, if any, will be as per the guidelines of the Ministry of Finance, Department of Economic Affairs, North Block, New Delhi.

(viii) The approval is valid for a period of 3 years within which time effective steps shall be taken to implement the project. The validity period may be extended by the Board of Approvals on merits.

(ix) This approval is liable to be withdrawn on infringement of any of the terms and conditions stipulated herein.

(x) The operation and maintenance of the facility will be made as per the standards specified in the proposal and to the satisfaction of the users.

(xi) The promoter shall maintain adequate manpower to provide the facility.

(xii) The user charges will be finalised in consultation with the Zone administration and the users. This shall be subject to revision as per the agreed terms.

(xiii) The operation and maintenance of the facility shall be undertaken as per the proposal.

(xiv) The approval will be subject to cancellation in case of defective service or if the service is not up to the minimum standard specified.

3. Kindly convey your acceptance of all the terms and conditions indicated above within 30 days from the date of issue of this letter.

4. All future correspondence may be addressed to the Deputy Secretary/Director (EPZ/EOU), Department of Commerce, Udyog Bhavan, New Delhi-11.

5. You are requested to send exact details of the area for issue of notification of the same and also keep the Department of Commerce and Development Commissioner,________ informed about the progress made in the matter from time to time.

Yours faithfully,

Director

APPENDIX-14-II.P

(FORMAT FOR LETTER OF PERMISSION FOR OPERATION AND MAINTENANCE OF INFRASTRUCTURE FACILITIES IN SEZ)

Government of India
Ministry of Commerce & Industry
Department of Commerce
(EPZ Section)

To

Dated................

Sir,

Subject: Proposal for operation and maintenance of infrastructure facilities in Special Economic Zone at____

1. The undersigned is directed to refer to your proposal for operation and maintenance of infrastructure facilities in SEZ at __________ and to convey the approval of the Government of India to your proposal, the details of which are noted below:

(i) PROPOSAL: Operation and maintenance of...facility.

(ii) PROMOTER:

(iii) PROJECT DETAILS:

2. General conditions:

(i) The operation and maintenance of the facility will be made as per the standards specified in the proposal and to the satisfaction of the users.

(ii) It would be the responsibility of the developer to obtain required approval from various statutory authorities under relevant statutes and regulations of the Government of India and the State Government.

(iii) The promoter shall maintain adequate manpower to provide the facility.

(iv) The user charges will be finalised in consultation with the Zone administration and the users. This shall be subject to revision as per the agreed terms.

(v) The operation and maintenance of the facility shall be undertaken as per the proposal.

(vi) The approval will be subject to cancellation in case of defective service or if the service is not up to the minimum standard specified.

(vii) The funds required for the project will be fully raised by the promoter. The external borrowing, if any, will be as per the guidelines of the Ministry of Finance, Department of Economic Affairs, North Block, New Delhi.

(viii) The approval is valid for a period of 3 years within which time effective steps shall be taken to implement the project. The validity period may be extended by the Board of Approvals on merits.

(ix) This approval is liable to be withdrawn on infringement of any of the terms and conditions stipulated herein.

3. Kindly convey your acceptance of all the terms and conditions indicated above within 30 days from the date of issue of this letter.

4. All future correspondence may be addressed to the Deputy Secretary/Director (EPZ/EOU), Department of Commerce, Udyog Bhavan, New Delhi-11.

5. You are requested to send exact details of the area for issue of notification of the same and also keep the Department of Commerce and Development Commissioner, _______ informed about the progress made in the matter from time to time.

Yours faithfully,

Director

APPENDIX-14-II.Q

(ZONE DEVELOPMENT BOARD)

TO BE PUBLISHED IN THE GAZETTE OF INDIA EXTRAORDINARY, (PART I SECTION 1)

Government of India
Ministry of Commerce and Industry
(Department of Commerce)
New Delhi the 18th February, 2003

NOTIFICATION

No.F.2(1)/19/2002-EPZ:

1. The Government of India hereby constitutes a Special Economic Zone Development Board, (hereinafter called "Zone Development Board") for each of the Special Economic Zone consisting of the following members:

(1)	The Development Commissioner of the Zone.	Chairperson
(2)	Deputy/Assistant Commissioner of Customs posted in the Zone	Member
(3)	Two officials nominated by the State Government concerned	Members
(4)	A nominee of the developer	Member

The Zonal Board may co-opt any other department or agency and representatives from interested groups such as Units, residents within the Zone, as special invitees, as it deems fit, for any specific purpose.

Powers and functions of the Zone Development Board

2. To secure the development of the Special Economic Zone, the powers and functions of the Board shall be as under:

(a) to approve import or domestic procurement of goods and services for development, operation and maintenance of infrastructure in the Zone without payment of duty or tax;

(b) to monitor utilisation of materials imported/procured as per (a) above;

(c) to co-ordinate with other departments and other agencies for the smooth implementation of the projects;

(d) functions as may be delegated by the State Government or its agencies;

(e) any other function as may be notified by the Central Government.

The Development Commissioner shall exercise such powers and perform such duties as may be delegated to him by the Central Government or the State Government.

Joint Secretary

APPENDIX-14-II.R

(UNIT APPROVAL COMMITTEE)
TO BE PUBLISHED IN THE GAZETTE OF INDIA
EXTRAORDINARY, (PART I SECTION 1)

Government of India
Ministry of Commerce and Industry
(Department of Commerce)
New Delhi the 18th February, 2003

NOTIFICATION

NO.F.2(1)/19/2002-EPZ: The Government of India hereby constitutes a Unit Approval Committee for each of the Special Economic Zone consisting of the following members:

(1) Development Commissioner	Chairperson
(2) Officers of the Central Government nominated by it not	Members

exceeding two (from amongst the officers posted in the Zone)	
(3) Officers of the State Government nominated by it not exceeding two (from amongst the officers posted in the Zone)	Members
(4) The nominee of the Developer	Member

The Development Commissioner may co-opt nominees of any Department, agency, and interested group as special invitees as he deems fit.

Powers and functions of the Unit Approval Committee

The powers and functions of the Unit Approval Committee shall be as under:

(a) to consider applications for setting up of Units in Zone and grant or refuse approval;

(b) to monitor the performance of the Units and take action against the Units wherever necessary as prescribed under the rules;

(c) to take appropriate action in case of violation of the conditions of the approval;

(d) to supervise and monitor permission, clearances, licenses granted to the Units and take appropriate action in accordance with law;

(e) to call for information required to monitor the performance of the Unit under the permission, clearances, licenses granted to it;

(f) to perform any other function delegated by the Central Government or its agencies;

(g) to perform any other function as may be delegated by the State Governments or its agencies;

(h) to grant all approvals and clearances for the establishment and operation of Units in the Special Economic Zone;

(i) the Central Government and its agencies may delegate their powers to the Unit Approval Committee under the relevant laws so as to enable the Committee.

(a) to prescribe common application form for any license, permission or registration under one or more laws;

(b) to authorize Development Commissioner to exercise the powers of the Central Government or its agencies;

(c) to notify an officer or agency, including accredited private agencies for carrying out inspections under various laws;

(d) to exempt the Zone from one or more provisions of any Central Law;

(e) to prescribe single return for reporting under two or more Central Laws.

Joint Secretary

Foreign Trade Policy (2004-09) Related to Special Economic Zones

6

Special Economic Zones (SEZ) are growth engines that can boost manufacturing, augment exports and generate employment. The private sector has been actively associated with the development of SEZs. The SEZs require special fiscal and regulatory regime in order to impart a hassle-free operational regime encompassing the state-of-the-art infrastructure and support services. The proposed legislation on SEZs to be enacted in the near future would cover the concepts of the developer and co-developer, incorporate the provision of virtual SEZs, have fiscal concessions under the Income Tax and Customs Act, provide for Offshore Banking Units (OBUs), etc. A brief on the facilities available under the SEZ scheme is given as under:

Eligibility

7.1 (a) Special Economic Zone (SEZ) is a specifically delineated duty free enclave and shall be deemed to be foreign territory for the purposes of trade operations and duties and tariffs.

(b) Goods and services going into the SEZ area from DTA shall be treated as exports and goods coming from the SEZ area into DTA shall be treated as if these are being imported.

(c) SEZ units may be set up for manufacture of goods and rendering of services.

Export and Import of Goods

7.2 (a) SEZ units may export goods and services including agro-products, partly processed goods, sub-assemblies and components except prohibited items of exports in ITC (HS). The units may also export by-products, rejects, waste scrap arising out of the production process. Export of Special Chemicals, Organisms, Materials, Equipment and Technologies (SCOMET) shall be subject to fulfillment of the conditions indicated in the ITC (HS) Classification of Export and Import Items.

SEZ units, other than trading/service unit, may also export to Russian Federation in Indian Rupees against repayment of State Credit/Escrow Rupee Account of the buyer, subject to RBI clearance, if any.

(b) SEZ unit may import/procure from the DTA without payment of duty all types of goods and services, including capital goods, whether new or second-hand, required by it for its activities or in connection therewith, provided they are not prohibited items of imports in the ITC(HS). However, any permission required for import under any other law shall be applicable. Goods shall include raw material for making capital goods for use within the unit. The units shall also be permitted to import goods required for the approved activity, including capital goods, free of cost or on loan from clients.

(c) SEZ units may procure goods required by it without payment of duty, from bonded warehouses in the DTA set up under the Policy and/or under Section 65 of the Customs Act and from International Exhibitions held in India.

(d) SEZ units, may import/procure from DTA, without payment of duty, all types of goods for creating a central facility for use by units in SEZ. The Central facility for software development can also be accessed by units in the DTA for export of software.

(e) Gems & Jewellery units may also source gold/silver/ platinum through the nominated agencies.

(f) SEZ units may import/procure goods and services from DTA without payment of duty for setting up, operation and maintenance of units in the Zone.

Leasing of Capital Goods

7.3 SEZ unit may, on the basis of a firm contract between the parties, source the capital goods from a domestic/foreign leasing company. In such a case the SEZ unit and the domestic/foreign leasing company shall jointly file the documents to enable import/procurement of the capital goods without payment of duty.

Net Foreign Exchange Earning (NFE)

7.4 SEZ unit shall be a positive Net Foreign Exchange earner. Net Foreign Exchange Earning (NFE) shall be calculated cumulatively for a period of five years from the commencement of production according to the formula given in Appendix-4-II of the *Handbook* (Vol. I).

Monitoring of Performance

7.5 (a) The performance of SEZ units shall be monitored by the Unit Approval Committee.

(b) The performance of SEZ units shall be monitored as per the guidelines given in Appendix 14-II of Handbook (Vol-I).

Legal Undertaking

7.6 The unit shall execute a legal undertaking with the Development Commissioner concerned and in the event of failure to achieve positive foreign exchange earning it shall be liable to penalty in terms of the legal undertaking or under any other law for the time being in force.

Approvals and Applications

7.7 (a) Applications for setting up a unit in SEZ other than proposals for setting up of unit in the services sector (except software and IT enabled services, trading or any other service activity as may be delegated by the BOA), shall be approved or rejected by the Unit Approval Committee within 15 days as per procedure indicated in Annexure to Appendix 14-II of Handbook (Vol. I). In other cases approval may be granted by the Board of Approval.

(b) Proposals for setting up units in SEZ requiring Industrial Licence may be granted approval by the Development Commissioner after clearance of the proposal by the SEZ Board of Approval and Department of Industrial Policy and Promotion within 45 days on merits.

DTA Sales and Supplies

7.8 (a) SEZ unit may sell goods, including by-products, and services in DTA in accordance with the import policy in force, on payment of applicable duty.

(b) DTA sale by service/trading unit shall be subject to achievement of positive NFE cumulatively. Similarly for units undertaking manufacturing and services/ trading activities against a single LOP, DTA sale shall be subject to achievement of NFE cumulatively.

(c) The following supplies effected in DTA by SEZ units will be counted for the purpose of fulfilment of positive NFE:

(i) Supplies effected in DTA in terms of Chapter 8 of the Policy.

(ii) Supplies made to bonded warehouses set up under the Policy and/or under Section 65 of the Customs Act.

(iii) Supplies to other EOU/SEZ/EHTP/STP units provided that such goods are permissible for procurement by units.

(iv) Supplies against special entitlement of duty free import of goods.

(v) Supplies of goods and services to such organizations which are entitled for duty-free import of such items in terms of general exemption notification issued by the Ministry of Finance.

(vi) Supply of services (by services units) relating to exports paid for in free foreign exchange or for such services rendered in Indian Rupees which are otherwise considered as having been paid for in free foreign exchange by RBI.

(vii) Supplies of Information Technology Agreement (ITA-1) items and notified zero duty telecom/electronic items indicated in the Appendix 14-II of Handbook.

Entitlement for Supplies from the DTA

7.9 Supplies from DTA to SEZ shall be entitled for the following:

(a) DTA supplier shall be entitled for:
   (i) Drawback
   or
   DEPB in lieu of Drawback
   (ii) Discharge of Export performance, if any, on the supplier.
(b) SEZ units shall be entitled for:
   (i) Exemption from Central Sales Tax;
   (ii) Exemption from payment of Central Excise Duty on all goods eligible for procurement by the unit.
   (iii) Reimbursement of Central Excise Duty, paid on bulk tea procured from the licensed auction centres by the Development Commissioner of concerned zone as long as levy on bulk tea in this regard is in force.
   (iv) Reimbursement of Duty paid on fuels or any other goods procured from DTA as per the rate of drawback notified by the Directorate General of Foreign Trade from the date of such notification.
(c) Supplier of precious and semi-precious stones, synthetic stones and processed pearls from Domestic Tariff Area to the units situated in SEZ shall be eligible for grant of Replenishment Licenses at the rates and for the items mentioned in the Handbook (Vol. I).
(d) The entitlements under paragraphs (a) and (b) (ii) above shall be available provided the goods supplied are manufactured in India.

Export through Status Holder

7.10 SEZ unit may also export goods manufactured/software developed by it through a merchant exporter/status holder recognized under this Policy or any other EOU/SEZ/EHTP/STP unit.

Inter-unit Transfer

7.11 (a) SEZ units may transfer manufactured goods, including partly processed/semi-finished goods and services from one SEZ unit to another SEZ/EOU/ EHTP/STP unit.

(b) Goods imported/procured by an SEZ unit may be transferred or given on loan to another unit within the same SEZ which shall be duly accounted for, but not counted towards discharge of export performance.

(c) Capital goods imported/procured may be transferred or given on loan to another SEZ/EOU/ EHTP/ STP unit with prior permission of the Development Commissioner and Customs authorities concerned.

(d) Transfer of goods in terms of sub-paras (a) and (b) above within the same SEZ shall not require any permission but the units shall maintain proper accounts of the transaction.

Other Entitlements

Other entitlements of SEZ units are indicated in the Appendix 14-II of the Handbook (Vol. 1).

Sub-contracting

7.12 (a) SEZ unit, may sub-contract a part of their production or production process through units in the DTA or through other SEZ/EOU/ EHTP/ STP, with the annual permission of Customs authorities. Sub-contracting of part of production process may also be permitted abroad with the approval of the Development Commissioner.

(b) Sub-contracting by SEZ gems and jewellery units through other SEZ units or EOUs or units in DTA shall be subject to following conditions:

(i) Goods, finished or semi-finished, including studded jewellery, taken outside the zone for sub-contracting shall be brought back to the unit within 30 days. No cut and polished diamonds, precious and semi-precious stones (except precious and semi-precious stones having zero duty) shall be allowed to be taken outside the zone for sub-contracting.

(ii) Receive plain gold/silver/platinum jewellery from DTA in exchange of equivalent quantity of gold/silver/platinum, as the case may be, contained in the said jewellery.

(iii) SEZ units shall be eligible for wastage as applicable for sub-contracting and against exchange.

(iv) The DTA unit undertaking job work or supplying jewellery against exchange of gold/silver/platinum shall not be entitled to export benefits.

(c) All units, including gem and jewellery, may sub-contract part of the production or production process through other units in the same SEZ without permission of Customs authorities subject to records being maintained by both the supplying and receiving units.

(d) SEZ units other than gem and jewellery units may be allowed to undertake job-work for export, on behalf of DTA exporter, provided the finished goods are exported directly from SEZ units. For such exports, the DTA units will be entitled for refund of duty paid on the inputs by way of Brand Rate of duty drawback.

(e) Scrap/waste/remnants generated through job work may either be cleared from the job worker's premises on payment of applicable duty or returned to the unit.

(f) SEZ units engaged in production/processing of agriculture/horticulture products, may on the basis of annual permission from the Customs authorities take out inputs and equipments to the DTA farm subject to the procedure indicated in Appendix 14-II of the Handbook (Vol. I).

Exit from SEZ Scheme

7.13 (a) SEZ unit may opt out of the scheme with the approval of the Development Commissioner. Such exit from the scheme shall be subject to payment of applicable Customs and Excise duties on the imported and indigenous capital goods, raw materials, etc. and finished goods in stock. In case the unit has not achieved positive NFE, the exit shall be subject to penalty, that may be imposed by the adjudicating authority under Foreign Trade (Development and Regulation) Act, 1992.

(b) SEZ unit may also be permitted by the Development Commissioner, as one time option, to exit from SEZ scheme on payment of duty on capital goods under the prevailing EPCG Scheme, subject to the unit satisfying the eligibility criteria of that Scheme and standard conditions for exit indicated in Appendix 14-II of Handbook (Vol. I).

Export through Exhibitions/Export PromotionTours/Export through Showrooms Abroad/Duty Free Shops

7.14 SEZ, units may:

(i) Export goods for holding/participating in exhibitions abroad with the permission of Development Commissioner.

(ii) Personal carriage of gold/ silver/ platinum jewellery, precious, semi-precious stones, beads and articles.

(iii) Export of jewellery is also permitted for display/ sale in the permitted shops set up abroad.

(iv) Display/sell in the permitted shops set up abroad or in the show rooms of their distributors/agents.

(v) Set up show rooms/retail outlets at the International Airports.

Personal Carriage of Export/Import Parcel

7.15 Import/export through personal carriage of gem and jewellery items may be undertaken as per the procedure prescribed by Customs. Import/export through personal carriage for units, other than gem and jewellery unit, shall be allowed provided the goods are not in commercial quantity.

Export/Import by Post/Courier

7.16 Goods including free samples, may be exported/imported by airfreight or through Foreign Post Office or through courier, subject to the procedure prescribed by Customs.

Disposal of Rejects/Scrap/Waste/Remnants

7.17 Rejects/scrap/waste/remnants arising out of production process or in connection therewith may be sold in the DTA on payment of applicable duty. No duty shall be payable in case scrap/waste/remnants/rejects are destroyed within the Zone after intimation to the Custom authorities or destroyed outside the SEZ with the permission of Custom authorities. Destruction as stated above shall not apply to gold, silver, platinum, diamond, precious and semi-precious stones.

Replacement/Repair of Goods

7.18 (a) The general provisions of Policy relating to export of replacement/repaired goods shall apply equally to SEZ units, save that, cases not covered by these provisions shall be considered on merits by the Development Commissioner.

(b) The goods sold in the DTA and found to be defective may be brought back for repair/ replacement under intimation to Development Commissioner.

(c) Goods or parts thereof, including gem stones and precious metal components for jewellery-making, on being imported/ indigenously procured and found defective or otherwise unfit for use or which have been damaged or become defective after import/ procurement may be returned and replacement obtained or destroyed. In the event of replacement, the goods may be brought back from the foreign suppliers or their authorised agents in India or the indigenous suppliers. Destruction shall however not apply to gem stones and precious metals.

(d) Goods may be transferred to DTA/abroad for repair/ replacement, testing or calibration, quality testing and R & D purpose under intimation to Customs authorities and subject to maintenance of records.

Management of SEZ

7.19 (a) SEZ will be under the administrative control of the Development Commissioner.

(b) All activities of SEZ units within the Zone, unless otherwise specified, including export and re-import of goods shall be through self-certification procedure.

Setting up of SEZ in Private/Joint/State Sector

7.20 An SEZ may be set up in the public, private, joint sector or by State Government as per details indicated in Appendix 14-II of the *Handbook of Procedures* (Vol. I).

Samples

7.21 SEZ units may, on the basis of records maintained by them, and on prior intimation to Customs authorities:

(i) supply or sell samples in the DTA for display/ market promotion on payment of applicable duties;

(ii) Remove samples without payment of duty, on furnishing a suitable undertaking to Customs authorities for bringing the goods back within a stipulated period;

(iii) Export free samples, without any limit, including samples made in wax moulds, silver mould and rubber moulds through all permissible modes of export including through couriers agencies/post.

Sale of Un-utilised Material/Obsolete goods

7.22 (a) In case an SEZ unit is unable, for valid reasons, to utilize the goods, including capital goods and spares, it may dispose them in the DTA in accordance with the import policy in force and on payment of applicable duties or export them.

(b) Capital goods and spares that have become obsolete/ surplus may either be exported or disposed of in the DTA on payment of applicable duties. The benefit of depreciation, as applicable, will be available in case of disposal in DTA.

(c) No duty shall be payable in case capital goods, raw material, consumables, spares, goods manufactured, processed or packaged and scrap/waste/remnants/rejects are destroyed within the Zone after intimation to the Custom authorities or destroyed outside the Zone with the permission of Custom authorities. However, destruction shall not apply to precious and semi-precious and precious metals

(d) SEZ unit may be allowed by Customs authorities concerned to donate imported/indigenously procured computer and computer peripherals without payment of duty, two years after their import/procurement and use by the units, to recognized non-commercial educational institutions, registered charitable hospitals, etc. as per the details given in Appendix 14-II in Handbook (Vol. I).

Entitlement for SEZ Developer

7.23 For development, operation and maintenance of infrastructure facilities in SEZs, the developer shall be eligible for the following entitlements:

(a) Income tax exemption as per 80 IA of the Income Tax Act.

(b) Import/procure goods without payment of Customs/ Excise duty.

(c) Exemption from Service tax.

(d) Exemption from CST.

The Special Economic Zones Act, 2005

7

An Act to provide for the establishment, development and management of the Special Economic Zones for the promotion of exports and for matters connected therewith or incidental thereto.

Be it enacted by Parliament in the Fifty-sixth Year of the Republic of India as follows:

CHAPTER I
PRELIMINARY

1. (*1*) This Act may be called the Special Economic Zones Act, 2005.

(*2*) It extends to the whole of India.

(*3*) It shall come into force on such date as the Central Government may, by notification in the Official Gazette, appoint, and different dates may be appointed for different provisions of this Act and any reference in any such provision to the commencement of this Act shall be construed as a reference to the coming into force of that provision.

2. In this Act, unless the context otherwise requires,

(*a*) "appointed day" with reference to a Special Economic Zone means the date on which the Special Economic Zone is notified by the Central Government under sub-section (*1*) of section 4;

(*b*) "Approval Committee" means an Approval Committee constituted under sub-section (*1*) of section 13;

(*c*) "authorised operations" means operations which may be authorised under sub-section (*2*) of section 4 and sub-section (*9*) of section 15;

(*d*) "Authority" means a Special Economic Zone Authority constituted under sub-section (*1*) of section 31;

(*e*) "Board" means the Board of Approvals constituted under sub-section (*1*) of section 8;

(*f*) "Co-Developer" means a person who, or a State Government which, has been granted by the Central Government a Letter of Approval under sub-section (*12*) of section 3;

(*g*) "Developer" means a person who, or a State Government which, has been granted by the Central Government a Letter of Approval under sub-section (*10*) of section 3 and includes an Authority and a Co-Developer;

(*h*) "Development Commissioner" means the Development Commissioner appointed for one or more Special Economic Zones under sub-section (*1*) of section 11;

(*i*) "Domestic Tariff Area" means the whole of India (including the territorial waters and continental shelf) but does not include the areas of the Special Economic Zones;

(*j*) "entrepreneur" means a person who has been granted a letter of approval by the Development Commissioner under sub-section (*9*) of section 15;

(*k*) "existing Special Economic Zone" means every Special Economic Zone which is in existence on or before the commencement of this Act;

(*l*) "existing unit" means every Unit which has been set up on or before the commencement of this Act;

(*m*) "export" means:

(*i*) taking goods, or providing services, out of India, from a Special Economic Zone, by land, sea or air or by any other mode, whether physical or otherwise; or

(*ii*) supplying goods, or providing services, from the Domestic Tariff Area to a Unit or Developer; or

(*iii*) supplying goods, or providing services, from one Unit to another Unit or Developer, in the same or different Special Economic Zone;

(*n*) "Free Trade and Warehousing Zone" means a Special Economic Zone wherein mainly trading and warehousing and other activities related thereto are carried on;

(*o*) "import" means:

(*i*) bringing goods or receiving services, in a Special Economic Zone, by a Unit or Developer from a place outside India by land, sea or air or by any other mode, whether physical or otherwise; or

(*ii*) receiving goods, or services by, Unit or Developer from another Unit or Developer of the same Special Economic Zone or a different Special Economic Zone;

(*p*) "infrastructure facilities" means industrial, commercial or social infrastructure or other facilities necessary for the development of a Special Economic Zone or such other facilities which may be prescribed;

(*q*) "International Financial Services Centre" means an International Financial Services Centre which has been approved by the Central Government under sub-section (*1*) of section 18;

(*r*) "manufacture" means to make, produce, fabricate, assemble, process or bring into existence, by hand or by machine, a new product having a distinctive name, character or use and shall include processes such as refrigeration, cutting, polishing, blending, repairing, remaking, re-engineering and includes agriculture, aquaculture, animal husbandry, floriculture, horticulture, pisciculture, poultry, sericulture, viticulture and mining;

(*s*) "notification" means a notification published in the Official Gazette and the expression "notify" shall be construed accordingly;

(*t*) "notified offences" means the offences specified as such under sub-section (*1*) of section 21;

(*u*) "Offshore Banking Unit" means a branch of a bank located in a Special Economic Zone and which has obtained the permission under clause (*a*) of sub-section (*1*) of section 23 of the Banking Regulation Act, 1949;

(*v*) "person" includes an individual, whether resident in India or outside India, a Hindu undivided family, co-operative society, a company, whether incorporated in India or outside India, a firm, proprietary concern, or an association of persons or body of individuals, whether incorporated or not, local authority and any agency, office or branch owned or controlled by such individual, Hindu undivided family, co-operative, association, body, authority or company;

(*w*) "prescribed" means prescribed by the rules made by the Central Government under this Act;

(*x*) "Reserve Bank" means the Reserve Bank of India constituted under section 3 of the Reserve Bank of India Act, 1934;

(*y*) "Schedule" means Schedules to this Act;

(*z*) "services" means such tradable services which:

(*i*) are covered under the General Agreement on Trade in Services annexed as IB to the Agreement establishing the World Trade Organisation concluded at Marrakes on the 15th day of April, 1994;

(*ii*) may be prescribed by the Central Government for the purposes of this Act; and

(*iii*) earn foreign exchange;

(*za*) "Special Economic Zone" means each Special Economic Zone notified under the proviso to sub-section (*4*) of section 3 and sub-section (*1*) of section 4 (including Free Trade and Warehousing Zone) and includes an existing Special Economic Zone;

(*zb*) "State Government" means a State Government of the State in which a Special Economic Zone is established or proposed to be established;

(*zc*) "Unit" means a Unit set up by an entrepreneur in a Special Economic Zone and includes an existing Unit, an Offshore Banking Unit and a Unit in an International Financial Services Centre, whether established before or established after commencement of this Act;

(*zd*) all other words and expressions used and not defined in this Act but defined in the Central Excise Act, 1944, the Industries (Development and Regulation) Act, 1951, the Income Tax Act, 1961, the Customs Act, 1962 and the Foreign Trade (Development and Regulation) Act, 1992 shall have the meanings respectively assigned to them in those Acts.

CHAPTER II

ESTABLISHMENT OF SPECIAL ECONOMIC ZONE

3. (*1*) A Special Economic Zone may be established under this Act, either jointly or severally by the Central Government, State Government, or any person for manufacture of goods or rendering services or for both or as a Free Trade and Warehousing Zone.

(*2*) Any person, who intends to set up a Special Economic Zone, may, after identifying the area, make a proposal to the State Government concerned for the purpose of setting up the Special Economic Zone.

(*3*) Notwithstanding anything contained in sub-section (*2*), any person, who intends to set up a Special Economic Zone, may, after identifying the area, at his option, make a proposal directly to the Board for the purpose of setting up the Special Economic Zone:

Provided that where such a proposal has been received directly from a person under sub-section, the Board may grant approval and after receipt of such approval, the person concerned shall obtain the concurrence of the State Government within the period, as may be prescribed.

(*4*) In case a State Government intends to set up a Special Economic Zone, it may after identifying the area, forward the proposal directly to the Board for the purpose of setting up the Special Economic Zone:

Provided that the Central Government may:

(*a*) after consulting the State Government concerned;

(*b*) without referring the proposal for setting up the Special Economic Zone to the Board; and

(*c*) after identifying the area;

suo moto set up and notify the Special Economic Zone

(*5*) Every proposal under sub-sections (*2*) to (*4*) shall be made in such form and manner containing such particulars as may be prescribed.

(6) The State Government may, on receipt of the proposal made under sub-section (*2*), forward the same together with its recommendations to the Board within such period as may be prescribed.

(*7*) Without prejudice to the provisions contained in sub-section (8), the Board may, after receipt of the proposal under sub-section (*2*) to (*4*), approve the proposal subject to such terms and conditions as it may deem fit to impose, or modify or reject the proposal.

(*8*) The Central Government may prescribe the following requirement for establishment of a Special Economic Zone, namely:

(a) the minimum area of land and other terms and conditions subject to which the Board shall approve, modify or reject any proposal received by it under sub-section (*2*) to (*4*); and

(b) the terms and conditions, subject to which the Developer shall undertake the authorised operations and his obligations and entitlements.

Provided that different minimum are of land and other terms and conditions referred to in clause (*a*) may be prescribed by the Central Government for a class or classes of Special Economic Zones.

(*9*) If the Board:

(*a*) approves without any modification, the proposal received under sub-section (2) to (*4*), it shall communicate the same to the Central Government;

(*b*) approves with modifications the proposal received under sub-section (2) to (*4*), it shall, communicate such modifications to the person or the State Government concerned and if such modifications have been accepted by such person or the State Government, the Board shall communicate the approval to the Central Government;

(*c*) rejects the proposal, received under sub-section (2) to (*4*), it shall record the reasons therefor and communicate the rejection to the Central Government which shall intimate to the State Government or the person concerned.

(*10*) The Central Government shall, on receipt of communication under clause (*a*) or clause (*b*) of sub-section (*9*), grant, within such time as may be prescribed, a letter of approval on such terms and conditions and obligations and entitlements as may be approved by the Board, to the Developer, being the person or the State Government concerned:

Provided that the Central Government may, on the basis of approval of the Board, approve more than one Developer in a Special Economic Zone in cases where one Developer does not have in his possession the minimum area of contiguous land, as may be prescribed, for setting up a Special Economic Zone and in such cases, each Developer shall be considered as a Developer in respect of the land in his possession.

(*11*) Any person who, or a State Government which intends to provide any infrastructure facilities in the identified area referred to in sub-section (*2*) to (*4*), or undertake any authorised operation may, after entering into an agreement with the Developer referred to in sub-section (*10*), make a proposal for the same to the Board for its approval and the provisions of sub-section (*5*) and sub-sections (*7*) to (*10*) shall, as far as may be, apply to the said proposal made by such person or State Government.

(*12*) Every person or a State Government referred to in sub-section (*11*), whose proposal has been approved by the Board and who, or which, has been granted the letter of approval by the Central Government, shall be considered as a Co-Developer of the Special Economic Zone.

(*13*) Subject to the provisions of this section and the letter of approval granted to a Developer, the Developer may allocate space or built up area or provide infrastructure services to the approved units in accordance with the agreement entered into by him with the entrepreneurs of such Units.

4. (*1*) The Developer shall, after the grant of letter of approval under sub-section (*10*) of section 3, submit the exact particulars of the identified area referred to in sub-section (*2*) to (*4*) of that section, to the Central Government and thereupon that Government may, after satisfying that the requirements, under sub-section (*8*) of section 3 and other requirements, as may be prescribed, are fulfilled, notify the specifically identified area in the State as a Special Economic Zone:

Provided that an existing Special Economic Zone shall be deemed to have been notified and established in accordance with the provisions of this Act and the provisions of this Act shall, as far as may be, apply to such Zone accordingly:

Provided further that the Central Government may, after notifying the Special Economic Zone, if it considers appropriate, notify subsequently any additional area to be included as a part of that Special Economic Zone.

(2) After the appointed day, the Board may, authorise the Developer to undertake in a Special Economic Zone, such operations which the Central Government may authorise.

5. (*1*) The Central Government, while notifying any area as a Special Economic Zone or an additional area to be included in the Special Economic Zone and discharging its functions under this Act, shall be guided by the following, namely:

(*a*) generation of additional economic activity;

(*b*) promotion of exports of goods and services;

(*c*) promotion of investment from domestic and foreign sources;

(*d*) creation of employment opportunities;

(*e*) development of infrastructure facilities; and

(*f*) maintenance of sovereignty and integrity of India, the security of the State and friendly relations with foreign States.

6. The areas falling within the Special Economic Zones may be demarcated by the Central Government or any authority specified by it as:

(*a*) the processing area for setting up Units for activities, being the manufacture of goods, or rendering services; or

(*b*) the area exclusively for trading or warehousing purposes; or

(*c*) the non-processing areas for activities other than those specified under clause (*a*) or clause (*b*).

7. Any goods or services exported out of, or imported into, or procured from the Domestic Tariff Area by:

(*i*) a Unit in a Special Economic Zone; or

(*ii*) a Developer;

shall, subject to such terms, conditions and limitations, as may be prescribed, be exempt from the payment of taxes, duties or cess under all enactments specified in the First Schedule.

CHAPTER III
CONSTITUTION OF BOARD OF APPROVALS

8. (*1*) The Central Government shall, within fifteen days of the commencement of this Act, by notification, constitute, for the purposes of this Act, a Board to be called the Board of Approval.

(2) The Board shall consist of:

(*a*) an officer not below the rank of an Additional Secretary to the Government of India in the Ministry or Department of the Central Government dealing with Commerce—Chairperson, ex officio;

(*b*) two officers, not below the rank of a Joint Secretary to the Government of India, to be nominated by the Central Government to represent the Ministry or Department of the Central Govt. dealing with revenue—Members, ex officio;

(*c*) one officer not below the rank of Joint Secretary to the Government of India to be nominated by the Central Government the Ministry or Department of the Central Government dealing with economic affairs (financial services)—Members, ex officio;

(*d*) such number of officers, not exceeding ten, not below the rank of the Joint Secretary to the Government of India, to be nominated by the Central Government to represent the Ministries or Departments of the Central Government dealing with commerce, industrial policy and promotion, science and technology, small scale industries and agro and rural industries, home affairs, defence, environment and forests, law, overseas Indian affairs and urban development—Members, ex officio;

(*e*) a nominee of the State Government concerned—Member, ex officio;

(*f*) the Director General of Foreign Trade or his nominee —Member, ex officio;

(g) the Development Commissioner concerned—Member, ex officio;

(*h*) a Professor in the Indian Institute of Management, being a society registered under the Societies Registration Act, 1860 or the Indian Institute of Foreign Trade, being a society registered under the Societies Registration Act, 1860, as may be, nominated by the Central Government—Member, ex officio;

(*i*) an officer not below the rank of Deputy Secretary to the Government of India dealing with the Special Economic Zones in the Ministry or Department of the Central Government, dealing with commerce to be nominated by the Central Government—Member-Secretary, ex-officio:

Provided that the member, being the Joint Secretary nominated under clauses (*b*) to (*d*) of this sub-section, may, if he is unable to attend the meeting of the Board, authorise any other officer to attend the meeting of the Board on his behalf.

(*3*) The term of office of an ex officio Member shall come to an end as soon as he ceases to hold the office by virtue of which he was so nominated.

(*4*) For the purpose of performing its functions, the Board may co-opt as members such number of persons as it deems fit who have special knowledge of, and practical experience in, matters relating to, or relevant to activity connected with the Special Economic Zones and any such person shall have the right to take part in the discussions of the Board but shall not be counted for the quorum and shall not be a member for any other purpose and such person shall be entitled to receive such allowances or fees, as the case may be, fixed by the Board.

(*5*) The Board shall meet at such times and places as may be appointed by it and shall have the power to regulate its own procedure.

(*6*) One-third of the total Members of the Board shall form a quorum, and all the acts of the Board shall be decided by a general consensus of the Members present.

(*7*) No act or proceeding of the Board shall be called in question on the ground merely of existence of any vacancy in, or any defect in the constitution of, the Board.

(*8*) All orders and decisions of the Board and all other instruments issued by it shall be authenticated by the signature of the Member-Secretary, or any other Member as may be authorised by the Board in this behalf.

9. (*1*) Subject to the provisions of this Act, the Board shall have the duty to promote and ensure orderly development of the Special Economic Zones.

(*2*) Without prejudice to the generality of the provisions contained in sub-section (*1*), the powers and functions of the Board shall include:

(*a*) granting of approval or rejecting proposal or modifying such proposals for establishment of the Special Economic Zones;

(*b*) granting approval of authorised operations to be carried out in the Special Economic Zones by the Developer;

(*c*) granting of approval to the Developers or Units (other than the Developers or the Units which are exempt from obtaining approval under any law or by the Central Government) for foreign collaborations and foreign direct investments, (including investments by a person resident outside India), in the Special Economic Zone for its development, operation and maintenance;

(*d*) granting of approval or rejecting of proposal for providing infrastructure facilities in a Special Economic Zone or modifying such proposals;

(*e*) granting, notwithstanding anything contained in the Industries (Development and Regulation) Act, 1951, a license to an industrial undertaking referred to in clause (*d*) of section 3 of that Act, if such undertaking is established, as a whole or part thereof, or proposed to be established, in a Special Economic Zone;

(*f*) suspension of the letter of approval granted to a Developer and appointment of an Administrator under sub-section (*1*) of section 10;

(*g*) disposing of appeals preferred under sub-section (*4*) of section 15;

(*h*) disposing of appeals preferred under sub-section (*4*) of section 16;

(*i*) performing such other functions as may be assigned to it by the Central Government.

(*3*) The Board may if so required for purposes of this Act or any other law for the time being in force relating to Special Economic Zones, by notification, decide as to whether a particular activity constitutes manufacture as defined in clause (*r*) of clause 2 and such decision of the Board shall be binding on all Ministries and Departments of the Central Government.

(*4*) The Board may delegate such powers and functions as it may deem fit to one or more Development Commissioners for effective and proper discharge of the functions of the Board.

(*5*) Without prejudice to the foregoing provisions of this Act, the Board shall, in exercise of its powers or the performance of its functions under this Act, be bound by such directions on the questions of policy as the Central Government may give in writing to it from time to time.

(*6*) The decision of the Central Government whether a question is one of policy or not shall be final.

10. (*1*) If at any time the Board is of the opinion that a Developer:

(*a*) is unable to discharge the functions or perform the duties imposed on him by or under the provisions of this Act or rules made thereunder; or

(*b*) has persistently defaulted in complying with any direction given by the Board under this Act; or

(*c*) has violated the terms and conditions of the letter of approval; or

(*d*) whose financial position is such that he is unable to fully and efficiently discharge the duties and obligations imposed on him by the letter of approval, and the circumstances exist which render it necessary for it in public interest to do so, the Board may, on application, or with the consent of the Developer, or otherwise, for reasons to be recorded in writing, suspend the letter of approval, granted to the Developer for a whole or part of his area established as Special Economic Zone, for a period not exceeding one year and appoint an Administrator to discharge the functions of the Developer in accordance with the terms and conditions of the letter of approval and manage the Special Economic Zone accordingly.

(*2*) Consequent upon appointment of an Administrator, the management of the Special Economic Zone of the Developer referred to in sub-section (*1*) shall vest in the Administrator.

(*3*) No letter of approval shall be suspended under sub-section (*1*) unless the Board has given to the Developer not less than three months' notice, in writing, stating the grounds on which it proposes to suspend the letter of approval, and has considered any cause shown by the Developer within the period of that notice, against the proposed suspension.

(*4*) The Board may, instead of suspending the letter of approval under sub-section (*1*), permit it to remain in force subject to such further terms and conditions as it thinks fit to impose, and any further terms or conditions so imposed shall be binding upon and be complied with by the Developer and shall be of like force and effect as if they were contained in the letter of approval.

(*5*) In case the Board suspends a letter of approval under this section, it shall serve a notice of suspension upon the Developer and fix a date on which the suspension shall take effect.

(*6*) Upon suspension of the letter of approval under sub-section (*1*), the Special Economic Zone of the Developer referred to in sub-section (*5*) shall vest in the Administrator under sub-section (*2*) for a period not exceeding one year or up to the date on which his letter of approval for such Special Economic Zone is transferred, whichever is earlier, in accordance with the provisions contained in sub-sections (*7*) and (*9*), as the case may be.

(*7*) Where the Board has given notice for suspension of letter of approval under sub-section (*5*), the Developer may, after prior approval of the Board, transfer his letter of approval to any person who is found eligible by the Board for grant of such approval.

(*8*) If at any time, it appears to the Board that the purpose of the order appointing the Administrator has been fulfilled or that for any reason it is undesirable that the order of appointment should remain in force, the Board may cancel the order and thereupon the Administrator shall be divested of the management of the Special Economic Zone which shall, unless otherwise directed by the Board, again vest in the person, being the Developer, in whom it was vested immediately prior to the date of appointment of the Administrator.

(*9*) Where the Board suspends the letter of approval, under this section, in respect of any Developer, the following provisions shall apply, namely:

(*a*) the Board shall invite applications for transferring the letter of approval of the Developer, whose approval has been suspended and select the person or persons, in accordance with the procedure as may be prescribed, to whom the letter of approval of the Developer in the Special Economic Zone may be transferred;

(*b*) upon selection of person or persons under sub-section (*a*), the Board may, by notice in writing, require the Developer to transfer his letter of approval in a Special Economic Zone to the person or the persons so selected and thereupon the Developer shall transfer his interests, rights and liabilities in the Special Economic Zone (hereafter in this section referred to as the "transferee") who has been selected by the Board on such terms and conditions and consideration as may be agreed upon between the Developer and the transferee;

(*c*) all the rights, duties, obligations and liabilities of the Developer, on and from the date of suspension of letter of approval or on and from the date, if earlier, on which his letter of approval in the Special Economic Zone of the Developer has been transferred to the transferee, shall cease absolutely except for any liabilities which have accrued prior to that date;

(*d*) the Board may make such interim arrangements in regard to the operation of the Special Economic Zone as may be considered appropriate;

(*e*) the Administrator shall exercise such powers and discharge such functions as the Board may direct.

(*10*) The Board may, in order to promote exports or to protect the interest of Units or in the public interest, issue such directions or formulate such scheme as it may consider necessary for operation of the Special Economic Zone.

CHAPTER IV
DEVELOPMENT COMMISSIONER

11. (*1*) The Central Government may appoint any of its officers not below the rank of Deputy Secretary to the Government of India as the Development Commissioner of one or more Special Economic Zones.

(*2*) The Central Government may appoint such officers and other employees as it considers necessary to assist the Development Commissioner in the performance of his functions in the Special Economic Zones established by a Developer (other than Central Government) under this Act on such terms and conditions as it deems fit.

(*3*) Every Development Commissioner, officers and other employee shall be entitled to such salary and allowances and subject to such terms and conditions of service in respect of leave, pension, provident fund and other matters as may, from time to time, be specified by the Central Government.

12. (*1*) Every Development Commissioner shall take all steps in order to discharge his functions under this Act to ensure speedy development of the Special Economic Zone and promotion of exports therefrom.

(2) Without prejudice to the generality of the foregoing provisions, the Development Commissioner shall:

(*a*) guide the entrepreneurs for setting up of Units in the Special Economic Zone;

(*b*) ensure and take suitable steps for effective promotion of exports from the Special Economic Zone;

(*c*) ensure proper co-ordination with the Central Government or State Government Departments concerned or agencies with respect to, or for the purposes, of clauses (*a*) and (*b*);

(*d*) monitor the performance of the Developer and the Units in a Special Economic Zone;

(*e*) discharge such other functions as may be assigned to him by the Central Government under this Act or any other law for the time being in force; and

(*f*) discharge such other functions as may be delegated to him by the Board.

(3) Every Development Commissioner shall be overall in charge of the Special Economic Zone and shall exercise administrative control and supervision over the officers and employees appointed under sub-section (2) of section 11 (including the officials deputed to such Special Economic Zone) to discharge any of the functions under this Act.

(*4*) Without prejudice to the provisions of sub-section (*1*) to (*3*), every Development Commissioner shall discharge such functions and exercise such powers as may be delegated to him by a general or special order by the Central Government or the State Government concerned, as the case may be.

(*5*) Every Development Commissioner may call for such information from a Developer or Unit from time to time as may be necessary to monitor the performance of the Developer or the Unit, as the case may be.

(*6*) The Development Commissioner, may, delegate any or all of his powers or functions to any of the officers employed under him.

CHAPTER V
SINGLE WINDOW CLEARANCE

13. (*1*) The Central Government shall:

(*a*) in the case of existing Special Economic Zones, within six months from the date of commencement of this Act;

(*b*) in case of other Special Economic Zones established after the commencement of this Act, within six months from the date of establishment of such Special Economic Zone,

by notification, constitute a Committee for every Special Economic Zone, to be called the Approval Committee to exercise the powers and perform the functions specified in section 14.

(*2*) Every Approval Committee shall consist of:

(*a*) the Development Commissioner—Chairperson, ex officio;

(*b*) two officers of the Central Government to be nominated by the Central Government—Members, ex officio;

(*c*) two officers of the Central Government to represent the Ministry or Department dealing with revenue—Members, ex officio;

(*d*) one officer of the Central Government to be nominated by that Government to represent the Ministry or Department dealing with the economic affairs (financial services)—Members, ex officio;

(*e*) two officers of the State Government concerned to be nominated by that Stated Government—Member, ex officio;

(*f*) a representative of the Developer concerned—Special invitee.

(*3*) For the purpose of exercising its powers and performing its functions, the Approval Committee may invite to its meetings, such persons as the Committee deems fit, whose assistance or advice it may consider necessary.

(*4*) Every Approval Committee shall meet at such times and places as it considers necessary and shall have the power to regulate its own procedure.

(*5*) One half of the total Members of the Approval Committee shall form a quorum, and all the acts of the Approval Committee shall be decided by a general consensus of the Members present.

Provided that in case the Approval Committee is unable to decide any matter by a general consensus, such matter shall stand referred to the Board of Approvals.

(*6*) No act of the Approval Committee shall be called in question on the ground merely of existence of any vacancy in, or any defect in the constitution of, the Approval Committee.

(*7*) All orders and decisions of the Approval Committee and all other communications issued by it shall be authenticated by the signature of the Chairperson or any other member as may be authorised by the Approval Committee in this behalf.

(*8*) The term of office of an ex officio Member shall come to an end as soon as he ceases to hold the office by virtue of which he was so nominated.

14. (*1*) Every Approval Committee may discharge the functions and exercise the powers in respect of the following matters, namely:

(*a*) approve the import or procurement of goods from the Domestic Tariff Area, in the Special Economic Zone for carrying on the authorised operations by a Developer;

(*b*) approve the providing of services by a service provider, from outside India, or from the Domestic Tariff Area, for carrying on the authorised operations by the Developer, in the Special Economic Zone;

(*c*) monitor the utilisation of goods or services or warehousing or trading in the Special Economic Zone;

(*d*) approve, modify or reject proposals for setting up Units for manufacturing or rendering services or warehousing or trading in the Special Economic Zone [other than the grant of licence under clause (*e*) of sub-section (*2*) of section 9] in accordance with the provisions of sub-section (*8*) of section 15;

Provided that where the Approval Committee is unable to decide whether a particular process constitutes manufacture or not, it shall refer the same to the Board of Approvals for a decision.

(*e*) allow, on receipt of approval under clause (*c*) of sub-section (*2*) of section 9, foreign collaborations and foreign direct investments (including investments by a person outside India) for setting up a Unit;

(*f*) monitor and supervise compliance of conditions subject to which the letter of approval or permission, if any, has been granted to the Developer or entrepreneur; and

(*g*) perform such other functions as may be entrusted to it by the Central Government or the State Government concerned, as the case may be.

(*2*) The Approval Committee shall not discharge such functions and exercise such powers in relation to a Developer, being the Central Government, as may be specified by notification by the Central Government.

Provided that till such time, the Approval Committee is constituted, the concerned Development Commissioner shall discharge all functions and exercise all powers of the Approval Committee.

15. (*1*) Any person, who intends to set up a Unit for carrying on the authorised operations in a Special Economic Zone, may submit a proposal to the Development Commissioner concerned in such form and manner containing such particulars as may be prescribed:

Provided that an existing Unit shall be deemed to have been set up in accordance with the provisions of this Act and such Units shall not require approval under this Act.

(*2*) On receipt of the proposal under sub-section (*1*), the Development Commissioner shall submit the same to the Approval Committee for its approval.

(*3*) The Approval Committee may, either approve the proposal without modification, or approve the proposal with modifications subject to such terms and conditions as it may deem fit to impose, or reject the proposal in accordance with the provisions of sub-section (*8*):

Provided that in case of modification or rejection of a proposal, the Approval Committee shall afford a reasonable opportunity of being heard to the person concerned and after recording the reasons, either modify or reject the proposal.

(*4*) Any person aggrieved, by an order of the Approval Committee, made under sub-section (*3*), may prefer an appeal to the Board within such time as may be prescribed.

(*5*) No appeal shall be admitted if it is preferred after the expiry of the time prescribed therefor:

Provided that an appeal may be admitted after the expiry of the period prescribed therefor if the appellant satisfies the Board that he had sufficient cause for not preferring the appeal within the prescribed time.

(*6*) Every appeal made under sub-section (*4*) shall be in such form and shall be accompanied by a copy of the order appealed against and by such fees as may be prescribed.

(*7*) The procedure for disposing of an appeal shall be such as may be prescribed:

Provided that before disposing of an appeal, the appellant shall be given a reasonable opportunity of being heard.

(*8*) The Central Government may prescribe:

(*a*) the requirements (including the period for which a Unit may be set up) subject to which the Approval Committee shall approve, modify or reject any proposal referred to in sub-section (3);

(*b*) the terms and conditions, subject to which the Unit shall undertake the authorised operations and its obligations and entitlements.

(9) The Development Commissioner may, after approval of the proposal referred to in sub-section (*3*), grant a letter of

approval to the person concerned to set up a Unit and undertake such operations which the Development Commissioner may authorise and every such operation so authorised shall be mentioned in the letter of approval.

16. (*1*) The Approval Committee may, at any time, if it has any reason or cause to believe that the entrepreneur has persistently contravened any of the terms and conditions or its obligations subject to which the letter of approval was granted to the entrepreneur, cancel the letter of approval:

Provided that no such letter of approval shall be cancelled unless the entrepreneur has been afforded a reasonable opportunity of being heard.

(*2*) Where the letter of approval has been cancelled under sub-section (*1*), the Unit shall not from the date of such cancellation, be entitled to any exemption, concession, benefit or deduction available to it, being a Unit, under this Act.

(*3*) Without prejudice to the provisions of this Act, the entrepreneur whose letter of approval has been cancelled under sub-section (*1*), shall remit, the exemption, concession, drawback and any other benefit availed by him in respect of the capital goods, finished goods lying in stock and unutilised raw materials relatable to his Unit, in such manner as may be prescribed.

(*4*) Any person aggrieved by an order of the Approval Committee made under sub-section (*1*), may prefer an appeal to the Board within such time as may be prescribed.

(*5*) No appeal shall be admitted if it is preferred after the expiry of the time prescribed therefor:

Provided that an appeal may be admitted after the expiry of the period prescribed therefor if the appellant satisfies the Board that he had sufficient cause for not preferring the appeal within the prescribed time.

(*6*) Every appeal made under sub-section (*4*) shall be in such form and shall be accompanied by a copy of the order appealed against and by such fees as may be prescribed.

(*7*) The procedure for disposing of an appeal shall be such as may be prescribed:

Provided that before disposing of an appeal, the appellant shall be given a reasonable opportunity of being heard.

17. (*1*) An application for setting up and operation of an Offshore Banking Unit in a Special Economic Zone may be made to the Reserve Bank in such form and manner as may be prescribed.

(2) On receipt of an application under sub-section (*1*), the Reserve Bank shall, if it is satisfied that the applicant fulfills all the conditions specified under sub-section (*3*), grant permission to such applicant for setting up and operation of an Off-shore Banking Unit.

(*3*) The Reserve Bank may, by notification, specify the terms and conditions subject to which an Offshore Banking Unit may be set up and operated in the Special Economic Zone.

18. (*1*) The Central Government may approve the setting up of an International Financial Services Centre in a Special Economic Zone and may prescribe the requirements for setting up and operation of such Centre:

Provided that the Central Government shall approve only one International Financial Services Centre in a Special Economic Zone.

(2) The Central Government may, subject to such guidelines as may be framed by the Reserve Bank, the Securities and Exchange Board of India, the Insurance Regulatory and Development Authority and such other concerned authorities, as it deems fit, prescribe the requirements for setting up and the terms and conditions of the operation of Units in an International Financial Services Centre.

19. Notwithstanding anything contained in any other law for the time being in force, the Central Government may, if required:

(*a*) prescribe a single application form for obtaining any licence, permission or registration or approval by a Developer, or an entrepreneur under one or more Central Acts;

(*b*) authorise the Board, the Development Commissioner or Approval Committee, to exercise the powers of the Central Government on matters relating to the development of a Special Economic Zone; or setting up and operation of units;

(*c*) prescribe a single form for furnishing returns or information by a Developer or an entrepreneur under one or more Central Acts.

20. Notwithstanding anything contained in any other law for the time being in force, the Central Government may, by notification, specify any officer or agency to carry out surveys or inspections for securing of compliance with the provisions of any Central Act by a Developer or an entrepreneur, as the case may be, and such officer or agency shall submit verification and compliance reports, in such manner and within such time as may be specified in the said notification.

21. (*1*) The Central Government may, by notification, specify any act or omission made punishable under any Central Act, as notified offence for purposes of this Act.

(*2*) The Central Government may, by general or special order, authorise any officer or agency to be the enforcement officer or agency in respect of any notified offences or committed in a Special Economic Zone.

(*3*) Every officer or agency authorised under sub-section (*2*) shall have all the corresponding powers of investigation, inspection or search or seizure as is provided under the relevant Central Act in respect of the notified offences.

22. The agency or officer, specified under section 20 or section 21, may, with prior intimation to the Development Commissioner concerned, carry out the investigation or search or seizure in the Special Economic Zone or in a Unit if such agency or officer has reasons to believe (reasons to be recorded in writing) that a notified offence has been committed or is likely to be committed in the Special Economic Zone:

Provided that no investigation, search or seizure shall be carried out in a Special Economic Zone by any agency or officer other than those referred to in sub-section (*2*) of section 21 without prior approval of the Development Commissioner concerned.

Provided further that any officer of agency, if so authorised by the Central Government, may carry out the investigation, inspection, search or seizure in the Special Economic Zone or Unit without prior intimation or approval of the Development Commissioner.

23. (*1*) The State Government, in which the Special Economic Zone is situated, may, with the concurrence of the Chief Justice of the High Court of that State, designate one or more courts:

(*a*) to try all suits of a civil nature arising in the Special Economic Zone; and

(*b*) to try notified offences committed in the Special Economic Zone.

(2) No court, other than the court designated under sub-section (*1*), shall try any suit or conduct the trial of any notified offence referred to in that sub-section:

Provided that the courts, in which any suit of a civil nature in a Special Economic Zone had been filed before the commencement of this Act, shall continue to try such suit after such commencement:

Provided further that the courts in which any trial of any notified offence is being conducted before the commencement of this Act, shall continue to conduct the trial of such offence after the commencement of this Act:

Provided also that the courts competent to try any notified offence before the commencement of this Act, shall conduct the trial in respect of such offence after the commencement of this Act until the courts have been designated under sub-section (*1*) and all such cases relating to such trials shall thereafter be transferred to such Courts so designated which shall conduct the trial from the stage at which such cases were so transferred.

24. Any person aggrieved, by any decision or order of the court designated under sub-section (*1*) of section 23, may file an appeal to the High Court within sixty days from the date of communication of the decision or order of the Courts so designated to him on any question of fact or law arising out of such orders:

Provided that the High Court may, if it is satisfied that the appellant was prevented by sufficient cause from filing an appeal within the said period, allow it to be filed within a further period not exceeding sixty days.

Explanation. In section 23 and this section "High Court" means the High Court of the State in which the Special Economic Zone is situated.

25. (*1*) Where an offence has been committed by a company, every person, who at the time the offence was committed was in charge of, and was responsible to, the company for the conduct of the business of the company, as well as the company, shall be deemed to be guilty of the offence and shall be liable to be proceeded against and punished accordingly:

Provided that nothing contained in this sub-section shall render any such person liable to any punishment provided for the offence, if he has proved that the offence was committed without his knowledge or that he had exercised all due diligence to prevent the commission of such offence.

(2) Notwithstanding anything contained in sub-section (*1*), where an offence has been committed by a company and it is proved that the offence has been committed with the consent or connivance of, or is attributable to any neglect on the part of, any director, manager, secretary or other officer of the company, such director, manager, secretary or other officer shall also be deemed to be guilty of the offence and shall be liable to be proceeded against and punished accordingly.

Explanation. For the purposes of this section:

(*a*) "company" means any body corporate and includes a firm or other association of individuals; and

(*b*) "director", in relation to a firm, means a partner in the firm.

CHAPTER VI

SPECIAL FISCAL PROVISIONS FOR SPECIAL ECONOMIC ZONES

26. (*1*) Subject to the provisions of sub-section (*2*), every Developer and the entrepreneur shall be entitled to the following exemptions, drawbacks and concessions, namely:

(*a*) exemption from any duty of customs, under the Customs Act, 1962 or the Custom Tariff Act, 1975 or any other law for the time being in force, on goods imported into, or service provided in, a Special Economic Zone or a Unit, to carry on the authorised operations by the Developer or entrepreneur;

(*b*) exemption from any duty of customs, under the Customs Act, 1962 or the Customs Tariff Act, 1975 or any other law for the time being in force, on goods exported from, or services provided, from a Special Economic Zone or from a Unit, to any place outside India:

(*c*) exemption from any duty of excise, under the Central Excise Act, 1944 or the Central Excise Tariff Act, 1985 or any other law for the time being in force, on goods brought from Domestic Tariff Area to a Special Economic Zone or Unit, to carry on the authorised operations by the Developer or entrepreneur;

(*d*) drawback or such other benefits as may be admissible from time to time on goods brought or services provided from the Domestic Tariff Area into a Special Economic Zone or Unit or services provided in a Special Economic Zone or Unit by the service providers located outside India to carry on the authorised operations by the Developer or entrepreneur;

(*e*) exemption from service tax under Chapter-V of the Finance Act, 1994 on taxable services provided to a Developer or Unit to carry on the authorised operations in a Special Economic Zone;

(*f*) exemption from the securities transaction tax leviable under section 98 of the Finance (No. 2) Act, 2004 in case the taxable securities transactions are entered into by a non-resident through the International Financial Services Centre;

(*g*) exemption from the levy of taxes on the sale or purchase of goods other than newspapers under the Central Sales Tax Act, 1956 if such goods are meant to carry on the authorised operations by the Developer or entrepreneur.

(2) The Central Government may prescribe the manner in which, and the terms and conditions subject to which, the exemptions, concessions, drawback or other benefits shall be granted to the Developer or entrepreneur under sub-section (*1*).

27. The provisions of the Income Tax Act, 1961, as in force for the time being, shall apply to, or in relation to, the Developer or entrepreneur for carrying on the authorised operations in a Special Economic Zone or Unit, subject to the modifications specified in the Second Schedule.

28. The Central Government may prescribe the period during which any goods brought into, or services provided in, any Unit or Special Economic Zone without payment of taxes, duties or cess shall remain or continue to be provided in such Unit or Special Economic Zone.

29. The transfer of ownership in any goods brought into, or produced or manufactured in, any Unit or Special Economic Zone or removal thereof from such Unit or Zone shall be allowed, subject to such terms and conditions as the Central Government may prescribe.

30. Subject to the conditions specified in the rules made by the Central Government in this behalf:

(*a*) any goods removed from a Special Economic Zone to the Domestic Tariff Area shall be chargeable to duties of customs including anti-dumping, countervailing and safeguard duties under the Customs Tariff Act, 1975, where applicable, as leviable on such goods when imported; and

(*b*) the rate of duty and tariff valuation, if any, applicable to goods removed from a Special Economic Zone shall be at the rate and tariff valuation in force as on the date of such removal, and where such date is not ascertainable, on the date of payment of duty.

CHAPTER VII
SPECIAL ECONOMIC ZONE AUTHORITY

31. (*1*) The Central Government shall, by notification in the Official Gazette, constitute, for every Special Economic Zone established by it before the commencement of this Act or which may be established by it after such commencement by the Central Government, an Authority to be called the…(name of the Special Economic Zone) Authority to exercise the powers conferred on, and discharge the functions assigned to it under this Act:

Provided that in respect of existing Special Economic Zone established by the Central Government, such Authority shall be constituted by the Central Government within six months from the date of commencement of this Act:

Provided further that until such Authority is constituted, the person or the authority including the Development Commissioner exercising control over such existing Special Economic Zones shall continue to exercise such control over the Special Economic Zones till the Authority is constituted.

(*2*) Every Authority shall be a body corporate by the name aforesaid, having perpetual succession and a common seal, with a power, subject to the provisions of this Act, to acquire, hold and dispose of property, both movable and immovable, and to contract and shall, by the said name, sue and be sued.

(*3*) The head office of every Authority shall be at such place as the Central Government may specify in the notification referred to in sub-section (*1*).

(*4*) Any Authority may, with the previous approval of the Central Government, establish branch offices at other places in India.

(*5*) Every Authority shall consist of:

(*a*) the Development Commissioner of the Special Economic Zone over which the Authority exercises its jurisdiction—Chairperson, ex officio;

(*b*) two officers of the Central Government to be nominated by that Government having knowledge of, or experience in, dealing with matters relating to Special Economic Zones—Members, ex officio;

(*c*) an officer of the Government of India in the Ministry or Department dealing with Commerce on matters relating to Special Economic Zone—Member, ex officio;

(*d*) not more than two persons being entrepreneurs or their nominees, to be nominated by the Central Government—Members, ex officio;

(*6*) The term of office of the Members of an Authority (other than ex officio Members) and the manner of filling of vacancies shall be such as may be prescribed.

(*7*) An Authority may associate with itself in such manner, subject to such conditions and for such purposes as may be prescribed, any person whose assistance or advice it requires in discharging its functions effectively and that person shall be entitled to receive such allowances or fees as may be fixed by the Authority.

(*8*) One third of the total Members of the Authority shall form a quorum, and all the acts of the Authority shall be decided by a majority of the Members present.

(*9*) No act or proceeding of an Authority shall be invalidated merely by reason of:

(*a*) any vacancy in, or any defect in the constitution of, the Authority; or

(*b*) any defect in the appointment of a person acting as a Member of the Authority; or

(*c*) any irregularity in the procedure of the Authority not affecting the merits of the case.

(*10*) Every Authority shall meet at such times and places and shall observe such rules of procedure in regard to the transaction of business at its meetings (including quorum at such meetings) as may be prescribed.

32. (*1*) Every Development Commissioner of the Special Economic Zone for which he is appointed as such shall be the chief executive of the Authority concerned and exercise such powers and perform such functions as may be prescribed.

(*2*) Every Authority may, in addition to the officers and employees transferred to it under section 33, appoint such other officers and employees, as it considers necessary for the efficient discharge of its functions under this Act.

(*3*) The method of appointment, the conditions of service and the scales of pay and allowances of such other officers and employees appointed under sub-section (2) shall be such as may be prescribed.

33. (*1*) It shall be lawful for the Central Government to transfer to each Authority, by order, and with effect from such date or dates, as may be specified in the order, any officer or other employee holding office as such (except officers or other employees on deputation) in the existing Special Economic Zone concerned:

Provided that the scale of pay of the post to which such officer or other employee is transferred shall not be lower than the scale of pay of the post which he was holding immediately before such transfer and the other terms and conditions of service (including pension, leave, provident fund and medical benefits) of the post to which he is transferred shall not be less favourable than the terms and conditions of service in relation to the post held by him immediately before such transfer:

Provided further that if, immediately before the date of his transfer, any such officer or other employee is officiating in a higher post under the Central Government either in a leave vacancy or in any vacancy of a specified duration, his pay and other allowances, if any, on transfer, shall be protected for the unexpired period of such vacancy and thereafter he shall be entitled to the scale of pay applicable to the post under the Central Government to which he would have reverted but for his transfer to the Authority.

(2) If any question arises as to whether the prescribed terms and conditions of service in respect of any matter, including remuneration, pension, leave, provident fund and medical benefits, are less favourable than those attached to the post held by an officer or other employee immediately before his transfer to the Authority, the decision of the Central Government in the matter shall be final.

34. (*1*) Subject to the provisions of this Act, it shall be the duty of each Authority to undertake such measures as it thinks fit for the development, operation and management of the Special Economic Zone for which it is constituted.

(2) Without prejudice to the generality of the provisions of sub-section (*1*), the measures referred to therein may provide for:

(*a*) the development of infrastructure in the Special Economic Zone;

(*b*) promoting exports from the Special Economic Zone;

(*c*) reviewing the functioning and performance of the Special Economic Zone;

(*d*) levy user or service charges or fees or rent for the use of properties belonging to the Authority;

(*e*) performing such other functions as may be prescribed.

35. The Central Government may, after due appropriation made by Parliament by law in this behalf, make to every Authority by way of grants and loans such sums of money as that Government may think fit for being utilised for the purposes of this Act.

36. (*1*) There shall be established by every Authority, a Fund to be called the...(the name of the Special Economic Zone concerned) Authority Fund and there shall be credited thereto:

(*a*) all sums of money, which the Central Government may, after due appropriation made by Parliament by law in this behalf, provide to the Authority;

(*b*) all grants or loans that may be made to the Authority under this Act;

(*c*) all sums received on account of user or service charges or fees or rent for the use of properties belonging to the Authority;

(*d*) all sums received by the Authority from such other sources as may be decided upon by the Central Government.

(2) The Fund shall be applied for meeting:

(*a*) the salaries, allowances and other remuneration of the members, officers and other employees of the Authority;

(*b*) the expenses of the Authority in the discharge of its functions under section 34;

(*c*) repayment of any loan;

(*d*) the expenses on objects and for purposes authorised by this Act;

(*e*) meeting any other administrative expenses of the Authority.

37. (*1*) Every Authority shall maintain proper accounts and other relevant records and prepare an annual statement of accounts in such form as may be prescribed by the Central Government, in consultation with the Comptroller and Auditor-General of India.

(2) The accounts of every Authority shall be audited by the Comptroller and Auditor-General of India at such intervals as may be specified by him and any expenditure incurred in connection with such audit shall be payable by the Authority to the Comptroller and Auditor-General of India.

(*3*) The Comptroller and Auditor-General of India or any person appointed by him in connection with the audit of the accounts of the Authority shall have the same rights and privileges and authority in connection with such audit as the Comptroller and Auditor-General generally has in connection with the audit of the Government accounts and, in particular, shall have the right to demand the production of books, accounts, connected vouchers and other documents and papers and to inspect any of the offices of the Authority.

(*4*) The accounts of every Authority as certified by the Comptroller and Auditor-General of India or any other person appointed by him in this behalf together with the audit report thereon shall be forwarded annually to the Central Government and the Central Government shall cause the same to be laid before each House of Parliament.

38. Every Authority shall be bound to carry out such directions as may be issued to it from time to time by the Central Government for the efficient administration of this Act.

39. (*1*) Every Authority shall furnish to the Central Government at such time and in such form and manner as may be prescribed or as the Central Government may direct, such returns and statements and such particulars in regard to the promotion and development of exports and the operation and maintenance of the Special Economic Zone and Units as the Central Government may, from time to time, require.

(*2*) Without prejudice to the provisions of sub-section (*1*), every Authority shall, as soon as possible, after the end of each financial year, submit to the Central Government a report in such form and before such date, as may be prescribed, giving a true and full account of its activities, policy and programmes during the previous financial year.

(*3*) A copy of every report received under sub-section (*2*) shall be laid, as soon as may be, after it is received, before each House of Parliament.

40. (*1*) If at any time the Central Government is of the opinion that an Authority is unable to perform, or has persistently made default in the performance of, the duty imposed on it by or under this Act or has exceeded or abused its powers, or has wilfully or without sufficient cause, failed to comply with any direction issued by the Central Government under section 38, the Central Government may, by notification, supersede that Authority for such period not exceeding six months, as may be specified in the notification:

Provided that before issuing a notification under this sub-section, the Central Government shall give reasonable time to that Authority to make representation against the proposed supersession and shall consider the representations, if any, of the Authority.

(*2*) Upon the publication of a notification under sub-section (*1*) superseding the Authority:

(*a*) the Chairperson and other Members of the Authority shall, notwithstanding that their term of office has not expired as from the date of supersession, vacate their offices as such;

(*b*) all the powers, functions and duties which may, by or under the provisions of this Act, be exercised or discharged by or on behalf of the Authority shall, during the period of supersession, be exercised and performed by such person or persons as the Central Government may direct;

(*c*) all property vested in the Authority shall, during the period of supersession, vest in the Central Government.

(*3*) On the expiration of the period of supersession specified in the notification issued under sub-section (*1*), the Central Government may:

(*a*) extend the period of supersession for such further period not exceeding six months; or

(*b*) reconstitute the Authority in the manner provided in section 31.

41. All Members, officers and other employees of every Authority, shall, when acting or purporting to act in pursuance of any of the provisions of this Act or the rules made thereunder, be deemed to be public servants within the meaning of section 21 of the Indian Penal Code.

CHAPTER VIII
MISCELLANEOUS

42. (*1*) Notwithstanding anything contained in any other law for the time being in force, if:

(*a*) any dispute of civil nature arises among two or more entrepreneurs or two or more Developers or between an entrepreneur and a Developer in the Special Economic Zone; and

(*b*) the court or the courts to try suits in respect of such dispute had not been designated under sub-section (*1*) of section 23,

such dispute shall be referred to arbitration:

Provided that no dispute shall be referred to the arbitration on or after the date of the designation of court or courts under sub-section (*1*) of section 23.

(2) Where a dispute has been referred to arbitration under sub-section (*1*), the same shall be settled or decided by the arbitrator to be appointed by the Central Government.

(*3*) Save as otherwise provided under this Act, the provisions of the Arbitration and Conciliation Act, 1996 shall apply to all arbitration under this Act as if the proceedings for arbitration were referred in settlement or decision under provisions of the Arbitration and Conciliation Act, 1996.

43. (*1*) The period of limitation in the case of any dispute which is required to be referred to arbitration shall be regulated by the provisions of the Limitation Act, 1963, as if the dispute was a suit and the arbitrator is civil court.

(2) Notwithstanding anything contained in sub-section (*1*), the arbitrator may admit a dispute after the expiry of the period of limitation, if the applicant satisfies the arbitrator that he had sufficient causes for not referring the dispute within such period.

44. All the provisions of this Act (except sections 3 and 4) shall, as far as may be, apply to every existing Special Economic Zones.

45. A communication by any competent authority or person under this Act may be sent to the person who has the ultimate control over the affairs of the Special Economic Zone or Unit or where the said affairs are entrusted to a manager, director, chairperson, or managing director, or to any other officer, by whatever name called, such communication may be sent to such manager, director, chairperson, or managing director, or any other officer.

46. Every person, whether employed or residing or required to be present in a Special Economic Zone, shall be provided an identity card by every Development Commissioner of such Special Economic Zone, in such form and containing such particulars as may be prescribed.

47. Any authority which has been conferred upon any power, or, is, required for discharging any function under any Central or State Act, may, subject to the provisions of this Act, exercise such powers or discharge such function in any Special Economic Zone under that Act.

48. No suit, prosecution or other legal proceeding shall lie against the Central Government or any Chairperson, Member, officer or other employee of the Board Approval Committee or the Authority or Development Commissioner for anything done or intended to be done in good faith under this Act.

49. (*1*) The Central Government may, by notification, direct that any of the provisions of this Act (other than sections 54 and 56) or any other Central Act or any rules or regulations made thereunder or any notification or order issued or direction given thereunder (other than the provisions relating to making of the rules or regulations) specified in the notification:

(*a*) shall not apply to a Special Economic Zone or a class of Special Economic Zones or all Special Economic Zones; or

(*b*) shall apply to a Special Economic Zone or a class of Special Economic Zones or all Special Economic Zones only with such exceptions, modifications and adaptation, as may be specified in the notification.

Provided that nothing contained in this section shall apply to any modifications of any Central Act or any rules or regulations made thereunder or any notification or order issued or direction given or scheme made thereunder so far as such modification, rule, regulation, notification, order or direction or scheme relates to the matters relating to trade unions, industrial and labour disputes, welfare of labour including conditions of work, provident funds, employers' liability, workmen's compensation, invalidity and old age pensions and maternity benefits applicable in any Special Economic Zones.

(2) A copy of every notification proposed to be issued under sub-section (*1*), shall be laid in draft before each House of Parliament, while it is in session, for a total period of thirty days which may be comprised in one session or in two or more successive sessions, and if, before the expiry of the session immediately following the session or the successive sessions aforesaid, both Houses agree in disapproving the issue of the notification or both Houses agree in making any modification in the notification, the notification shall not be issued or, as the case may be, shall be issued only in such modified form as may be agreed upon by both the Houses.

50. The State Government may, for the purposes of giving effect to the provisions of this Act, notify policies for Developers and Units and take suitable steps for enactment of any law:

(a) granting exemption from the State taxes, levies and duties to the Developer or the entrepreneur;

(b) delegating the powers conferred upon any person or authority under any State Act to the Development Commissioner in relation to the Developer or the entrepreneur.

51. (*1*) The provisions of this Act shall have effect, notwithstanding anything inconsistent therewith contained in any other law for the time being in force or in any instrument having effect by virtue of any law other than this Act.

52. The provision contained in the Chapter X-A of the Customs Act, 1962 and the Special Economic Zones Rules, 2003 and the Special Economic Zones (Customs Procedure) Regulations, 2003 made thereunder shall not, with effect from such date as the Central Government by notification appoint, apply to the Special Economic Zones.

(2) Notwithstanding anything contained in sub-section (*1*), all offences committed before the commencement of this Act, under any provisions of Customs Act, 1962 and the Special Economic Zones Rules, 2003 and the Special Economic Zones (Customs Procedure) Regulations, 2003 made thereunder, shall

continue to be governed by the said Act or rules, as the case may be.

(*3*) Anything done or any action taken or purported to have been done or taken including any rule, notification, inspection, order or notice made or issued or any permission, authorisation or exemption granted or any document or instrument executed under the said provisions of the Act, rules and regulations referred to in sub-section (*1*) shall, in so far as they are not inconsistent with the provisions of this Act, be deemed to have been done or taken or made or issued or granted under the corresponding provisions of the Act or rules referred to in that sub-section.

53. A Special Economic Zone shall, on and from the appointed day, be deemed to be a territory outside the customs territory of India for the purposes of undertaking the authorized operations.

(2) A Special Economic Zone shall, with effect from such date as Central Government may notify, be deemed to be a port, inland container depot, land station and land customs stations, as the case may be, under section 7 of the Customs Act, 1962:

Provided that for the purposes of this section, the Central Government may notify different dates for different Special Economic Zones.

54. (*1*) The Central Government may, having regard to the objects of this Act, and if it considers necessary or expedient so to do, by notification add to, or as the case may be, omit from the First Schedule any enactment specified therein.

(2) A copy of every notification proposed to be issued under sub-section (*1*), shall be laid in draft before each House of Parliament, while it is in session, for a total period of thirty days which may be comprised in one session or in two or more successive sessions, and if, before the expiry of the session immediately following the session or the successive sessions aforesaid, both houses agree in disapproving the issue of the notification or both Houses agree in making any modification in the notification, the notification shall not be issued or, as the case may be , shall be issued only in such modified form as may be agreed upon by both the House.

55. (*1*) The Central Government may, by notification, make rules for carrying out the provisions of this Act.

(*2*) In particular, and without prejudice to the generality of the foregoing power, such rules may provide for all or any of the following matters, namely:

(*a*) the infrastructure facilities necessary for the development of the Special Economic Zones under clause (*p*) and services in the Special Economic Zones under clause (*z*) of section 2;

(*b*) the period within which the person concerned shall obtain the concurrence of the State Government under sub-section (*3*) of section 3;

(*c*) the form and the manner in which a proposal may be made and the particulars to be contained therein under sub-section (*5*) of section 3;

(*d*) the period within which the State Government may forward the proposal together with its recommendation under sub-section (*6*) of section 3;

(*e*) the requirements subject to which the Board may approve, modify or reject the proposal under sub-section (*8*) of section 3;

(*f*) the period within which the grant of letter of approval shall be communicated to the State Government or Developer or entrepreneur under sub-section (*10*) of section 3;

(*g*) the other requirements for notifying the specifically identified area in a State as a Special Economic Zone under sub-section (*1*) of section 4;

(*h*) the terms, conditions and limitations subject to which the goods or services exported out of, or imported into, or procured from the Domestic Tariff Area to, a Special Economic Zone, be exempt from payment of taxes, duties or cess under section 7;

(*i*) the procedure for transfer of letter of approval in case of suspension of letter of approval of a Developer under clause (*a*) of sub-section (*9*) of section 10;

(*j*) the form and the manner in which a proposal may be submitted and the particulars to be contained therein under sub-section (*1*) of section 15;

(*k*) the time within which a person aggrieved by the order of the Approval Committee may prefer an appeal under sub-section (*4*) of section 15;

(*l*) the form in which the appeal shall be made and the fees for making such appeal under sub-section (*6*) of section 15;

(*m*) the procedure for disposing of an appeal under sub-section (*7*) of section 15;

(*n*) the requirements (including the period for which a unit may be set up) subject to which the proposal may be approved, modified or rejected under clause (*a*) of sub-section (*8*) of section 15;

(*o*) the terms and conditions, for the Unit subject to which it shall undertake authorised operations under clause (*b*) of sub-section (*8*) of section 15 and the obligations and entitlements of the Unit;

(*p*) the time within which a person aggrieved by the order of the Approval Committee may prefer an appeal under sub-section (*4*) of section 16;

(*q*) the form in which the appeal shall be made and the fees for making such appeal under sub-section (*6*) of section 16;

(*r*) the procedure for disposing of an appeal under sub-section (*7*) of section 16;

(*s*) the form and the manner in which an application may be made for setting up of an Offshore Banking Unit in a Special Economic Zone under sub-section (*1*) of section 17; and

(*t*) the requirements for setting up and operation of an International Financial Services Centre in a Special Economic Zone under sub-section (*1*) of section 18;

(*u*) the requirements and terms and conditions subject to which a Unit in the International Financial Services

Centre may be set up and operated in Special Economic Zone under sub-section (2) of section 18;

(*v*) the form of single application for obtaining any licence, permission or registration or approval under clause (*a*) of section 19;

(*w*) the form of single return or information to be furnished by an entrepreneur or Developer under clause (*c*) of section 19;

(*x*) the manner in which and the terms and the conditions subject to which the exemptions concessions, draw back or other benefits shall be granted to every Developer and entrepreneur under sub-section (2) of section 26;

(*y*) the period during which any goods brought into, or services provided in, any Special Economic Zone shall remain or continue to be provided in such Unit or Special Economic Zone under section 28;

(*z*) the terms and conditions subject to which transfer in ownership of any goods brought into, or produced or manufactured in, any Unit or Special Economic Zone, or removal thereof from such Unit or the Zone, shall be allowed under section 29;

(*za*) the conditions subject to which the Units shall be entitled to sell the goods manufactured in a Special Economic Zone to the Domestic Tariff Area under section 30;

(*zb*) the term of office of the Members, other than ex officio Members, of every Authority and the manner of filling of vacancies under sub-section (6) of section 31;

(*zc*) the manner in which and the conditions subject to which and the purposes for which any person may be associated under sub-section (7) of section 31;

(*zd*) the times and the places of meetings and the procedure to be followed in the transaction of business meeting under sub-section (*10*) of section 31;

(*ze*) the powers and the functions of every Development Commissioner under sub-section (*1*) of section 32;

(*zf*) the method of appointment of officers and other employees of every Authority, conditions of their service and the scale of pay and allowances under sub-section (*3*) of section 32;

(*zg*) the other functions to be performed by the Authority under clause (*e*) of sub-section (2) of section 34;

(*zh*) the form in which the accounts and other relevant records of every Authority shall be maintained and annual statement of accounts shall be prepared under sub-section (*1*) of section 37;

(*zi*) the form and the manner in which and the time at which every Authority shall furnish returns and statements and other particulars to the Central Government under sub-section (*1*) of section 39;

(*zj*) the form in which and the date before which every Authority shall furnish to the Central Government the report of its activities, policy and programmes under sub-section (*2*) of section 39;

(*zk*) the form in which and the particulars to be contained in the identity cards under section 46;

(*zl*) any other matter which is to be, or may be, prescribed.

(*3*) Every rule made by the Central Government under this Act shall be laid, as soon as may be after it is made, before each House of Parliament while it is in session, for a total period of thirty days which may be comprised in one session or in two or more successive sessions, and if, before the expiry of the session immediately following the session or the successive sessions aforesaid, both Houses agree in making any modification in the rule or both Houses agree that the rule should not be made, the rule shall thereafter have effect only in such modified form or be of no effect, as the case may be; so however, that any such modification or annulment shall be without prejudice to the validity of anything previously done under that rule.

56. (*1*) If any difficulty arises in giving effect to the provisions of this Act, the Central Government may, by order published in the Official Gazette, make such provisions not inconsistent with the provisions of this Act, as may appear to it to be necessary or expedient for removing the difficulty:

Provided that no such order shall be made under this section after the expiration of two years from the date of commencement of this Act.

(2) Every order made under this section shall be laid, as soon as may be after it is made, before each House of Parliament.

57. With effect from such date as the Central Government may by notification appoint, the enactments specified in the Third Schedule shall be amended in the manner specified therein:

Provided that different dates may be appointed on which the amendments specified in the Third Schedule shall apply to a particular Special Economic Zone or a class of Special Economic Zones or all Special Economic Zones.

58. All rules made or purporting to have been made or all notifications issued or purporting to have been issued under any Central Act relating to the Special Economic Zone shall, in so far as they relate to matters for which provision is made in this Act or rules made or notification issued thereunder and are not inconsistent therewith, be deemed to have been made or issued under this Act as if this Act had been in force on the date on which such rules were made or notifications were issued and shall continue to be in force unless and until they are superseded by any rules made or notifications issued under this Act.

THE FIRST SCHEDULE

(See sections 7 and 54)

Enactments

1. The Agricultural Produce Cess Act, 1940 (27 of 1940).
2. The Coffee Act, 1942 (7 of 1942).
3. The Mica Mines Labour Welfare Fund Act, 1946 (22 of 1946).
4. The Rubber Act, 1947 (24 of 1947).
5. The Tea Act, 1953 (29 of 1953).

6. The Salt Cess Act, 1953 (49 of 1953).
7. The Medicinal and Toilet Preparations (Excise Duties) Act, 1955 (16 of 1955).
8. The Additional Duties of Excise (Goods of Special Importance) Act, 1957 (58 of 1957).
9. The Sugar (Regulation of Production) Act, 1961 (55 of 1961).
10. The Textiles Committee Act, 1963 (41 of 1963).
11. The Produce Cess Act, 1966 (15 of 1966).
12. The Marine Products Export Development Authority Act, 1972 (13 of 1972).
13. The Coal Mines (Conservation and Development Act, 1974 (28 of 1974).
14. The Oil Industry (Development) Act, 1974 (47 of 1974).
15. The Tobacco Cess Act, 1975 (26 of 1975).
16. The Additional Duties of Excise (Textile and Textile Articles) Act, 1978 (40 of 1978).
17. The Sugar Cess Act, 1982 (3 of 1982).
18. The Jute Manufactures Cess Act, 1983 (28 of 1983).
19. The Agricultural and Processed Food Products Export Cess Act, 1985 (3 of 1986).
20. The Spices Cess Act, 1986 (11 of 1986).
21. The Research and Development Cess Act, 1986 (32 of 1986).

THE SECOND SCHEDULE

(See section 27)

MODIFICATIONS TO THE INCOME-TAX ACT, 1961.

(43 of 1961)

(a) in section 10:

(A) in clause (*15*), after sub-clause (vii), the following clause shall be inserted at the end, namely:

"(*viii*) any income by way of interest received by a non-resident or a person who is not ordinarily resident, in India on a deposit made on or after the 1st day of April, 2005 in an Offshore Banking Unit referred to in clause (u) of section 2 of the Special Economic Zones Act, 2005;"

(B) in clause (*23G*), after the words, brackets, figures and letters "sub-section (*4*) of section 80-IA", the words brackets, figures and letters "or sub -section (*3*) of section 80-IAB." shall be inserted;

(C) in clause (*34*), the following Explanation shall be inserted, namely:

"*Explanation.* For the removal of doubts, it is hereby declared that the dividend referred to in section 115-O shall not be included in the total income of the assessee, being a Developer or entrepreneur."

(b) in section 10A, *after* sub-section (*7A*), the following sub-section shall be inserted, namely:

"(*7B*) The provisions of this section shall not apply to any undertaking, being a Unit referred to in clause (*zc*) of section 2 of the Special Economic Zones Act, 2005, which has begun or begins to manufacture or produce articles or things or computer software during the previous year relevant to the assessment year commencing on or after the 1st day of April, 2006 in any Special Economic Zone."

(c) after section 10A, the following section shall be inserted, namely:

'10AA. (*1*) Subject to the provisions of this section, in computing the total income of an assessee, being an entrepreneur as referred to in clause (*j*) of section (2) of the Special Economic Zones Act, 2005, from his Unit, who begins to manufacture or produce articles or things or provide any services during the previous year relevant to any assessment year commencing on or after the 1st day of April, 2006, a deduction of:

(*i*) hundred per cent of profits and gains derived from the export, of such articles or things or from services for a period of five consecutive assessment years beginning with the assessment year relevant to the previous year in which the Unit begins to manufacture or produce such articles or things or provide services, as the case may be, and fifty per cent of such profits and gains for further five assessment years and thereafter;

(*ii*) for the next five consecutive assessment years, so much of the amount not exceeding fifty per cent of the profit as is debited to the profit and loss account of the previous year in respect of which the deduction is to be allowed and credited to a reserve account (to be called the "Special Economic Zone Re-investment Reserve Account") to be created and utilised for the purposes of the business of the assessee in the manner laid down in sub-section (*2*).

(*2*) The deduction under clause (*ii*) of sub-section (*1*) shall be allowed only if the following conditions are fulfilled, namely:

(*a*) the amount credited to the Special Economic Zone Re-investment Reserve Account is to be utilised:

(*i*) for the purposes of acquiring machinery or plant which is first put to use before the expiry of a period of three years following the previous year in which the reserve was created; and

(*ii*) until the acquisition of the machinery or plant as aforesaid, for the purposes of the business of the undertaking other than for distribution by way of dividends or profits or for remittance outside India as profits or for the creation of any asset outside India;

(*b*) the particulars, as may be specified by the Central Board of Direct Taxes in this behalf, under clause (b) of sub-section (IB) of section 10A have been furnished by the assessee in respect of machinery or plant along with the return of income for the assessment year relevant to the previous year in which such plant or machinery was first put to use.

(*3*) Where any amount credited to the Special Economic Zone Re-investment Reserve Account under clause (*ii*) of sub-section (*1*),:

(*a*) has been utilised for any purpose other than those referred to in sub-section (2), the amount so utilised; or

(*b*) has not been utilised before the expiry of the period specified in sub-clause (*i*) of clause (*a*) of sub-section (2), the amount not so utilised,

shall be deemed to be the profits,-

(*i*) in a case referred to in clause (*a*), in the year in which the amount was so utilised; or

(*ii*) in a case referred to in clause (*b*), in the year immediately following the period of three years specified in sub-clause (*i*) of clause (*a*) of sub-section (2),

and shall be charged to tax accordingly:

Provided that where in computing the total income of the Unit for any assessment year, its profits and gains had not been included by application of the provisions of sub-section (7B) of section 10A, the undertaking being the Unit shall be entitled to deduction referred to in this sub-section only for the unexpired period of ten consecutive assessment years and thereafter it shall be eligible for deduction from income as provided in clause (*ii*) of sub-section (*1*):

Explanation. For the removal of doubts, it is hereby declared that an undertaking being the Unit, which had already availed before the commencement of the Special Economic Zone Act, 2005, the deductions referred to in section 10A for ten consecutive assessment years, such Unit shall not be eligible for deduction from income under this section.

Provided further that where a Unit initially located in any free trade zone or export processing zone is subsequently located in a Special Economic Zone by reason of conversion of such free trade zone or export processing zone into a Special Economic Zone, the period of ten consecutive assessment years referred to above shall be reckoned from the assessment year relevant to the previous year in which the Unit began to manufacture, or produce or process such articles or things or services in such free trade zone or export processing zone:

Provided also that where a Unit initially located in any free trade zone or export processing zone is subsequently located in a Special Economic Zone by reason of conversion of such free trade zone or export processing zone into a Special Economic Zone and has completed the period of ten consecutive assessment years referred to above, it shall not be eligible for deduction from income as provided in clause (ii) of sub-section (*1*) with effect from the 1st day of April, 2006.

(*4*) This section applies to any undertaking being the Unit, which has begun or begins to manufacture or produce articles or things or services during the previous year relevant to the assessment year commencing on or after the 1st day of April, 2006, in any Special Economic Zone;

(*5*) Where any undertaking being the Unit which is entitled to the deduction under this section is transferred, before the expiry of the period specified in this section, to another undertaking, being the Unit in a scheme of amalgamation or demerger:

(*a*) no deduction shall be admissible under this section to the amalgamating or the demerged Unit, being the company for the previous year in which the amalgamation or the demerger takes place; and

(*b*) the provisions of this section shall, as they would have applied to the amalgamating or the demerged Unit being the company as if the amalgamation or demerger had not taken place.

(6) Loss referred to in sub-section (*1*) of section 72 or sub-section (*1*) or sub-section (*3*) of section 74, in so far as such loss relates to the business of the undertaking, being the Unit shall be allowed to be carried forward or set off.

(7) For the purposes of sub-section (*1*), the profits derived from the export of articles or things or services (including computer software) shall be the amount which bears to the profits of the business of the undertaking, being the Unit, the same proportion as the export turnover in respect of such articles or things or services bears to the total turnover of the business carried on by the assessee.

(8) The provisions of sub-sections (*5*) and (*6*) of section 10A shall apply to the articles or things or services referred to in sub-section (*1*) as if:

(*a*) for the figures, letters and word "1st April, 2001", the figures, letters and word "1st April, 2006" had been substituted;

(*b*) for the word "undertaking", the words "undertaking, being the Unit" had been substituted.

(9) The provisions of sub-section (*8*) and sub-section (*10*) of section 80-IA shall, so far as may be, apply in relation to the undertaking referred to in this section as they apply for the purposes of the undertaking referred to in section 80-IA.

Explanation 1. For the purposes of this section:

(*i*) "export turnover" means the consideration in respect of export by the undertaking, being the Unit of articles or things or services received in, or brought into, India by the assessee but does not include freight, telecommunication charges or insurance attributable to the delivery of the articles or things outside India or expenses, if any, incurred in foreign exchange in rendering of services (including computer software) outside India;

(*ii*) "export" in relation to the Special Economic Zones means taking goods or providing services out of India from a Special Economic Zone by land, sea, air, or by any other mode whether physical or otherwise;

(*iii*) "manufacture" shall have the same meaning as assigned to it in clause (*r*) of section 2 of the Special Economic Zones Act, 2005;

(i*v*) "relevant assessment year" means any assessment year falling within a period of fifteen consecutive assessment years referred to in this section;

(*v*) "Special Economic Zone" and "Unit" shall have the same meanings as assigned to them under clause (za) and (zc) of section 2 of the Special Economic Zones Act, 2005.

Explanation 2. For the removal of doubts, it is hereby declared that the profits and gains derived from on site development of computer software (including services for development of software) outside India shall be deemed to be the profits and gains derived from the export of computer software outside India;

(d) after section 54G, the following section shall be inserted, namely:

"54GA. (*1*) Notwithstanding anything contained in section 54G, where the capital gain arises from the transfer of a capital asset, being machinery or plant or building or land or any rights in building or land used for the purposes of the business of an industrial undertaking situate in an urban area, effected in the course of, or in consequence of the shifting of such industrial undertaking to any Special Economic Zone, whether developed in any urban area or any other area and the assessee has within a period of one year before or three years after the date on which the transfer took place:

(*a*) purchased machinery or plant for the purposes of business of the industrial undertaking in the Special Economic Zone to which the said undertaking is shifted;

(*b*) acquired building or land or constructed building for the purposes of his business in the Special Economic Zone;

(*c*) shifted the original asset and transferred the establishment of such undertaking to the Special Economic Zone; and

(*d*) incurred expenses on such other purposes as may be specified in a scheme framed by the Central Government for the purposes of this section,

then, instead of the capital gain being charged to income-tax as income of the previous year in which the transfer took place, it shall, subject to the provisions of sub-section (2), be dealt with in accordance with the following provisions of this section, that is to say:

(*i*) if the amount of the capital gain is greater than the cost and expenses incurred in relation to all or any of the purposes mentioned in clauses (*a*) to (*d*) (such cost and expenses being hereafter in this section referred to as the new asset), the difference between the amount of the capital gain and the cost of the new asset shall be charged under section 45 as the income of the previous year; and for the purpose of computing in respect of the new asset any capital gain arising from its transfer within a period of three years of its being purchased, acquired, constructed or transferred, as the case may be, the cost shall be nil; or

(*ii*) if the amount of the capital gain is equal to, or less than, the cost of the new asset, the capital gain shall not be charged under section 45; and for the purpose of computing in respect of the new asset any capital gain arising from its transfer within a period of three years of its being purchased, acquired, constructed or transferred, as the case may be, the cost shall be reduced by the amount of the capital gain.

Explanation. In this sub-section:

(*a*) "Special Economic Zone" shall have the meaning assigned to it in clause (*za*) of the Special Economic Zones Act, 2005;

(*b*) "urban area" means any such area within the limits of a municipal corporation or municipality as the Central Government may, having regard to the population, concentration of industries, need for proper planning of the area and other relevant factors, by general or special order, declare to be an urban area for the purposes of this sub-section.

(*2*) The amount of capital gain which is not appropriated by the assessee towards the cost and expenses incurred in relation to all or any of the purposes mentioned in clauses (*a*) to (*d*) of sub-section (*1*) within one year before the date on which the transfer of the original asset took place, or which is not utilised by him for all or any of the purposes aforesaid before the date of furnishing the return of income under section 139, shall be deposited by him before furnishing such return [such deposit being made in any case not later than the due date applicable in the case of the assessee for furnishing the return of income under sub-section (*1*) of section 139] in an account in any such bank or institution as may be specified in, and utilised in accordance with, any scheme which the Central Government may, by notification, frame in this behalf and such return shall be accompanied by proof of such deposit; and, for the purposes of sub-section (*1*), the amount, if any, already utilised by the assessee for all or any of the aforesaid purposes together with the amount so deposited shall be deemed to be the cost of the new asset:

Provided that if the amount deposited under this sub-section is not utilised wholly or partly for all or any of the purposes mentioned in clauses (*a*) to (*d*) of sub-section (*1*) within the period specified in that sub-section, then:

(*i*) the amount not so utilised shall be charged under section 45 as the income of the previous year in which the period of three years from the date of the transfer of the original asset expires; and

(*ii*) "the assessee shall be entitled to withdraw such amount in accordance with the scheme aforesaid";

(*e*) in section 80-IA, *after* sub-section (*12*), the following section shall be inserted, namely:

"(13) nothing contained in this section shall apply to any Special Economic Zones notified on or after the 1st day of April, 2005 in accordance with the scheme referred to in sub-clause (iii) of clause (*c*) of sub-section (*4*)".

(*f*) *after* section 80-IA, the following section shall be inserted, namely:

"80-I AB. (*1*) Where the gross total income of an assessee, being a Developer, includes any profits and gains derived by an undertaking or an enterprise from any business of developing a Special Economic Zone, notified on or after the 1st day of April, 2005 under the Special Economic Zone Act, 2005, there shall, in accordance with and subject to the provisions of this section, be allowed, in computing the total income of the assessee, a deduction of an amount equal to one hundred per cent of the profits and gains derived from such business for ten consecutive assessment years.

(*2*) The deduction specified in sub-section (*1*) may, at the option of the assessee, be claimed by him for any ten consecutive assessment years out of fifteen years beginning from the year in which a Special Economic Zone has been notified by the Central Government:

Provided that where in computing the total income of any undertaking, being a Developer for any assessment year, its profits and gains had not been included by application of the provisions of sub-section (*13*) of section 80-1A, the undertaking being the Developer shall be entitled to deduction referred to in this section only for the unexpired period of ten consecutive assessment years and thereafter it shall be eligible for deduction from income as provided in sub-section (*1*) or sub-section (2) as the case may be:

Provided further that in a case where an undertaking, being a Developer who develops a Special Economic Zone on or after the 1st day of April, 2005 and transfers the operation and maintenance of such Special Economic Zone to another Developer (hereafter in this section referred to as the transferee Developer), the deduction under sub-section (*1*) shall be allowed to such transferee Developer for the remaining period in the ten consecutive assessment years as if the operation and maintenance were not so transferred to the transferee Developer.

(3) The provisions of sub-sections (*5*) and sub-sections (*7*) to (*12*) of section 80-IA shall apply to the Special Economic Zones for the purpose of allowing deductions under sub-section (*1*).

Explanation. For the purposes of this section, "Developer" and "Special Economic Zone" shall have the same meanings respectively as assigned to them in clauses (*g*) and (*za*) of section 2 of the Special Economic Zones Act, 2005";

(g) for section 80LA, the following section shall be substituted, namely:

'80LA. (*1*) Where the gross total income of an assessee:

(*i*) being a scheduled bank, or, any bank incorporated by or under the laws of a country outside India; and having an Offshore Banking Unit in a Special Economic Zone; or

(*ii*) being a Unit of an International Financial Services Centre,

includes any income referred to in sub-section (2), there shall be allowed, in accordance with and subject to the provisions of this section, a deduction from such income, of an amount equal to:

(*a*) one hundred per cent of such income for five consecutive assessment years beginning with the assessment year relevant to the previous year in which the permission, under clause (*a*) of sub-section (*1*) of section 23 of the Banking Regulation Act, 1949 or permission or registration under the Securities and Exchange Board of India Act, 1992 or any other relevant law was obtained, and thereafter;

(*b*) fifty per cent of such income for five consecutive assessment years.

(2) The income referred to in sub-section (*1*) shall be the income:

(*a*) from an Offshore Banking Unit in a Special Economic Zone; or

(*b*) from the business referred to in sub-section (*1*) of section 6 of the Banking Regulation Act, 1949 with an undertaking located in a Special Economic Zone or any other undertaking which develops, develops and operates or develops, operates and maintains a Special Economic Zone; or (*c*) from any Unit of the International Financial Services Centre from its business for which it has been approved for setting up in such a Centre in a Special Economic Zone.

(*3*) No deduction under this section shall be allowed unless the assessee furnishes along with the return of income:

(*i*) the report, in the form specified by the Central Board of Direct Taxes under clause (i) of sub-section (2) of section 80LA, as it stood immediately before its substitution by this section, of an accountant as defined in the Explanation below sub-section (2) of section 288, certifying that the deduction has been correctly claimed in accordance with the provisions of this section; and

(*ii*) a copy of the permission obtained under clause (*a*) of sub-section (*1*) of section 23 of the Banking Regulation Act, 1949.

Explanation. For the purposes of this section:

(*a*) "International Financial Services Centre" shall have the same meaning as assigned to it in clause (*q*) of section 2 of the Special Economic Zones Act, 2005;

(*b*) "scheduled bank" shall have the same meaning as assigned to it in clause (e) of section 2 of the Reserve Bank of India Act, 1934;

(*c*) "Special Economic Zone" shall have the same meaning as assigned to it in clause (*za*) of section 2 of the Special Economic Zones Act, 2005;

(*d*) "Unit" shall have the same meaning as assigned to it in clause (*zc*) of section (2) of the Special Economic Zones Act, 2005;

(*e*) in section 115JB, after sub-section (*5*), the following sub-section shall be inserted, namely:

"(6) The provisions of this section shall not apply to the income accrued or arising on or after the 1st day of April, 2005 from any business carried on, or services rendered, by an entrepreneur or a Developer, in a Unit or Special Economic Zone, as the case may be."

(*i*) in section 115-0, after sub-section (*5*), the following sub-section shall be inserted, namely:

"(*6*) Notwithstanding anything contained in this section, no tax on distributed profits shall be chargeable in respect of the total income of an undertaking or enterprise engaged in developing or developing and operating or developing, operating and maintaining a Special Economic Zone for any assessment year on any amount declared, distributed or paid by such Developer or enterprise, by way of dividends (whether interim or otherwise) on or after the 1st day of April, 2005 out of its current income either in the hands of the Developer or enterprise or the person receiving such dividend not falling under clause (23*G*) of section 10";

(*j*) in section 197A, after sub-section (*1C*), the following sub-section shall be inserted, namely:

'(*1D*) Notwithstanding anything contained in this section, no deduction of tax shall be made by the Offshore Banking Unit from the interest paid:

(*a*) on deposit made on or after the 1st day of April, 2005, by a non-resident or a person not ordinarily resident in India; or

(*b*) on borrowings, on or after the 1st day of April, 2005, from a non-resident or a person not ordinarily resident in India.

Explanation. For the purposes of this sub-section "Offshore Banking Unit" shall have the same meaning as assigned to it in clause (u) of section 2 of the Special Economic Zones Act, 2005.'

THE THIRD SCHEDULE

(See section 56)

AMENDMENT TO CERTAIN ENACTMENTS

PART I
AMENDMENT TO THE INSURANCE ACT, 1938 (4 OF 1938)

1. In section 2C, in sub-section (*1*), after the third Proviso, insert:

"Provided also an insurer being an Indian Insurance Company, insurance co-operative society or a body corporate referred to in clause (*c*) of this sub-section carrying on the business of insurance, may carry on any business of insurance in any Special Economic Zone as defined in clause (*za*) of section 2 of the Special Economic Zones Act, 2005."

Power of Central Government to apply provisions of this Act to Special Economic zones.

2. After section 2C insert:

"2CA. The Central Government may, by notification, direct that any of the provisions of this Act:

(a) shall not apply to insurer, being an Indian Insurance Company, insurance co-operative society or a body corporate referred to in clause (c) of this sub-section (*1*) of section 2C, carrying on the business of insurance, in any Special Economic Zone as defined in clause (*za*) of section 2 of the Special Economic Zones Act, 2005; or

(b) shall apply to any insurer being an Indian Insurance Company, insurance co-operative society or a body corporate referred to in clause

(c) of sub-section (*1*) of section 2C, carrying on the business of insurance, in any Special Economic Zone as defined in clause (za) of section 2 of the Special Economic Zones Act, 2005 only with such exceptions, modifications and adaptations as may be specified in the notification."

PART II
AMENDMENTS TO THE BANKING REGULATION ACT, 1949 (10 OF 1949)

1. Section 53 shall be renumbered as sub-section (*1*) thereof and in sub-section (*1*) as so re-numbered, for "banking company or institution or to any class of banking companies", substitute:

"banking company or institution or to any class of banking companies or any of their branches functioning or located in any Special Economic Zone established under the Special Economic Zones Act, 2005."

2. After sub-section (*1*) as so numbered, the following sub-section shall be inserted, namely:

"(2) A copy of every notification proposed to be issued under sub-section (*1*), shall be laid in draft before each House of Parliament, while it is in session, for a total period of thirty days which may be comprised in one session or in two or more successive sessions, and if, before the expiry of the session immediately following the session or the successive sessions aforesaid, both Houses agree in disapproving the issue of the notification or both Houses agree in making any modification in the notification, the notification shall not be issued or, as the case may be, shall be issued only in such modified form as may be agreed upon by both the Houses.".

PART III
AMENDMENT TO THE INDIAN STAMP ACT, 1899 (2 OF 1899)

In section 3, in the proviso, after clause (2), insert:

"(3) any instrument executed, by, or, on behalf of, or, in favour of the Developer, or Unit or in connection with the carrying out of purposes of the Special Economic Zone.

Explanation. For the purposes of this clause, the expressions "Developer", "Special Economic Zone" and "Unit" shall have meanings respectively assigned to them in clause (g), (za) and (zc) of section 2 of the Special Economic Zones Act, 2005."

AMENDMENTS TO THE ACT VIDE SEZ RULES, 2006 PUBLISHED IN THE GAZETTE OF INDIA, EXTRAORDINARY, PART II, SECTION 3, SUB-SECTION (I) DATED THE 10TH AUGUST 2006

Government of India, Ministry of Commerce and Industry,
(Department of Commerce)

Notification

G.S.R.470 (E). In exercise of the powers conferred by section 55 of the Special Economic Zones Act, 2005 (28 of 2005), the

Central Government hereby makes the following rules to amend the Special Economic Zones Rules, 2006, namely:

1. (1) These rules may be called the Special Economic Zones (Amendment) Rules, 2006.

(2) They shall come into force on the date of their publication in the Official Gazette.

2. In the Special Economic Zones Rules, 2006 (hereinafter referred to as the principal rules), in sub-rule (2) of rule 5:

(1) in clause (a), for the third proviso, the following proviso shall be substituted, namely:

"Provided also that at least thirty-five per cent of the area shall be earmarked for developing the processing area, which may be relaxed upto twenty-five per cent by the Central Government on recommendations of the Board for the reasons to be recorded in writing;"

(2) In clause (b) in the second proviso, for the words "the area shall be ten hectares or more", the following shall be substituted, namely:

"the area shall be ten hectares or more with a minimum built up area as under:

(i) forty thousand square meters in case of a Special Economic Zone proposed to be set up exclusively for bio-technology and non-conventional energy sectors, including solar energy equipments/cells but excluding a Special Economic Zone set up for non-conventional energy production and manufacturing;

(ii) fifty thousand square meters in case of a Special Economic Zone proposed to be set up exclusively for the gems and jewellery sector:"

(3) in clause (c):

(i) for the first proviso, the following proviso shall be substituted, namely:

"Provided that in a stand alone Free Trade and Warehousing Zone at least fifty per cent of the area shall be earmarked for developing processing area:

Provided further that a Free Trade and Warehousing Zone may also be set up as part of a Special Economic Zone for multi-product:"

(ii) in the second proviso, for the words "provided further", the words "provided also" shall be substituted.

3. After rule 5 of the principal rules, the following rule shall be inserted, namely:

"5A. Infrastructure requirements relating to information technology:

In case of a Special Economic Zone relating to information technology, the following facilities shall be ensured, namely:

(a) twenty-four hours uninterrupted power supply at stable frequency in the Zone;

(b) reliable connectivity for uninterrupted and secure data transmission;

(c) provision for central air-conditioning system; and

(d) a ready to use, furnished plug and pay facility for end users."

4. For sub-rule (10) of rule 11 of the principal rules, the following subrule shall be substituted, namely:

"(10) No vacant land in the non-processing area shall be leased for business and social purposes such as educational institutions, hospitals, hotels, recreation and entertainment facilities, residential and business complexes, to any person except a co-developer approved by the Board:

Provided that the developer or co-developer may lease the completed infrastructure along with the vacant land appurtenant thereto for such purposes:

Provided further that infrastructure for business or social purposes in the Special Economic Zone, as may be approved by the Board, shall be eligible for exemptions, concessions and drawback."

5. In sub-rule (4) of rule 18 of the principal rules, after clause (f), the following clause shall be inserted, namely:

"(g) the use of any plant or machinery previously used for any purpose in Domestic Tariff Area."

6. In rule 76 of the principal rules:

(i) for the words "sub-clause", the word "clause" shall be substituted;

(ii) the following Explanation shall be inserted at the end, namely:

"*Explanation*. The expression "Trading", for the purposes of the Second Schedule of the Act, shall mean import for the purposes of re-export."

(F.No. F.1/6/2006-SEZ)

AMENDMENTS TO THE ACT VIDE SEZ RULES, 2007 PUBLISHED IN THE GAZETTE OF INDIA, EXTRAORDINARY, PART-II SECTION-3, SUB-SECTION (II)

Government of India, Ministry of Commerce and Industry, (Department of Commerce), New Delhi, dated the 16th March, 2007

Notification

S.O. 393 (E). In exercise of the powers conferred by section 55 of the Special Economic Zones Act, 2005(28 of 2005), the Central Government hereby makes the following rules to amend the Special Economic Zones Rules, 2006, namely:

1. (1) These rules may be called the Special Economic Zones (Second Amendment) Rules, 2007

(2) They shall come into force on the date of their publication in the Official Gazette.

2. In the Special Economic Zones Rules, 2006 (hereinafter referred to as the principal rules), in sub-rule (1) rule 2, for clause (b), following shall be substituted:

"Advance License" means Advanse License issued under the Duty Exemption and Remission Scheme of the Foreign Trade Policy and includes advance authorisation.

3. In the principal rules in rule 5, in sub-rule (2):

(i) in clause (a):

(A) the first proviso shall be deleted;

(B) the fourth proviso shall be deleted.

(ii) in clause (b), for the words "A Special Economic Zone for a specific sector or in a port or airport," the words "A Special Economic Zone for a specific sector or for one or more services or in a port or airport" shall be substituted;

(iii) after clause (c), the following clause shall be added, namely:

"(d) If a Developer subsequent to approval or notification of a Special Economic Zone acquires more contiguous and vacant land which makes the total area available, including the area already notified as Special Economic Zone, more than the minimum area required for another class of SEZ, the Board may consider such cases on a case to case basis for allowing conversion to another class of Special Economic Zone by subsuming such already approved or notified Special Economic Zone."

4. In the principal rules, in rule 6:

(i) for sub-rule (1), the following shall be substituted, namely:

"(1) The Central Government shall, within a period of thirty days of the communication received by it under clause (a) or clause (b) of sub-section (9) of section 3 of the Act grant following approvals:

(a) formal approval in the cases where land is in possession of the developer in Form-B to the person or the State Government concerned or in Form-C, if the approval is for providing infrastructural facilities in the Special Economic Zone, incorporating additional conditions, if any, specified by the Board while approving the proposal;

(b) in-principle approval in other cases in Form-B 1 to the person or the State Government concerned, incorporating additional conditions, if any, specified by the Board while approving the proposal."

(ii) for sub-rule (2), the following shall be substituted, namely:

"(2) (a) The letter of approval of a Developer granted under clause (a) of sub-rule (1) shall be valid for a period of three years within which time, effective steps shall be taken by the Developer to implement the approved proposal:

Provided that the Board may, on an application by the developer or co-developer, for reasons to be recorded in writing, extend the validity period for a further period not exceeding two years.

(b) The letter of approval of a Developer granted under clause (b) of sub-rule (1) shall be valid for a period of one year within which time, the Developer shall submit suitable proposal for formal approval in Form "A" as prescribed under the provisions of rule 3:

Provided that the Board may, on an application by the developer or co-developer for reasons to be recorded in writing, extend the validity period for a further period, not exceeding two years, upon a request made in writing by the Developer or Co-developer."

5. In the principal rules, in rule 7:

(i) for sub-rule (1), the following shall be substituted, namely:

"(1) The Developer shall furnish to the Central Government, particulars required under sub-section (1) of section 4 with regard to the area referred to in sub-section (2) or sub-section (4) of section 3, (hereinafter referred to as identified area), with a certificate from the concerned State Government or its authorized agency stating that the developer(s) have legal possession and irrevocable rights to develop the said area as SEZ and that the said area is free from all encumbrances:

Provided that where the Developer has leasehold rights over the identified area, the lease shall be for a period not less than twenty years."

(ii) in sub-rule (2), the words, brackets and figures "subject to third proviso to clause (a) of sub-rule (2) of rule 5" shall be deleted.

(iii) in sub-rule (2), the following proviso shall be inserted:

"Provided that the Board may relax any or all of the conditions, except the condition regarding identified area to be a vacant land, specified in this sub-rule on a case-to-case basis on merits for reasons to be recorded in writing and with such conditions as the Board may decide."

6. In the principal rules, in rule 11,

(i) for sub-rule (2), following shall be substituted, namely:

"(2) The processing area and Free Trade and Warehousing Zone shall have specified entry and exit points and be fully secured by taking such measures as approved by the Board of Approvals."

(ii) in sub-rule (5), for the words, "the lease period shall be co-terminus with the validity of Letter of Approval", the following shall be substituted, namely:

"the lease period shall not be less than five years but notwithstanding any other condition in the lease deed, the lease rights would cease to exist in case of the expiry or cancellation of the Letter of Approval."

(iii) in sub-rule (10), for the second proviso, following shall be substituted:

"Provided further that infrastructure for business or social purposes in the Special Economic Zone, as may be approved by the Board, shall be eligible for exemptions, concessions, drawback and any such infrastructure created in addition or in excess thereof shall not be eligible for any exemptions, concessions and drawback."

7. In the principal rules, in rule 27, after sub-rule (1), the following provisos shall be inserted:

"Provided that exemptions from payment of duty, taxes or cess, drawbacks and concessions on all types of goods and services, required for setting up and maintenance of the factory building, allowed to a unit shall also be available to the contractors appointed by such unit and all the documents in such cases shall bear the name of the unit along with the contractor and these shall be filed jointly in the name of the unit and the contractor:

Provided further that the unit shall be responsible and liable for proper utilization of such goods and services in all cases."

8. In the principal rules, in rule 41, after sub-rule (2), the following sub-rule shall be inserted:

"(3) A Developer or a co-developer or on their behalf their contractor, as the case may be, may also temporarily remove the goods, procured or imported duty free by them for their authorized operations, to a place in the Domestic Tariff Area or a unit in the same or another Special Economic Zone or Export Oriented Unit or a unit in Electronic Hardware Technology Park unit or Software Technology Park unit or Bio-technology Park unit, for sub-contracting a process, with prior permission of and subject to such conditions as may be prescribed by the Approval Committee."

9. In the principal rules, in rule 42, after sub-rule (4), the following sub-rule shall be inserted:

"(5) The Developer or a co-developer or on their behalf their contractor, as the case may be, shall follow the same procedure for sub-contracting in Domestic Tariff Area or in a Unit in other Special Economic Zones or in a Export Oriented Unit or in an Electronic Hardware Technology Park Unit or a Software Technology Park Unit as prescribed for sub-contracting by SEZ Units in subrules (1) above:

Provided that the Bank Guarantee to cover the duty foregone on the materials being sent for sub-contracting shall apply only in case of temporary removal of goods by the contractor."

10. In the principal rules:

(i) in Form-A, after point No. VI, the following shall be inserted:

"VIA. Foreign Direct Investment (FDI)

(a) Extent of FDI (if any) in million U.S. Dollars;

(b) Source of FDI (Country and Company details may be provided)";

(ii) in Form-A, at the end, the following shall be deleted, namely:

"*Note*: Furnish 25 copies of the application with project report"

11. In the principal rules, in Form A, after the "Undertaking", the following shall be added, namely:

"Check List

(1) Name of the Developer.

(2) Proposed area of the location of the SEZ.

(3) Status of recommendation of the proposal by the State Government (if available).

(4) Whether proposal is for formal or in-principle approval. (In case land is in possession of the promoter, it is considered for formal approval)

(5) Is it a multi-product SEZ?

(6) If it is a sector specific SEZ, mention the sector the sector.

(7) Whether it meets the area requirements.

(8) Area of the SEZ (in hectares)

(9) Whether Form-A has been filed?

(10) Whether undertaking and affidavit have been submitted.

(11) Whether project report has been submitted.

(12) Whether land is owned/leased and is in possession of the Developer.

(13) Does the proposal meet the area requirements of the Rules?

(14) Whether the land has existing structures or is vacant.

(15) Whether the land is contiguous.

(16) Projected investment in the project.

(17) Projected exports from the project.

(18) Projected employment from the project.

(19) Share capital and Reserves of the Developer Company.

(20) Source of funds for the project.

(21) Net worth of the Applicant (including Group companies) duly supported by Audited Accounts of the Developer for last 3 Years (for all the constituents in case the Developer is an SPV). If the company is a new company, audited accounts of Flagship Company/ promoters may be provided.

(22) Extent of FDI (if any) in million US Dollars

(23) Source of FDI (Country and Company details may be provided)

(24) Whether provisions contained in the Press Note No. 5 (2005 Series), issued by the Ministry of Commerce and Industry have been followed in respect of Telecom/IT SEZ development."

11. In the principal rules, in Form-B, in the first line, for the word "EPZ", the word "SEZ" shall be substituted;

12. In the principal rules, after Form-B, the following form shall be inserted, namely:

"Form- B 1

No. F. ____________ -SEZ

Government of India

Ministry of Commerce & Industry

Department of Commerce

(SEZ Section)

Dated, the ________________

To

____

____

____

Subject: Setting up of a ________ Special Economic Zone at ____________ by M/s.______ – Reg.

Reference: Your application dated _______.

Sir(s),

With reference to your above-mentioned application, Government of India is pleased to grant "in-principle" approval to your proposal for development, operation and maintenance of a Special Economic Zone (SEZ), as per details given below:

I. Proposal and Project Details: To set up a ___________ Special Economic Zone over an area of _________ hectares ___________ by M/s._______________.

II. General Conditions:

(i) This "in-principle" approval is valid for a period of one year within which time the applicant shall submit suitable proposal for formal approval in Form "A" as prescribed under the provisions of Rule 3 of the SEZ Rules 2006, alongwith proof of land possession/ leasehold rights, updated Project Report and Check List. Fifteen copies of the application and other enclosures prescribed shall be submitted to the Director (SEZ), Department of Commerce, Udyog Bhavan, New Delhi-110 011 directly or through the State Government concerned. The applicant should be in possession of the identified area either by way of ownership or by way of leasehold rights valid for twenty years or more on the date of application.

(ii) The Developer shall obtain the required approval from various statutory authorities under relevant statutes and regulations of the Government of India and the State Government and local bodies.

(iii) The Developer shall make adequate provision for rehabilitation of the displaced persons as per the RR policy of the State Government.

(iv) The project shall be implemented and operated in terms of the Special Economic Zones Act, 2005 and the rules and orders made thereunder.

(v) The Developer shall conform to the environmental requirements.

(vi) The Developer shall abide by the local laws, rules, regulations or bye-laws in regard to area planning, sewage disposal, pollution control, labour laws and the like as may be locally applicable.

(vii) The Developer shall raise the required funds for the project. External commercial borrowing, if any, will be as per the guidelines of the Ministry of Finance, Department of Economic Affairs, Government of India, New Delhi.

(viii) The Developer shall obtain the approval of Board for specific activities proposed to be undertaken for development, operation and maintenance of Special Economic Zone.

(ix) Any request for extension, for a period not exceeding two years, may be submitted with valid reasons and details of steps taken for implementation, which may be considered by the Board, on merits. Such request shall be submitted to the Government two months before expiry of the approval period.

2. This approval shall be also subject to other conditions as prescribed by the Board.

3. The Developer may convey acceptance of all the terms and conditions indicated above within thirty days from the date of issue of this letter. All future correspondence may be addressed to the Director (SEZ), Department of Commerce, Udyog Bhavan, New Delhi-11.

Yours faithfully,
Sd/-
Director/Deputy Secretary
Department of Commerce"
(F.2/633/2006-SEZ)

Guidelines for SEZ Developers

8

Ministry of Commerce and Industry Department of Commerce Notification dated 24th January 2002

S.O. No. 100(E): In exercise of the powers conferred under Section 80 IA of the Income Tax Act, 1961, read with sub rule (2) of rule 18 C of the Income Tax Rules, 1962, the Central Government hereby makes the following scheme to develop, operate and maintain Special Economic Zones for the period beginning on the 1st day of April, 2001 for the Zones developed on or before 31.3.2006.

1. Objectives of the Scheme

(a) The scheme shall aim at development of integrated world class infrastructure for exports including carrying out manufacture of goods, rendering of services or in connection therewith and would include industrial, commercial and social infrastructure. Components of a Special Economic Zone shall include roads, airports, ports, transport system, generation and distribution of power, telecom, hospitals, hotels, educational institutions, leisure and entertainment units, residential/industrial/commercial complexes, water supply, sanitation and sewerage system and any other facility required for development of the Zone.

(b) Special Economic Zones may be developed and managed in the private sector or jointly by State Government and a private agency or exclusively by the State Government or their agencies. In the case of privately developed Zones, the investors could be either Indian individuals, NRIs, Indian or foreign companies.

(c) New infrastructural development works such as construction of Standard Design Factory Building, etc. and operation and maintenance of infrastructure in the Zones may also be undertaken through private/joint/State sector in the Export Processing Zones converted into Special Economic Zones.

2. Criteria for Approval

Proposals for setting up SEZ in the public/private/joint/State sector are required to meet the following conditions:

(i) Minimum size of the SEZ shall not be less than 1000 hectares. This would however, not apply to existing EPZs converted into SEZs as such or for notifying additional area as a part of such SEZ or to product specific SEZs or port/airport-based SEZs, on a case to case basis.

(ii) The SEZ and units therein shall abide by local laws, rules, regulations or bye-laws in regard to area planning, sewerage disposal, pollution control and the like. They shall also comply with industrial and labour laws and such other laws/rules and regulations as may be locally applicable.

(iii) Such SEZ shall make adequate arrangements to fulfill all the requirements of the laws, rules and procedures applicable to such SEZ.

(iv) Only units approved under the SEZ Scheme would be permitted to be located in these SEZs. At least 25% area of the SEZ shall be used for developing industrial area for setting up of such units.

(v) The predominant objective of development of an SEZ would be to create infrastructure, which would facilitate setting up of industrial area for units therein as indicated in the para (iv) above.

3. Procedure for Approval

3.1 Applications (15 copies) indicating the name and address of the applicant, status of the promoter (whether individual/private company/State Government/NRIs, etc.) along with a project report covering the following particulars shall be submitted to the Chief Secretary of the State:

(i) Location of the proposed zone with details of existing and proposed infrastructure;

(ii) Area of the proposed SEZ and its distance from the nearest Sea Port/Airport/Rail/Road head, etc.;

(iii) Financial details including investment proposed, mode of financing the project and viability of the project;

(iv) Details of foreign equity and repatriation of dividends, etc., if any;

(v) Whether the Zone will allow only certain specific industries or will be a multi-product zone.

3.2 The State Government shall, forward it along with their commitment to the following, to the Department of Commerce, Government of India:

(i) The area incorporated in the proposed Special Economic Zone is free from environmental prohibition;

(ii) Water, electricity and other services would be provided as required;

(iii) Full exemption in electricity duty and tax on sale of electricity for self-generated and purchased power;

(iv) To allow generation, transmission and distribution of power within the SEZ;

(v) Exemption from State Sales Tax, octroi, mandi tax, turnover tax and taxes, duty, cess, levies on supply of goods from Domestic Tariff Area to SEZ units;

(vi) For units inside the Zone, the powers under the Industrial Disputes Act and other related Acts would be delegated to the Development Commissioner;

(vii) The Zone will be declared as a Public Utility Service under the Industrial Disputes Act;

(viii) Single point clearances system would be provided to the units in the Zone under State Laws/Rules.

3.3 The Government may grant in-principle approval to proposals for setting up of SEZs. The in-principle approval shall be valid for a period of one year. The validity period may be extended by the Department of Commerce, on a case to case basis.

3.4 On acceptance of the proposal by the BOA, the Department of Commerce will issue a Letter of Permission to the applicant, hereafter referred to as "developer".

3.5 The approval shall be valid for a period of 3 years within which time effective steps shall be taken by the developer to implement the project. The validity period may be extended by the Department of Commerce, on a case to case basis. Provided that commercial, residential and recreational facilities shall be approved only if the applicant has at least 26% equity in such entities.

3.6 In case of converted EPZ into SEZ, approval for development, operation and maintenance of requirements in infrastructure will have to be obtained from BOA on case to case basis. Para 3.5 shall *mutatis mutandis*, apply to creation of new infrastructure in the converted SEZs.

4. General Conditions

(1) The undertaking applying for approval shall undertake to continue to operate under the SEZ scheme during the period in which benefits under Section 80 IA of the Income Tax Act are to be availed.

(2) The Central Government may withdraw the approval given to an undertaking for setting up of SEZ if the undertaking fails to comply with any of the conditions of approval.

5. Agreement with Central Government

The Letter of Permission issued by the Government of India (Department of Commerce) to the developer for setting up of Special Economic Zone shall be treated as 'Agreement' for availing exemption under the Section 80-IA of the Income Tax Act.

Facilities for Developers

Developer of SEZ may import/procure goods without payment of duty for the development, operation and maintenance of SEZ.

Income tax exemption for a block of 10 year in 15 years at the option of developer as per section 80-IA of the Income Tax Act read with Appendix 14-II-N of *Handbook of Procedure*.

Full freedom in allocation of developed plots to approved SEZ units on purely commercial basis.

Full authority to provide services like water, electricity, security, restaurants, recreation centres, etc. on commercial lines.

Foreign investment permitted to develop township within the SEZ with residential areas, markets, playgrounds, clubs, recreation centers, etc.

Develop Standard Design Factory (SDF) building in exiting Special Economic Zones. Guildlines at Appendix 14-II-N

Income Tax exemption to Investor's in SEZs under section 10 (23) G of Income Tax Act.

Exemption from Service Tax

Investment made by individuals, etc. in SEZ company also eligible for exemption u/s 88 of IT Act.

Development promoted to transfer infrastructure facility for operations and maintenance u/s 80-I-A of IT Act.

Generation, Transmission and Distribution of Power in SEZs allowed.

Terms and Conditions

SEZ units have to be a positive Net Foreign Exchange Earner.

Performance of the unit will be monitored by a committee consisting of Development Commissioner of the Zone and Customs.

Units shall maintain proper accounts and furnish details regarding value of import, export, etc. to Development Commissioner on a quaterly basis.

For detail please see chapter 7 of *Export and Import Policy* and chapter 7 *Handbook of Procedure.*

How to Apply

Applications (15 copies) indicating the name and address of the applicant, status of the promoter (whether individual/private company/State Government/NRIs, etc.) alongwith a project report covering the following particulars shall be submitted to the Chief Secretary of the State:

(i) Location of the proposed zone with details of existing and proposed infrastructure.

(ii) Area of the proposed SEZ and its area distance from the nearest Sea Port/Airport/Rail/Road head, etc.

(iii) Financial details including investment proposed, mode of financing the project and viability of the project.

(iv) Details of foreign equity and repatriation o: dividends etc., if any.

(v) Whether the Zone will allow only certain specific industries or will be a multi-product Zone or it is a port/airport based Zone.

The State Government shall, forward it alongwith their commitment to the following, to the Department of Commerce, Government of India:

The area incorporated in the proposed Special Economic Zone is free from environmental prohibition; water, electricity and other services would be provided as required;

Full exemption in electricity duty and tax on sale of electricity for self generated and purchased power; To allow generation, transmission and distribution of power within SEZ;

(vi) Exemption from State Sales Tax, octroi, mandi tax, turnover tax and taxes, duty, cess, levies on supply of goods from Domestic Tariff Area to SEZ units;

(vii) For units inside the Zone, the powers under the Industrial Disputes Act and other related Acts would be delegated to the Development Commissioner.

(viii) The Zone will be declared as a Public Utility Service under Industrial Disputes Act.

(ix) Single point clearances system would be provided to the units in the Zone under State Laws/Rules.

The proposal incorporating the commitments of the State Government shall be considered by the Board of Approvals (BOA) as notified vide notification No 14/1/2001-EPZ dated 7.8.2001. (Appendix 14-I-D)

On acceptance of the proposal by the BOA, the Department of Commerce will issue a Letter of Permission to the applicant;

For full details see guidelines at Appendix 14-II-N

15 Days Prior Notice for Approval of SEZ Projects

PRESS NOTE

Proposals received for setting up of Special Economic Zones (SEZs) are considered by an Inter-Ministerial Committee known as the Board of Approvals (BOA), in its meeting held every month. The promoters of the SEZs are also invited to such meetings to explain the salient features of their proposals and to furnish clarifications, wherever required.

Suggestions have been received from the concerned Ministries/ Departments requesting for 15 days' time for examination of the proposals. Accordingly, it has been decided that the proposals that have been received up to 15 days prior to the scheduled meeting of the Board of Approvals, will be placed for its consideration and any proposals received thereafter will be considered in the next meeting.

The next meeting of the Board of Approvals is scheduled to be held on 25th November, 2005 and proposals for setting up of Special Economic Zones received till 11/11/2005 would be taken up for consideration in the proposed meeting.

Ministry of Finance, Notifications on Income Tax

9

NOTIFICATION

Dated 13th November, 2003

S.O. 1397 (E). In exercise of powers conferred by section 295, read with section 80LA of the Income Tax Act, 1961 (43 of 1961), the Central Board of Direct Taxes hereby makes the following rules further to amend the Income Tax Rules, 1962, namely:

1. (1) These rules may be called the Income Tax (26th Amendment) Rules, 2003

   (2) They shall come into force on the date of issue of this notification.

2. In the Income Tax Rules, 1962,

   (i) after the rule-19AD, the following shall be inserted, namely:

   "19-AE. The report of the accountant, which is required to be furnished by the assessee under sub-section (3) of section 80-LA shall be in Form No. 10-CCF."

   (ii) in Appendix-II after Form No. 10CCE, the following shall be inserted, namely:

NOTIFICATION

Dated 13th November, 2003 the 25th September, 2003

S.O.1110(E)—In exercise of powers conferred by section 295, read with section 80HHC of the Income-tax Act, 1961 (43 of 1961), the Central Board of Direct Taxes hereby makes the following rules further to amend the Income Tax Rules, 1962, namely:

1. (1) These rules may be called the Income Tax (21 st Amendment) Rules, 2003

   - They shall come into force on the date of their publication in the Official Gazette.
   - In the Income-tax Rules, 1962,-

     (a) in part IV, in rule 18-BBA, after sub-rule(2), the following sub-rule shall be inserted, namely:-

"(2A) The certificate from the undertaking in the Special Economic Zone which is required to be furnished under proviso to Sub-section (4) of section 80HHC by an undertaking referred to in sub-section (4C) of that section shall be in Form No.10CCABA";

(b) in the Appendix-II,

- after the Form No.10CCAB, the following form shall be inserted, namely:

....

NOTIFICATION

26th August, 2003

1. S.O. 972(E)—In exercise of the powers conferred by Section 295, read with clause (b) of sub-section (1B) of section 10A of the Income Tax Act, 1961 (43 of 1961), the Central Board of Direct Taxes hereby makes the following rules further to amend the Income Tax Rules, 1962, namely:

(1) These rules may be called the Income Tax (15th Amendment) Rules, 2003.

(2) They shall come into force on the date of their publication in the Official Gazette.

2. In the Income Tax Rules, 1962:

(i) after the rule 16D, the following rule shall be inserted, namely:

"16DD. Form of particulars to be furnished along with return of income for claiming deduction under clause (b) of sub-section (1B) of section 10A.

The particulars, which are required to be furnished by the assessee along with the return of income under clause (b) of sub-section (1B) of section 10A shall be in Form No. 56FF";

(ii) in Appendix II, after Form No.56F, the following Form shall be inserted, namely:

....

NOTIFICATION

Dated 23rd May, 2003

GSR.————(E): In exercise of the powers conferred by section 13 of the Central Sale Tax Act, 1956 (74 of 1956), the Central Government hereby makes the following rules further to amend the Central Sales Tax (Registration and Turnover) Rules, 1957, namely:

1. Short title and commencement—(1) These Rules may be called the Central Sale Tax (Registration and Turnover) Second Amendment Rules, 2003.

(2) They shall come into force on the date of their publication in the Official Gazette.

2. In the Central Sales Tax (Registration and Turnover) Rules, 1957,-

(a) in rule 12',-

(i) in sub-rule (10), the proviso to clause (a) shall be omitted;

(ii) after sub-rule (10), the following sub-rule shall be inserted, namely:

"(11) The dealer, selling goods in the course of inter-State trade or commerce to a registered dealer under sub-section (6) or under sub-section (8) of section 8 sub-section (1) or section 5 of the Central Sales Tax Act, 1956, read with section 76A of the Customs Act, 1962 (52 of 1962), shall furnish a declaration for the purpose of sub-section (8) of the said section 8 in "Form I" duly countersigned and certified by the Authority specified by the Central Government authorising the establishment of the unit in the Special Economic Zone (notified under section 76A of the Customs Act, 1962 (52 of 1962) that the sale of goods is for the purpose of establishing a unit in such Zone",

(b) after Form 'H', the following form shall be inserted, namely:

....

NOTIFICATION: NO. S.O. 890(E)

"In exercise of the powers conferred by clause (b) of item (i) of *Explanation* 2 of section 10A of the Income Tax Act, 1961 (43 of 1961), the Central Board of Direct Taxes hereby specifies the following Information Technology enabled products or services, as the case may be, for the purpose of said clauses, namely:

1. Back-office Operations
2. Call Centres;
3. Content Development or Animation;
4. Data Processing;
5. Engineering and Design;
6. Geographic Information System Services;
7. Human Resource Services;
8. Insurance Claim Processing;
9. Legal Databases;
10. Medical Transcription;
11. Payroll;
12. Remote Maintenance;
13. Revenue Accounting;
14. Support Centres, and
15. Website Services: Notification: No. S.O. 890(E), dated 26.9.2000."

Income Tax Rules/Sections Relating to Special Economic Zones

10

INCOME TAX RULE 18-C

Eligibility of Industrial Parks and Special Economic Zone for benefits under section 80-IA(4(iii)) of the Income Tax Act, 1961 as amended vide notification no 183/2002/dated 23rd July 2002

1. The undertaking shall begin to develop or develop and operate or maintain and operate a Special Economic Zone any time during the period beginning of 1st day of April, 2001 and ending on 31st day of March 2006.

2. The undertaking shall be duly approved by the Ministry of Commerce and Industry in the Central Government under the scheme for industrial park or Special Economic Zones notified by that Ministry.

3. The undertaking shall continue to fulfil the conditions envisaged in the scheme.

4. On approval under sub-rule (2), the Central Board of Direct Taxes, shall notify industrial parks of Special Economic Zone for benefit under section 80-IA.

EXPLANATORY MEMORANDUM

Under section 10A of the Income Tax Act, 1961 undertaking operating from a Special Economic Zone (SEZ) which manufactures articles/things or computer software is eligible for deduction of export profits. For undertaking commencing operation from the notified Special Economic Zones (SEZs) on or after 1st April, 2002, the tax holiday is available for a total period of seven assessment years, comprising of a deduction of 100% of export for five years followed by deduction of 50% of export profits for subsequent two years.

2. Under 80-IA (4) (iii) of the Income Tax Act, 1961 tax holiday equal to 100% of eligible profit for 10 out of initial 15 years is available to any undertaking which, develops, or develops and operates or maintains and operates a Special Economic Zone notified by the Central Government in accordance with the scheme framed and notified by the Government for the period beginning on the first day of April, 1997 and ending of the 31st day of March 2006.

3. Rule 18C of the Income Tax Rules, 1962, provides Income Tax for eligibility of industrial parks for benefit under section 80-IA (4) (iii) of the Income Tax Act 18C is being amended to enable notification of Special Economic Zones for the purpose of benefit to developers of Special Economic Zones under section 80-IA of the Income Tax Act.

4. These changes will come into force with retrospective effect from 1st of April 2001.

5. It is certified that the above-mentioned amendment to the said rule 18C shall not prejudicially affect the interest of any assessee.

INCOME TAX SECTION 88

88. (1) Subject to the provisions of this section, an assessee, being an individual, or a Hindu Undivided Family, shall be entitled to a deduction, from the amount of income tax (as computed before allowing the deductions under this Chapter) on his total income with which he is chargeable for any assessment year, of an amount equal to:

(i) in the case of an individual or a Hindu Undivided Family, whose gross total income before giving effect to deductions under Chapter VI-A, is one lakh fifty thousand rupees or less, twenty per cent of the aggregate of the sums referred to in sub-section (2):

Provided that an individual shall be entitled to a deduction of an amount equal to thirty per cent of the aggregate of the sums referred to in sub-section (2) if his income under the head "Salaries":

(a) does not exceed one lakh rupees during the previous year before allowing the deduction under section 16; and

(b) is not less than ninety per cent of his gross total income, as defined in sub-section (5) of section 80B.

(ii) in the case of an individual or a Hindu Undivided Family, whose gross total income before giving effect to deductions under chapter VI-A, is more than one lakh fifty thousand rupees but does not exceed five lakh rupees, fifteen per cent of the aggregate of the sums referred to in sub-section (2);

(iii) in the case of an individual or a Hindu Undivided Family, whose gross total income before giving effect to deductions under Chapter VI-A, exceeds five lakh rupees, nil.

(2) The sums referred to in sub-section (1) shall be any sums paid or deposited in the previous year by the assessee 7a [out of his income chargeable to tax]....

[(xvi) as subscription to equity shares or debentures forming part of any eligible issue of capital approved by the Board on an application made by a public company [or as subscription to any eligible issue of capital by any public financial institution] in the prescribed form:

Provided that where a deduction is claimed and allowed under this clause with reference to the cost of any equity shares or debentures, the cost of such shares or debentures shall not be taken into account for the purposes of sections 54EA and 54EB].

Explanation. For the purposes of this clause:

(i) "eligible issue of capital" means an issue made by a public company formed and registered in India or a public financial institution and the entire proceeds of the issue are utilised wholly and exclusively for the purposes of any business referred to in sub-section (4) of section 80-IA;

(ii) "public company" shall have the meaning assigned to it in section 3 of the Companies Act, 1956;

(iii) "public financial institution" shall have the meaning assigned to it in section 4A of the Companies Act, 1956.

INCOME TAX 80-IA

Deductions in respect of profits and gains from industrial undertakings or enterprises engaged in infrastructure development, etc.

80-IA. (1) Where the gross total income of an assessee includes any profits and gains derived by an undertaking or an enterprise from any business referred to in sub-section (4) (such business being hereinafter referred to as the eligible business), there shall, in accordance with and subject to the provisions of this section, be allowed, in computing the total income of the assessee, a deduction of an amount equal to hundred per cent of profits and gains derived from such business for ten consecutive assessment years.

(2) The deduction specified in sub-section (1) may, at the option of the assessee, be claimed by him for any ten consecutive assessment years out of fifteen years beginning from the year in which the undertaking or the enterprise develops and begins to operate any infrastructure facility or starts providing telecommunication service or develops an industrial park or develops a Special Economic Zone referred to in clause (iii) of sub-section (4) or generates power or commences transmission or distribution of power:

Provided that where the assessee develops or operates and maintains or develops, operates and maintains any infrastructure facility referred to in clause (a) or clause (b) or clause (c) of the Explanation to clause (i) of sub-section (4), the provisions of this sub-section shall have effect as if for the words "fifteen years", the words "twenty years" had been substituted.

(2A) Notwithstanding anything contained in sub-section (1) or sub-section (2), the deduction in computing the total income of an undertaking providing telecommunication services, specified in clause (ii) of sub-section (4), shall be hundred per cent of the profits and gains of the eligible business for the first five assessment years commencing at any time during the periods as specified in sub-section (2) and thereafter, thirty per cent of such profits and gains for further five assessment years.

(3) This section applies to an undertaking referred to in clause (iv) of sub-section (4) which fulfils all the following conditions, namely:

(i) it is not formed by splitting up, or the reconstruction, of a business already in existence:

Provided that this condition shall not apply in respect of an undertaking which is formed as a result of the re-establishment, re-construction or revival by the assessee of the business of any such one undertaking as is referred to in section 33B, in the circumstances and within the period specified in that section;

(ii) it is not formed by the transfer to a new business of machinery or plant previously used for any purpose.

Explanation 1. For the purposes of clause (ii), any machinery or plant which was used outside India by any person other than the assessee shall not be regarded as machinery or plant previously used for any purpose, if the following conditions are fulfilled, namely:

(a) such machinery or plant was not, at any time previous to the date of the installation by the assessee, used in India;

(b) such machinery or plant is imported into India from any country outside India; and

(c) no deduction on account of depreciation in respect of such machinery or plant has been allowed or is allowable under the provisions of this Act in computing the total income of any person for any period prior to the date of the installation of machinery or plant by the assessee.

Explanation 2. Where in the case of an undertaking , any machinery or plant or any part thereof previously used for any purpose is transferred to a new business and the total value of the machinery or plant or part so transferred does not exceed twenty per cent of the total value of the machinery or plant used in the business, then, for the purposes of clause (ii) of this sub-section, the condition specified therein shall be deemed to have been complied with.

(4) This section applies to-

(i) any enterprise carrying on the business of (i) developing; or (ii) operating and maintaining; or (iii) developing, operating and maintaining any infrastructure facility which fulfils all the following conditions, namely:

(a) it is owned by a company registered in India or by a consortium of such companies;

(b) it has entered into an agreement with the Central Government or a State Government or a local authority or any other statutory body for (i) developing; or (ii) operating and maintaining; or (iii) developing, operating and maintaining a new infrastructure facility;

(c) it has started or starts operating and maintaining the infrastructure facility on or after the 1st day of April, 1995:

Provided that where an infrastructure facility is transferred on or after the 1st day of April, 1999 by an enterprise which developed such infrastructure facility (hereafter referred to in this section as the transferor enterprise) to another enterprise (hereafter in this section referred to as the transferee enterprise) for the purpose of operating and maintaining the infrastructure facility on its behalf in accordance with the agreement with the Central Government, State Government, local authority or statutory body, the provisions of this section shall apply to the transferee enterprise as if it were the enterprise to which this clause applies and the deduction from profits and gains would be available to such transferee enterprise for the unexpired period during which the transferor enterprise would have been entitled to the deduction, if the transfer had not taken place.

Explanation. For the purposes of this clause, "infrastructure facility" means:

(a) a road including toll road, a bridge or a rail system;

(b) a highway project including housing or other activities being an integral part of the highway project;

(c) a water supply project, water treatment system, irrigation project, sanitation and sewerage system or solid waste management system;

(d) a port, airport, inland waterway or inland port;

(ii) any undertaking which has started or starts providing telecommunication services whether basic or cellular, including radio paging, domestic satellite service, network of trunking, broadband network and internet services on or after the 1st day of April, 1995, but on or before the 31st day of March, 2003;

(iii) any undertaking which develops, develops and operates or maintains and operates an industrial park or special economic zone notified by the Central Government in accordance with the scheme framed and notified by that Government for the period beginning on the 1st day of April, 1997 and ending on the 31st day of March 10, 2006:

Provided that in case where an undertaking develops an industrial park on or after the 1st day of April, 1999 or a Special Economic Zone on or after 1st day of April, 2001 and transfer the operation and maintenance of such industrial park or such Special Economic Zone, as the case may be , to another undertaking (hereafter in this section referred to as the transferee undertaking), the deduction under sub-section (1) shall be allowed to such transferee undertaking for the remaining period in the ten consecutive assessment years as if the operation and maintenance were not so transferred to the transferee undertaking. (Incorporated vide Finance Bill, 2003)

(iv) an undertaking which,-

(a) is set up in any part of India for the generation or generation and distribution of power if it begins to generate power at any time during the period beginning on the 1st day of April, 1993 and ending on the 31st day of March, 2006;

(b) starts transmission or distribution by laying a network of new transmission or distribution lines at any time during the period beginning on the 1st day of April, 1999 and ending on the 31st day of March, 2006:

Provided that the deduction under this section to an undertaking under sub-clause (b) shall be allowed only in relation to the profits derived from laying of such network of new lines for transmission or distribution.

(5) Notwithstanding anything contained in any other provision of this Act, the profits and gains of an eligible business to which the provisions of sub-section (1) apply shall, for the purposes of determining the quantum of deduction under that sub-section for the assessment year immediately succeeding the initial assessment year or any subsequent assessment year, be computed as if such eligible business were the only source of income of the assessee during the previous year relevant to the initial assessment year and to every subsequent assessment year up to and including the assessment year for which the determination is to be made.

(6) Notwithstanding anything contained in sub-section (4), where housing or other activities are an integral part of the highway project and the profits of which are computed on such basis and manner as may be prescribed, such profit shall not be liable to tax where the profit has been transferred to a special reserve account and the same is actually utilised for the highway project excluding housing and other activities before the expiry of three years following the year in which such amount was transferred to the reserve account; and the amount remaining unutilised shall be chargeable to tax as income of the year in which such transfer to reserve account took place.

(7) Where the assessee is a person other than a company or a co-operative society, the deduction under sub-section (1) from profits and gains derived from an undertaking shall not be admissible unless the accounts of the undertaking for the previous

year relevant to the assessment year for which the deduction is claimed to have been audited by an accountant, as defined in the Explanation below sub-section (2) of section 288, and the assessee furnishes, along with his return of income, the report of such audit in the prescribed form 14 duly signed and verified by such accountant.

(8) Where any goods or services held for the purposes of the eligible business are transferred to any other business carried on by the assessee, or where any goods or services held for the purposes of any other business carried on by the assessee are transferred to the eligible business and, in either case, the consideration, if any, for such transfer as recorded in the accounts of the eligible business does not correspond to the market value of such goods or services as on the date of the transfer, then, for the purposes of the deduction under this section, the profits and gains of such eligible business shall be computed as if the transfer, in either case, had been made at the market value of such goods or services as on that date:

Provided that where, in the opinion of the Assessing Officer, the computation of the profits and gains of the eligible business in the manner hereinbefore specified presents exceptional difficulties, the Assessing Officer may compute such profits and gains on such reasonable basis as he may deem fit.

Explanation: For the purposes of this sub-section, "market value", in relation to any goods or services, means the price that such goods or services would ordinarily fetch in the open market.

(9) Where any amount of profits and gains of an undertaking or of an enterprise in the case of an assessee is claimed and allowed under this section for any assessment year, deduction to the extent of such profits and gains shall not be allowed under any other provisions of this Chapter under the heading "C.- Deductions in respect of certain incomes", and shall in no case exceed the profits and gains of such eligible business of undertaking or enterprise, as the case may be.

(10) Where it appears to the Assessing Officer that, owing to the close connection between the assessee carrying on the eligible

business to which this section applies and any other person, or for any other reason, the course of business between them is so arranged that the business transacted between them produces to the assessee more than the ordinary profits which might be expected to arise in such eligible business, the Assessing Officer shall, in computing the profits and gains of such eligible business for the purposes of the deduction under this section, take the amount of profits as may be reasonably deemed to have been derived therefrom.

(11) The Central Government may, after making such inquiry as it may think fit, direct, by notification in the Official Gazette, that the exemption conferred by this section shall not apply to any class of industrial undertaking or enterprise with effect from such date as it may specify in the notification.

(12) Where any undertaking of an Indian company which is entitled to the deduction under this section is transferred, before the expiry of the period specified in this section, to another Indian company in a scheme of amalgamation or demerger:

(a) no deduction shall be admissible under this section to the amalgamating or the demerged company for the previous year in which the amalgamation or the demerger takes place; and

(b) the provisions of this section shall, as far as may be, apply to the amalgamated or the resulting company as they would have applied to the amalgamating or the demerged company if the amalgamation or demerger had not taken place.

SECTION 80-HHC

(Deduction in respect of profits retained for export business.)

(1) Where an assessee, being an Indian company or a person (other than a company) resident in India, is engaged in the business of export out of India of any goods or merchandise to which this section applies, there shall, in accordance with and subject to the provisions of this section, be allowed, in computing the total income of the assessee, a deduction to the extent of profits, referred to in sub-section(1B), derived by the assessee from the export of such goods or merchandise:

Provided that if the assessee, being a holder of an Export House Certificate or a Trading House Certificate (hereafter in this section referred to as an Export House or a Trading House, as the case may be), issues a certificate referred to in clause (b) of sub-section (4A), that in respect of the amount of the export turnover specified therein, the deduction under this sub-section is to be allowed to a supporting manufacturer, then the amount of deduction in the case of the assessee shall be reduced by such amount which bears to the total profits derived by the assessee from the export of trading goods, the same proportion as the amount of export turnover specified in the said certificate bears to the total export turnover of the assessee in respect of such trading goods.

(1A) Where the assessee, being a supporting manufacturer, has, during the previous year, sold goods or merchandise to any Export House or Trading House in respect of which the Export House or Trading House has issued a certificate under the proviso to sub-section (1), there shall, in accordance with and subject to the provisions of this section, be allowed in computing the total income of the assessee, a deduction to the extent of profits, referred to in sub-section (1B), derived by the assessee from the sale of goods or merchandise to the Export House or Trading House in respect of which the certificate has been issued by the Export House or Trading House.

(1B) For the purposes of sub-section (1) and (1A), the extent of deduction of the profits shall be an amount equal to-

(i) eighty per cent thereof for an assessmet year beginning on the 1st day of April, 2001;

(ii) seventy per cent thereof for an assessment year beginning on the 1st day of April, 2002;

(iii) fifty per cent thereof for an assessment year beginning on the 1st day of April, 2003;

(iv) thirty per cent thereof for an assessment year beginning on the 1st day of April, 2004, and no deductions shall be allowed in respect of the assessment year beginning on the 1st day of April, 2005 and any subsequent assessment year.

(2) (a) This section applies to all goods or merchandise, other than those specified in clause (b), if the sale proceeds of such goods or merchandise exported out of India are received in, or brought into, India by the assessee (other than the supporting manufacturer) in convertible foreign exchange within a period of six months from the end of the previous year or, within such further period as the competent authority may allow in this behalf.

Explanation. For the purposes of this clause, the expression "competent authority" means the Reserve Bank of India or such other authority as is authorised under any law for the time being in force for regulating payments and dealings in foreign exchange;

(b) This section does not apply to the following goods or merchandise, namely:

(i) mineral oil; and

(ii) minerals and ores (other than processed minerals and ores specified in the Twelfth Schedule).

Explanation 1: The sale proceeds referred to in clause (a) shall be deemed to have been received in India where such sale proceeds are credited to a separate account maintained for the purpose by the assessee with any bank outside India with the approval of the Reserve Bank of India.

Explanation 2: For the removal of doubts, it is hereby declared that where any goods or merchandise are transferred by an assessee to a branch, office, warehouse or any other establishment of the assessee situate outside India and such goods or merchandise are sold from such branch, office, warehouse or establishment, then, such transfer shall be deemed to be export out of India of such goods and merchandise and the value of such goods or merchandise declared in the shipping bill or bill of export as referred to in sub-section (1) of section 50 of the Customs Act, 1962 (52 of 1962), shall, for the purposes of this section, be deemed to be the sale proceeds thereof.

(3) For the purposes of sub-section (1),-

(a) where the export out of India is of goods or merchandise manufactured or processed by the assessee, the profits derived from such export shall be the amount which bears to the profits of the business, the same proportion as the export turnover in respect of such goods bears to the total turnover of the business carried on by the assessee;

(b) where the export out of India is of trading goods, the profits derived from such export shall be the export turnover in respect of such trading goods as reduced by the direct costs and indirect costs attributable to such export;

(c) where the export out of India is of goods or merchandise manufactured or processed by the assessee and of trading goods, the profits derived from such export shall, -

(i) in respect of the goods or merchandise manufactured or processed by the assessee, be the amount which bears to the adjusted profits of the business, the same proportion as the adjusted export turnover in respect of such goods bears to the adjusted total turnover of the business carried out by the assessee; and

(ii) in respect of trading goods, be the export turnover in respect of such trading goods as reduced by the direct and indirect costs attributable to export of such trading goods:

Provided that the profits computed under clause (a) or clause (b) or clause (c) of this sub-section shall be further increased by the amount which bears to ninety per cent of any sum referred to in clause (iiia) (not being profits on sale of a license acquired from any other person), and clauses (iiib) and (iiic) of section 28, the same proportion as the export turnover bears to the total turnover of the business carried out by the assessee.

Explanation: For the purposes of this sub-section,-

(a) "adjusted export turnover" means the export turnover as reduced by the export turnover in respect of trading goods;

(b) "adjusted profits of the business" means the profits of the business as reduced by the profits derived from the business of export out of India of trading goods as computed in the manner provided in clause (b) of sub-section (3);

(c) "adjusted total turnover" means the total turnover of the business as reduced by the export turnover in respect of trading goods;

(d) "direct costs" means costs directly attributable to the trading goods exported out of India including the purchase price of such goods;

(e) "indirect costs" means costs, not being direct costs, allocated in the ratio of the export turnover in respect of trading goods to the total turnover;

(f) "trading goods" means goods which are not manufactured or processed by the assessee.

(3A) For the purposes of sub-section (1A), profits derived by a supporting manufacturer from the sale of goods or merchandise shall be,

(a) in a case where the business carried out by the supporting manufacturer consists exclusively of sale of goods or merchandise to one or more Export Houses or Trading Houses, the profits of the business;

(b) in a case where the business carried out by the supporting manufacturer does not consist exclusively of sale of goods or merchandise to one or more Export Houses or Trading Houses, the amount which bears to the profits of the business the same proportion as the turnover in respect of sale to the respective Export House or Trading House bears to the total turnover of the business carried on by the assessee.

(4) The deduction under sub-section (1) shall not be admissible unless the assessee furnishes in the prescribed form, along with the return of income, the report of an accountant, as defined in the Explanation below sub-section (2) of section 288, certifying that the deduction has been correctly claimed in accordance with the provisions of this section.

Provided that in the case of an undertaking referred to in sub-section (4C), the assessee shall also furnish along with the return of income, a certificate from the undertaking in the Special Economic Zone containing such particulars as may be prescribed, duly certified by the auditor auditing the accounts of the undertaking in the Special Economic Zone under the provisions of this Act or under any other law for this time being in force." (inserted vide Finance Bill, 2003)

(4A) The deduction under sub-section (1A) shall not be admissible unless the supporting manufacturer furnishes in the prescribed form along with his return of income,-

(a) the report of an accountant, as defined in the Explanation below sub-section (2) of section 288, certifying that the deduction has been correctly claimed on the basis of the profits of the supporting manufacturer in respect of his sale of goods or merchandise to the Export House or Trading House; and

(b) a certificate from the Export House or Trading House containing such particulars as may be prescribed and verified in the manner prescribed that in respect of the export turnover mentioned in the certificate, the Export House or Trading House has not claimed the deduction under this section:

Provided that the certificate specified in clause (b) shall be duly certified by the auditor auditing the accounts of the Export House or Trading House under the provisions of this Act or under any other law.

(4B) For the purposes of computing the total income under sub-section (1) or sub-section (1A), any income not charged to tax under this Act shall be excluded.

(4C) The provisions of this section shall apply to an assessee,-

(a) for an assessment year beginning after the 31st day of March, 2004 and ending before the 1st day of April, 2005;

(b) who owns any undertaking which manufactures or produces goods or merchandise anywhere in India (outside any Special Economic Zone) and sells the same to any undertaking situated in a Special

Economic Zone which is eligible for deduction under section 10A and such sale shall be deemed to be export out of India for the purposes of this section;

(c) in the Explanation occurring at the end, after clause (d), the following clause shall be inserted, namely:

"(e) "Special Economic Zone" shall have the meaning assigned to it in clause (viii) of the Explanation 2 to section 10A." (inserted vide Finance Bill, 2003)

Explanation: For the purposes of this section,-

(a) "convertible foreign exchange" means foreign exchange which is for the time being treated by the Reserve Bank of India as convertible foreign exchange for the purposes of the Foreign Exchange Regulation Act, 1973 (46 of 1973), and any rules made thereunder;

(aa) "export out of India" shall not include any transaction by way of sale or otherwise, in a shop, emporium or any other establishment situate in India, not involving clearance at any customs station as defined in the Customs Act, 1962 (52 of 1962);

(b) "export turnover" means the sale proceeds, received in, or brought into, India by the assessee in convertible foreign exchange in accordance with clause (a) of sub-section (2) of any goods or merchandise to which this section applies and which are exported out of India, but does not include freight or insurance attributable to the transport of the goods or merchandise beyond the customs station as defined in the Customs Act, 1962 (52 of 1962);

(ba) "total turnover" shall not include freight or insurance attributable to the transport of the goods or merchandise beyond the customs station as defined in the Customs Act, 1962 (52 of 1962):

Provided that in relation to any assessment year commencing on or after the 1st day of April, 1991, the expression "total turnover" shall have effect as if it also excluded any sum referred to in clauses (iiia), (iiib) and (iiic) of section 28;

(baa) "profits of the business" means the profits of the business as computed under the head "Profits and gains of business or profession" as reduced by:

(1) ninety per cent of any sum referred to in clauses (iiia), (iiib) and (iiic) of section 28 or of any receipts by way of brokerage, commission, interest, rent, charges or any other receipt of a similar nature included in such profits; and

(2) the profits of any branch, office, warehouse or any other establishment of the assessee situate outside India;

(c) "Export House Certificate" or "Trading House Certificate" means a valid Export House Certificate or Trading House Certificate, as the case may be, issued by the Chief Controller of Imports and Exports, Government of India;

(d) "supporting manufacturer" means a person being an Indian company or a person (other than a company) resident in India, manufacturing (including processing) goods or merchandise and selling such goods or merchandise to an Export House or a Trading House for the purposes of export.

(e) "Special Economic Zone" shall have the meaning assigned to it in clause (viii) of the Explanation 2 to section 10A. (inserted vide Finance Bill, 2003).

SECTION 80-LA

1. 80LA (1) Where the gross total income of an assesse.

(i) being a scheduled bank (not being a bank incorporated by or under the laws of a country outside India);

(ii) owning an offshore banking unit in a Special Economic Zone, includes any income referred to in sub-section (2), there shall be allowed, in accordance with and subject to the provisions of this section, a deduction from such income, of an amount equal to-

(a) one hundred per cent of such income for three consecutive assessment years beginning with the assessment year relevant to the previous year in which the permission, under clause (a) of sub-section

(1) of section 23 of the Banking Regulation Act, 1949, was obtained, and thereafter;

(2) The income referred to in sub-section (1) shall be the income:

(a) from an offshore banking unit in a special economic zone;

(b) from the business, referred to in sub-section (1) of section 6 of the Banking Regulation Act, 1949, with an undertaking located in a Special Economic Zone or any other undertaking which develops, develops and operates or operates and maintains a Special Economic Zone;

(c) received in convertible foreign exchange, in accordance with the regulations made under the Foreign Exchange Management Act, 1999.

(3) No deduction under this section shall be allowed unless the assessee furnishes along with the return of income:

(i) in the prescribed form the report of an accountant as defined in the Explanation below sub-section (2) of section 2888, certifying that the deduction has been correctly claimed in accordance with the provisions of this section; and

(ii) a copy of the permission obtained under clause (a) of sub-section (1) of section 23 of the Banking Regulation Act, 1949.

Explanation: For the purposes of this section,-

(a) "convertible foreign exchange" shall have the same meaning assigned to it in clause (a) of the Explanation below sub-section (4C) of section 80HHC;

(b) "Offshore Banking Unit" means a branch of a bank in India located in the Special Economic Zone and has obtained the permission under clause (a) of sub-section (1) of section 23 of the Banking Regulation Act 1949;

(c) "scheduled bank" shall have the same meaning assigned to it in clause (e) of section 2 of the Reserve Bank of India Act, 1934;

(d) "Special Economic Zone" shall have the same meaning assigned to it in clause (viii) of the Explanation 2 to section 10A.

SECTION 10-A

Special provision in respect of newly established undertakings in Free Trade Zone, etc.

10A. (1) Subject to the provisions of this section, a deduction of such profits and gains as are derived by an undertaking from the export of articles or things or computer software for a period of ten consecutive assessment years beginning with the assessment year relevant to the previous year in which the undertaking begins to manufacture or produce such articles or things or computer software, as the case may be, shall be allowed from the total income of the assessee:

Provided that where in computing the total income of the undertaking for any assessment year, its profits and gains had not been included by application of the provisions of this section as it stood immediately before its substitution by the Finance Act, 2000, the undertaking shall be entitled to deduction referred to in this sub-section only for the unexpired period of the aforesaid ten consecutive assessment years:

Provided further that where an undertaking initially located in any Free Trade Zone or Export Processing Zone is subsequently located in a Special Economic Zone by reason of conversion of such Free Trade Zone or Export Processing Zone into a Special Economic Zone, the period of ten consecutive assessment years referred to in this sub-section shall be reckoned from the assessment year relevant to the previous year in which the undertaking began to manufacture or produce such articles or things or computer software in such Free Trade Zone or Export Processing Zone:

1[***] The following third proviso shall be inserted to sub-section (1) of section 10A by the Finance Act, 2002, w.e.f. 1-4-2003:

Provided also that for the assessment year beginning on the 1st day of April, 2003, the deduction under this sub-section shall be ninety per cent of the profits and gains derived by an undertaking from the export of such articles or things or computer software:

Provided also that no deduction under this section shall be allowed to any undertaking for the assessment year beginning on the 1st day of April, 2010 and subsequent years.

The following sub-section (1A) shall be inserted after sub-section (1) of section 10A by the Finance Act, 2002, w.e.f. 1-4-2003:

(1A) Notwithstanding anything contained in sub-section (1), the deduction, in computing the total income of an undertaking, which begins to manufacture or produce articles or things or computer software during the previous year relevant to any assessment year commencing on or after the 1st day of April, 2003, in any Special Economic Zone, shall be:

(i) hundred per cent of profits and gains derived from the export of such articles or things or computer software for a period of five consecutive assessment years beginning with the assessment year relevant to the previous year in which the undertaking begins to manufacture or produce such articles or things or computer software, as the case may be, and thereafter, fifty per cent of such profits and gains for further two assessment years, and thereafter;

(ii) for the next three consecutive assessment years, so much of the amount not exceeding fifty per cent. Of the profit as is debited to the profit and loss account of the previous year in respect of which the deduction is to be allowed and credited to a reserve account (to be called the "Special Economic Zone Re-investment Allowance Reserve Account") to be created and utilised for the purposes of the business of the assessee in the manner laid down in sub-section (1B).

(1B) The deduction under clause (ii) of sub-section (1A) shall be allowed only if the following conditions are fulfilled, namely:

(a) the amount credited to the Special Economic Zone Re-investment Allowance Reserve Account is to be utilised-

(i) for the purposes of acquiring new machinery or plant which is first put to use before the expiry of a period of three years next following the previous year in which the reserve was created; and

(ii) until the acquisition of new machinery or plant as aforesaid, for the purposes of the business of the undertaking other than for distribution by way of dividends or profits or for remittance outside India as profits or for the creation of any asset outside India;

(b) the particulars, as may be prescribed in this behalf, have been furnished by the assessee in respect of new machinery or plant along with the return of income for the assessment year relevant to the previous year in which such plant or machinery was first put to use.

(1C) Where any amount credited to the Special Economic Zone Re-investment Allowance Reserve Account under clause (ii) of sub-section (1A):

(a) has been utilised for any purpose other than those referred to in sub-section (1B), the amount so utilised; or (b) has not been utilised before the expiry of the period specified in sub-clause (I) of clause (a) of sub-section (1B), the amount not so utilised, shall be deemed to be the profits,-

(i) in a case referred to in clause (a), in the year in which the amount was so utilised; or

(ii) in a case referred to in cluase (b), in the year immediately following the period of three years specified in sub-clause (i) of clause (a) of sub-section (1B), and shall be charged to tax accordingly."

(ab) in sub-section (4), for the word, brackets and figures "sub-section (1)", the words, brackets, figures and letters "sub-sections (1) and (1A)" shall be substituted;'. (substituted vide Finance Bill, 2003)

(2) This section applies to any undertaking which fulfils all the following conditions, namely:

(i) it has begun or begins to manufacture or produce articles or things or computer software during the previous year relevant to the assessment year;

(a) commencing on or after the 1st day of April, 1981, in any Free Trade Zone; or

(b) commencing on or after the 1st day of April, 1994, in any electronic hardware technology park, or, as the case may be, software technology park;

(c) commencing on or after the 1st day of April, 2001 in any Special Economic Zone;

(ii) it is not formed by the splitting up, or the reconstruction, of a business already in existence:

Provided that this condition shall not apply in respect of any undertaking which is formed as a result of the re-establishment, reconstruction or revival by the assessee of the business of any such undertakings as is referred to in section 33B, in the circumstances and within the period specified in that section;

(iii) it is not formed by the transfer to a new business of machinery or plant previously used for any purpose.

Explanation: The provisions of *Explanation 1* and *Explanation 2* to sub-section (2) of section 80-I shall apply for the purposes of clause (iii) of this sub-section as they apply for the purposes of clause (ii) of that sub-section.

(3) This section applies to the undertaking, if the sale proceeds of articles or things or computer software exported out of India are received in, or brought into, India by the assessee in convertible foreign exchange, within a period of six months from the end of the previous year or, within such further period as the competent authority may allow in this behalf.

Explanation 1: For the purposes of this sub-section, the expression "competent authority" means the Reserve Bank of India or such other authority as is authorised under any law for the time being in force for regulating payments and dealings in foreign exchange.

Explanation 2: The sale proceeds referred to in this sub-section shall be deemed to have been received in India where such sale proceeds are credited to a separate account maintained for the purpose by the assessee with any bank outside India with the approval of the Reserve Bank of India.

2[(4) For the purposes of sub-section (1) and (IA), the profits derived from export of articles or things or computer software shall be the amount which bears to the profits of the business of the undertaking, the same proportion as the export turnover in respect of such articles or things or computer software bears to the total turnover of the business carried out by the undertaking.]

(5) The deduction under this section shall not be admissible for any assessment year beginning on or after the 1st day of April, 2001, unless the assessee furnishes in the prescribed Form 3, alongwith the return of income, the report of an accountant, as defined in the Explanation below sub-section (2) of section 288, certifying that the deduction has been correctly claimed in accordance with the provisions of this section.

(6) Notwithstanding anything contained in any other provision of this Act, in computing the total income of the assessee of the previous year relevant to the assessment year immediately succeeding the last of the relevant assessment years, or of any previous year, relevant to any subsequent assessment year,-

(i) section 32, section 32A, section 33, section 35 and clause (ix) of sub-section (1) of section 36 shall apply as if every allowance or deduction referred to therein and relating to or allowable for any of the relevant assessment years *ending before the 1st day of April, 2001* (inserted vide Finance Bill 2003) in relation to any building, machinery, plant or furniture used for the purposes of the business of the undertaking in the previous year relevant to such assessment year or any expenditure incurred for the purposes of such business in such previous year had been given full effect to for that assessment year itself and accordingly sub-section (2) of section 32, clause (ii) of sub-section (3) of section 32A, clause (ii) of sub-section (2) of section 33, sub-section (4) of section 35 or the second proviso to clause (ix) of sub-section (1) of section 36, as the case may be, shall not apply in relation to any such allowance or deduction;

(ii) no loss referred to in sub-section (1) of section 72 or sub-section (1) or sub-section (3) of section 74, in so far as such loss relates to the business of the undertaking, shall be carried forward or set off where such loss relates to any of the relevant assessment years *ending before the 1st day of April, 2001* (inserted vide Finance Bill 2003);

(iii) no deduction shall be allowed under section 80HH or section 80HHA or section 80-I or section 80-IA or section 80-IB in relation to the profits and gains of the undertaking; and

(iv) in computing the depreciation allowance under section 32, the written down value of any asset used for the purposes of the business of the undertaking shall be computed as if the assessee had claimed and been actually allowed the deduction in respect of depreciation for each of the relevant assessment years.

(7) The provisions of sub-section (8) and sub-section (10) of section 80-IA shall, so far as may be, apply in relation to the undertaking referred to in this section as they apply for the purposes of the undertaking referred to in section 80-IA.

(7A) where any undertaking of an Indian company which is entitled to the deduction under this section is transferred, before the expiry of the period specified in this section, to another Indian company in a scheme of amalgamation or demerger-

(a) no deduction shall be admissible under this section to the amalgamating or the demerged company for the previous year in which the amalgamation or the demerger takes place; and

(b) the provisions of this section shall, as far as may be, apply to the amalgamated or the resulting company as they would have applied to the amalgamating or the demerged company if the amalgamation or demerger had not taken place." (incorporated vide Finance Bill, 2003)

(8) Notwithstanding anything contained in the foregoing provisions of this section, where the assessee, before the due date for furnishing the return of income under sub-section (1) of section 139, furnishes to the Assessing Officer a declaration in writing that the provisions of this section may not be made applicable to him, the provisions of this section shall not apply to him for any of the relevant assessment years.

(9) omitted (vide Finance Bill, 2003)

(9A) omitted (vide Finance Bill, 2003)

Explanation 1: omitted (vide Finance Bill, 2003)

Explanation 2: For the purposes of this section,- (i) "computer software" means:

(a) any computer programme recorded on any disc, tape, perforated media or other information storage device; or

(b) any customized electronic data or any product or service of similar nature, as may be notified by the Board, which is transmitted or exported from India to any place outside India by any means;

(ii) "convertible foreign exchange" means foreign exchange which is for the time being treated by the Reserve Bank of India as convertible foreign exchange for the purposes of the Foreign Exchange Regulation Act, 1973 (46 of 1973), and any rules made thereunder or any other corresponding law for the time being in force;

(iii) "electronic hardware technology park" means any park set up in accordance with the Electronic Hardware Technology Park (EHTP) Scheme notified by the Government of India in the Ministry of Commerce and Industry;

(iv) "export turnover" means the consideration in respect of export 6[by the undertaking] of articles or things or computer software received in, or brought into, India by the assessee in convertible foreign exchange in accordance with sub-section (3), but does not include freight, telecommunication charges or insurance attributable to the delivery of the articles or things or computer software outside India or expenses, if any, incurred in foreign exchange in providing the technical services outside India.

(v) "Free Trade Zone" means the Kandla Free Trade Zone and the Santacruz Electronics Export Processing Zone and includes any other Free Trade Zone which the Central Government may, by notification in the Official Gazette, 7 specify for the purposes of this section;

(vi) "relevant assessment year" means any assessment year falling within a period of ten consecutive assessment years referred to in this section;

(vii) "software technology park" means any park set up in accordance with the Software Technology Park Scheme notified by the Government of India in the Ministry of Commerce and Industry;

(viii) "Special Economic Zone" means a zone which the Central Government may, by notification in the Official Gazette, specify as a Special Economic Zone for the purposes of this section.

7a [*Explanation* 3: For the removal of doubts, it is hereby declared that the profits and gains derived from on-site development of computer software (including services for development of software) outside India shall be deemed to be the profits and gains derived from the export of computer software outside India].

Explanation 4: For the purposes of this section, "manufacture or produce" shall include the cutting and polishing of precious and semi-precious stones." (incorporated vide Finance Bill, 2003).

INCOME TAX 10(23)-G

Any income by way of dividends, 48a[other than dividends referred to in section 115-O], interest or long-term capital gains of an infrastructure capital fund or an infrastructure capital company 49[or a co-operative bank] from investments made on or after the 1st day of June, 1998 by way of shares or long-term finance in 50 [any enterprise or undertaking wholly engaged in the business referred to in sub-section (4) of section 80-IA or a housing project referred to in sub-section (10) of section 80-IB] and which has been approved 51 by the Central Government on an application made by it in accordance with the rules 52 made in this behalf and which satisfies the prescribed conditions.

53 [*Explanation 1.*]—For the purposes of this clause,—

(a) "infrastructure capital company" means such company as has made investments by way of acquiring shares or providing long term finance to an enterprise wholly engaged 54[in the business of—

(i) developing; or

(ii) maintaining and operating; or

(iii) developing, maintaining and operating,

any infrastructure facility;]

(b) "infrastructure capital fund" means such fund operating under a trust deed registered under the provisions of the Registration Act, 1908 (16 of 1908) established to raise monies by the trustees for investment by way of acquiring shares or providing long-term finance to an enterprise wholly engaged 54[in the business of—

(i) developing; or

(ii) maintaining and operating; or

(iii) developing, maintaining and operating,

any infrastructure facility;]

(c) 55[***]

(d) "long-term finance" shall have the meaning assigned to it in clause (viii) of sub-section (1) of section 36;

56[(e) "co-operative bank"57 shall have the meaning assigned to it in clause (dd) of section 2 of the Deposit Insurance and Credit Guarantee Corporation Act, 1961 (47 of 1961);

(f) "interest" includes any fee or commission received by a financial institution for giving any guarantee to, or enhancing credit in respect of, an enterprise which has been approved by the Central Government for the purposes of this clause;]

58 [*Explanation 2.* For the removal of doubts, it is hereby declared that any income by way of dividends, interest or long-term capital gains of an infrastructure capital fund or an infrastructure capital company from investments made before the 1st day of June, 1998 by way of shares or long-term finance in any enterprise carrying on the business of developing, maintaining and operating any infrastructure facility shall not be included and the provisions of this clause as it stood immediately before its amendment by the Finance (No. 2) Act, 1998 (21 of 1998) shall apply to such income;]

Central Sales Tax Amendment in Budget 2004-05

11

CHAPTER VIII—Miscellaneous

In section 8 of the Central Sales Tax Act, 1956 (hereinafter referred to as the Central Sales Tax Act):

(a) for sub-section (6), the following sub-section shall be substituted, namely:

"(6) Notwithstanding anything contained in this section, no tax under this Act shall be payable by any dealer in respect of sale of any goods made by such dealer, in the course of inter-State trade or commerce to a registered dealer for the purpose of setting up, operation, maintenance, manufacture, trading, production, processing, assembling, repairing, reconditioning, reengineering, packaging or for use as packing material or packing accessories in a unit located in any Special Economic Zone or for development, operation and maintenance of Special Economic Zone by the developer of the Special Economic Zone, if such registered dealer has been authorized to establish such unit or to develop, operate and maintain such Special Economic Zone by the authority specified by the Central Government in this behalf."

(b) in sub-section (8), for the words, brackets and figures "authority referred to in sub-section (6) a declaration in the prescribed manner on the prescribed form obtained from the authority referred to in sub-section (5)", the following shall be substituted, namely:

"prescribed authority referred to in sub-section (4) a declaration in the prescribed manner on the prescribed form obtained from the authority specified by the Central Government under sub-section (6)".

EXTRACT OF CST ACT (AS NOW AMENDED)

8) Rates of tax on sales in the course of inter-State trade or commerce.

(6) Notwithstanding anything contained in this section, no tax under this Act shall be payable by any dealer in respect of sale of any goods made by such dealer, in the course of inter-State trade or commerce to a registered dealer for the purpose of setting up, operation, maintenance, manufacture, trading, production, processing, assembling, repairing, reconditioning, reengineering, packaging or for use as packing material or packing accessories in a unit located in any Special Economic Zone or for development, operation and maintenance of Special Economic Zone by the developer of the Special Economic Zone, if such registered dealer has been authorized to establish such unit or to develop, operate and maintain such Special Economic Zone by the authority specified by the Central Government in this behalf.

(7) The goods referred to in sub-section (6) shall be the goods of such class or classes of goods as specified in the certificate of registration of the registered dealer referred to in that sub-section.

(8) The provisions of sub-sections (6) and (7) shall not apply to any sale of goods made in the course of inter-State trade or commerce unless the dealer selling such goods furnishes to the prescribed authority referred to in sub-section (4) a declaration in the prescribed manner on the prescribed form obtained from the authority specified by the Central Government under sub-section (6), duly filled in and signed by the registered dealer to whom such goods are sold.

Explanation. For the purpose of sub-section (6) the expression "Special Economic Zone" has the meaning assigned to it in clause (iii) to Explanation 2 to the proviso to section 3 of the Central Excise Act, 1944.

Customs Chapter X-A, and Customs Circular No. 33 Dated 12th May 2004

12

Notification of Special Economic Zone

76A. The Central Government may, by notification in the Official Gazette, specify Special Economic Zones comprising specifically delineated areas where any goods admitted shall be regarded, in so far as duties of customs are concerned, as being outside the customs territory of India as provided in this Chapter.

Application of Provision

76B. The provisions of this Chapter and other Chapters shall apply to goods admitted to a Special Economic Zone but in the event of conflict between the provisions of this Chapter and other Chapters, the provisions of this Chapter shall prevail.

Establishment and Control

76C. (1) The Central Government may make rules specifying the requirements relating to goods or class of goods admissible to a Special Economic Zone, the nature of operations to which such goods or class of goods may be subjected to, the conditions to be subjected to, the conditions to be fulfilled and the procedures to be followed in this regard.

(2) The Board may specify, in the regulations made in this behalf, arrangements for customs control in a Special Economic Zone.

(3) The proper officer shall have the right to carry out checks, at any time. On the foods kept or stored in a Special Economic Zone.

Admission of goods

76D. Subject to such conditions as may be specified in the rules made in this behalf, any goods imported directly from outside India or procured from within India shall be authorized for admission to a Special Economic Zone.

Exemption from duties of customs

76E. Without prejudice to the provisions of sections 76F, 76G and 76H, any goods admitted to a Special Economic Zone shall be exempt from duties of customs.

Levy of duties of customs

76F. Subject to the conditions as may be specified in the rules made in this behalf:

(a) any goods admitted to a Special Economic Zone from the domestic tariff area shall be chargeable to export duties at such rates as are leviable on such goods when exported;

(b) any goods removed from a Special Economic Zone for home consumption shall be chargeable to duties of customs including anti-dumping, countervailing and safeguard duties under the Customs Tariff Act, 1975, where applicable, as leviable on such goods when imported; and

(c) the rate of duty and tariff valuation, if any, applicable to goods admitted to, or removed from, a Special Economic Zone shall be the rate and tariff valuation in force as on the date of such admission of removal, as the case may be, and where such date is not ascertainable, on the date of payment of the duty.

Authorised operations

76G. All goods admitted to a Special Economic Zone shall undergo such operations including processing or manufacturing as may be specified in the rules made in this behalf.

Goods utilized within a Special Economic Zone

76H.(1) The Central Government may make rules in this behalf to enumerate the cases in which goods to be utilized inside a Special Economic Zone may be admitted free of duties of customs and lay down the requirements which shall be fulfilled.

(2) Goods utilized contrary to the provisions of rules made under sub-section (1) shall be chargeable to duties of customs in the same manner as provided under clause (b) of Section 76F as if they have been removed for home consumption.

Drawback on goods admitted to a Special Economic Zone

76-L. Any goods admitted to a Special Economic Zone from the domestic tariff area for the purposes authorized under this Chapter shall be eligible for drawback under section 75 as if such goods are export goods for the purposes of that section.

Duration of stay

76J. Any goods admitted to Special Economic Zone shall not be allowed to remain within such Zone beyond such time as may be specified in the rules made in this behalf.

Security

76K. Any goods admitted free of duty to a Special Economic Zone or goods under transshipment to and from such zone without payment of duty shall be subject to execution of such bond and such surety or security as may be specified in the rules made in this behalf.

Transfer of ownership

76L. Any goods admitted to, or produced or manufactured in a Special Economic Zone shall be allowed for transfer of ownership subject to such conditions as may be specified in the rules made in this behalf.

Removal of goods

76M. Any goods admitted to, or produced or manufactured in a Special Economic Zone may be removed in accordance with such procedure as may be specified in the rules made in this behalf.

Closure of a Special Economic Zone

76N. In the event of closure of a Special Economic Zone by the Central government, by notification, goods produced or manufactured in, such Zone shall be removed within such time and in such manner as may be specified in the rules made in this behalf.

Customs Circular No. 33

Sub: Operationalisation of the Provisions of Chapter X A of the Customs Act, 1962—Issuance of SEZ Rules and Regulations

....The important features of these amendments are explained below:

3. The important features of amendments of SEZ Rules, 2003, are as under:

(i) Earlier Rule 9 provided that depreciation would be allowed @ 20% per annum for 'computer and computer peripherals' and for 'capital goods other than computer and computer peripherals', the rate of depreciation is @ 10% per annum. The rule has been amended to provide a different rate of depreciation now for which the notification may be referred to. The depreciation will be allowed in straight line method. For the purpose of computing rate of depreciation for any part of a quarter, full such quarter shall be taken into account. Value for charging duty at the time of removal of capital goods would be based on the depreciated value and not on the transaction value. There will be no upper limit for depreciation. In other words 100% depreciation is permissible.

(ii) Earlier it was provided that SEZ unit could transfer only manufactured goods and capital goods to EOU/EHTP/STP/SEZ. Rule 11 has now been amended to allow transfer of all goods to EOU/EHTP/STP/SEZ. However, transfer of raw materials to EOU/EHTP/STP and other SEZ should be allowed only in those cases where the SEZ units are unable to utilise the raw material for a valid reason [Also refer paras 7.11 and of the EXIM Policy, read with para 19.1, 19.2 and 28.1 of the *Handbook of Procedures*]. Sale of unutilized raw materials to a DTA unit or to another

EOU/EPZ/EHTP/STP unit can arise only in exceptional cases and cannot be a regular basis.

It has also been provided that in case the goods procured by SEZ Unit from DTA are transferred, directly or via another SEZ, to EOU/EHTP/STP, as it is, or after subjecting them to processes not amounting to manufacture, the SEZ units would be required to pay back the duty drawback or DEPB benefits which was taken at the time of procurement of such goods from DTA either by the DTA unit or the SEZ unit, as the case may be. This provision has been introduced to ensure that supplies from DTA to EOU/EHTP/STP do not get benefit of DBK or DEPB indirectly.

(iii) In rule 12, earlier there was a provision that in case of destruction of goods procured from DTA, the SEZ unit shall be liable to pay back the export benefits allowed against such goods. However, the rule has been amended so as to provide that where payment for such goods has already been made in foreign exchange, the SEZ unit will not be liable to pay back the export benefits taken against such goods. However, the scrap generated through such destruction would be assessed on merits, e.g. if the scrap is HMS it will pay duty under heading 7204.4900, if cleared to DTA.

(iv) The SEZ units are now not required to submit any separate return to the jurisdictional customs. They are only required to endorse a copy of the annual/quarterly return which they submit to the concerned Development Commissioner in the format as specified in Appendix 14-IF of HOP. Rule 14 has been amended to this effect.

(v) The SEZ unit or a developer would be required to execute a bond with the Deputy Commissioner or Assistant Commissioner of Customs instead of Commissioner of Customs. Rule 18 has been amended to this effect.

(vi) Monitoring of the SEZ would now be done by jurisdictional customs through the Unit Approval Committee of the Zone where the jurisdictional Commissioner of Customs will be represented. Rule 19 has been amended accordingly.

(vii) In the event of closure of an SEZ, goods may be transferred to EOU/EHTP/STP or another SEZ without payment of duty subject to restrictions as mentioned in clause 3(ii) above. Rule 20 has been amended accordingly.

4. The important features of amendments of SEZ Regulations, 2003, are as under:

(i) In the original SEZ regulations, it was provided that two or more zone units shall not be allowed to operate from the same 'premises'. Since the term premises is subject to different interpretations, Regulation 3 has been amended to provide that each unit would be 'a distinct establishment and identifiable or distinct and partitioned from other zone unit'.

(ii) Regulation 10 has been amended to provide that where goods are procured from DTA by SEZ unit or the developer and where no export benefit has been obtained or where such goods or sale proceeds are not counted towards fulfilment of export obligation under any export Promotion scheme, admission of goods would be allowed against 'Domestic procurement Certificate' and ARE-I and there would be no requirement for filing any Bill of Export. For detailed procedure the relevant provision of the regulations may please be referred to. However, where the duty paid goods are procured from Domestic Tariff Area and no duty concession or export incentives are being claimed against such supplies the goods shall be allowed admission into the Zone on the basis of invoice issued by the supplier of the goods and connected transport documents, if any.

(iii) The procedure for transfer of manufactured goods or capital goods from one Zone unit to another Zone unit as envisaged in earlier regulation 12 would also apply in case of transfer of raw material from one zone unit to another zone unit. Regulation 12 has been amended accordingly.

(iv) In respect of export of gems and jewellery through personal baggage, the SEZ unit shall not be required to submit advance remittance certificate . Regulation 15 has been accordingly amended.

(v) In respect of exchange of jewellery, wastage would be allowed. Regulation 20 stands amended to that effect.

(vi) As explained above at para 3(ii), rule 11 has been amended so as to provide transfer of raw material also alongwith manufactured goods and capital goods from a Zone unit to EOU/EHTP/STP/SEZ. Corresponding changes have been made in Regulation 21.

(vii) Goods procured by a Zone unit from DTA, when supplied back to DTA, are to be considered as re-import and all the procedures and conditions as applicable in case of normal re-import of goods would apply. However, when import duty on such goods is 'nil' and no export benefits were taken during procurement of such goods, in such cases, the goods may be allowed to be supplied back to DTA on the basis of invoice only and filing of Bill of Entry, etc. is not required. Regulation 22(6) has been amended accordingly.

(viii) In case of jobwork following important provisions have been introduced in regulation 25, namely:

(a) In the regulation 25(1) (iii), it was earlier provided that while considering application for jobwork the proper officer would ensure that there is no attempt to parcel out 'substantial manufacturing process' to DTA. The word 'substantial' has been substituted by the word 'entire'. This entails that the Zone unit would not be allowed to parcel out entire manufacturing activity in DTA in the name of jobwork.

(b) In addition to the status holders, units having unblemished track record, which have not come to the adverse notice of Customs authorities for a period of at least last two years are also exempted from furnishing security/bank guarantee for taking goods into DTA for the purpose of jobwork.

(c) Earlier, there was provision that SEZ unit could subcontract production only up to a limit of 50% of FOB value of exports made in the previous year. However, this limitation in respect of subcontracting of production has been withdrawn. However, the Zone unit should have the production facility in the Zone and only to meet excess demand, etc. sub-contracting of production should be allowed.

(ix) Where the duty-free goods procured from DTA are destroyed due to natural calamities and where export benefits have been allowed against such goods, the SEZ units would not be required to pay back the export benefits provided the payment for such goods has been made by the SEZ unit in foreign exchange. Regulation 28(2) has been amended to this effect.

(x) The bond executed by the SEZ unit would be a running bond. Debiting and crediting of the bond would now be done on quarterly basis instead of transaction basis. The bond value would be equal to 25% of duty forgone on the sanctioned requirement of capital goods to be procured or imported duty-free, plus duty on raw materials to be held in stock for three months by the Zone unit. The unit having a turnover of rupees one crore or above or a unit which is in existence for more than a period of three years with an unblemished track record, would be exempted from furnishing surety or security. Regulation 29 has been amended accordingly.

(xi) The developer of SEZ is now not required to apply to any Committee for duty-free import or procurement of goods. The requirement of goods shall be assessed by a Chartered Engineer and approval would be given by the concerned Development Commissioner. On the basis of approval given by the Development Commissioner, the jurisdictional Deputy Commissioner or Assistant Commissioner would allow duty-free import or procurement of goods by the developer for the purpose of authorized operations. The developer would be required to submit certificate of utilisation of duty-free goods from a Charterd Engineer other than one who assessed the requirement of goods, within six months of every import or procurement of goods, to the Development Commissioner. In addition, other conditions as specified in the regulation would be required to be followed. It may be noted that in the case of new Zones, there would be no regular Deputy Commissioner or Assistant Commissioner of Customs in the Zone. Hence all the functions of Deputy Commissioner or Assistant Commissioner under the regulation 33 would be exercised by the jurisdictional Deputy Commissioner or Assistant Commissioner customs. However, once a regular Deputy Commissioner or Assistant Commissioner of customs is posted in the Zone, such functions would be exercised by the Assistant Commissioner customs in the Zone.

5. In Circular No 68/2003-Cus dated 30-7-2003 it was clarified that motor vehicles for personal use or goods for consumption by the workers, staff and officials of the SEZ unit / SEZ developer cannot be admitted into the SEZ without payment of duty [Rule 5(2)]. Please note that there will be no restriction

on movement of duty paid vehicles in & out of the SEZ for use by the units or their employees. This position is once again reiterated.

6. Board's Circular 68/2003-Cus dated 30-7-2003 stands modified to the above extent.

7. In regulation 17, it has been provided that in case of export of goods for participation in exhibition abroad, the goods would be subject to examination following the same procedure as applicable in the case of normal import or export. It has been decided that in case of gems and jewellery consignments examination of goods would be restricted to 10% for both inwards and outwards consignments, at random. The other conditions remain unaltered.

8. Please note that on the operationalisation of Chapter XA of the Customs Act, 1962, along with the attendant Rules and Regulations, Drawback, DEPB and other export benefits would be available in respect of supplies from DTA to SEZ subject to fulfilment of relevant provisions of the EXIM Policy and Customs and Central Excise laws (including notifications).

9. For sanction and payment of Drawback your attention is invited to Board's Circular no 24/2003-Cus dated 1.4.2003.

10. Wide publicity may be given by issue of a Public Notice in this regard.

11. Kindly acknowledge receipt of this Circular.

Ministry of Finance, Department of Revenue Notifications, 2004

13

NOTIFICATION NO. 58/2004

In exercise of the powers conferred by sub-section (1) of section 156, read with Chapter XA of the Customs Act, 1962 (52 of 1962), the Central Government, hereby makes the following rules to amend the Special Economic Zones Rules, 2003, namely:

1. (1) These rules may be called the Special Economic Zones (Amendment) Rules, 2004.

(2) They shall come into force on the date of their publication in the Official Gazette.

2. In the Special Economic Zones Rules, 2003, in rule 1, in sub-rule (2), for the figures, letters and words "1st day of May, 2004", the figures, letters and words "11th day of May , 2004" shall be substituted.

Note: The principal notification No. 52/2003—Customs (N.T.), dated the 22nd July, 2003, was published in the *Gazette of India, Extraordinary*, Part II, Section 3, Sub-section (i) vide G.S.R 570 (E), dated the 22nd July, 2003 and was last amended by notification No. 47 /2004-CUSTOMS (N.T.), dated the 31st March, 2004 [G.S.R 240 (E), dated the 31st March, 2004].

NOTIFICATION NO. 59 /2004

In exercise of the powers conferred by sub-section (1) of section 157, read with sub-section (2) of section 76C of the Customs Act, 1962 (52of 1962), the Board hereby makes the following regulations to amend the Special Economic Zones (Customs Procedures) Regulations, 2003, namely:

1. (1) These regulations may be called the Special Economic Zones (Customs Procedures) (Amendment) Regulations, 2004.

(2) They shall come into force on the date of their publication in the Official Gazette.

2. In the Special Economic Zones (Customs Procedures) Regulations, 2003, in regulation 1, in sub-regulation (3), for the figures, letters and words "Ist day of May , 2004", the figures, letters and words "11th day of May, 2004 " shall be substituted.

Note: ...No. 48 /2004-CUSTOMS (N.T.), dated the 31st March, 2004 [G.S.R. 241(E), dated the 31st March, 2004].

NOTIFICATION NO. 61 /2004

In exercise of the powers conferred by sub-section (1) of section 156, read with Chapter XA of the Customs Act, 1962 (52 of 1962), the Central Government, hereby makes the following rules further to amend the Special Economic Zones Rules, 2003, namely:

1. (1) These rules may be called the Special Economic Zones (Fourth Amendment) Rules, 2004.

(2) They shall come into force on the date of their publication in the Official Gazette.

2. In the Special Economic Zones Rules, 2003,-

(A) in rule 2,-

(i) in clause (c), for the words "permitted by the Commissioner of Customs", the words, brackets, letter and figures "approved by the Board of Approvals as defined in clause (c) of regulation 2 of the Special Economic Zones (Customs Procedures) Regulations, 2003" shall be substituted.

(ii) after clause (i), the following clause shall be inserted, namely:

'(ii) " Unit Approval Committee", in respect of a Special Economic Zone, means a committee set up for the Special Economic Zone as notified in the Official Gazette by the

Central Government in the Ministry of Commerce and Industry';

(B) in rule 5, in sub-rule (4) , for the words "Commissioner of Customs", the words "Deputy Commissioner of Customs or Assistant Commissioner of Customs, as the case may be" shall be substituted;

(C) in rule 9, in sub rule (1),

(i) in clause (a), the words "or on the transaction value, whichever is higher" shall be omitted;

(ii) for clause (c), the following clause shall be substituted, namely:

"(c) the depreciation shall be allowed in straight line method as specified below, namely:

(i) for computer and computer peripherals:

for every quarter in the first year	@10%
for every quarter in the second year	@8%
for every quarter in the third year	@5%
for every quarter in the fourth and fifth year	@1%

(ii) for capital goods other than computer and computer peripherals:

for every quarter in the first year	@4%
for every quarter in the second year	@3%
for every quarter in the third year	@3%
for every quarter in the fourth and fifth year	@2.5%
and thereafter for every quarter	@2%

Explanation. For the purpose of computing rate of depreciation for any part of a quarter the full such quarter shall be taken into account; and";

(D) for rule 11, following rule shall be substituted, namely:

"11. Removal of goods from a Special Economic Zone unit to an export-oriented undertaking or software technology park unit or electronic hardware technology park unit or to other Special Economic Unit in the same or other Special Economic Zone. (1) With the prior permission of the Assistant Commissioner of Customs or Deputy Commissioner of Customs, as the case may be, goods may be allowed to be removed from a Special Economic Zone unit to an export-oriented undertaking or software technology park unit or electronic hardware technology park unit or to another Special Economic Zone unit in the same Special Economic Zone or in other Special Economic Zone without payment of duty for the purpose of carrying out authorised operations within the receiving export-oriented undertaking or software technology park unit or electronic hardware technology park unit or Special Economic Zone unit, as the case may be:

Provided that in case the goods admitted into Special Economic Zone unit from any domestic tariff area, on which benefit under duty exemption passbook scheme or dutydraw back has been availed, are removed as such or after subjecting them to a process not amounting to manufacture, to an export-oriented undertaking or software technology park unit or electronic hardware technology park unit directly by the Special Economic Zone unit or through any unit in the same Special Economic Zone or another Special Economic Zone, the duty equal to benefit availed under duty exemption passbook scheme or dutydrawback shall be liable to be paid.

(2) In case of clearance of goods by a Special Economic Zone unit to another Special Economic Zone unit within the same Special Economic Zone, no prior permission of Assistant Commissioner of Customs or Deputy Commissioner of Customs shall be required, but both supplying and receiving Special Economic Zone units shall be required to maintain records for such transaction."

(E) in rule 12, in sub-rule (1), for clause (i), the following clause shall be substituted, namely:

"(i) in case of destruction of goods procured from domestic tariff area, the Special Economic Zone unit shall be required to pay back the export benefits taken by the domestic tariff area supplying unit or taken by the Special Economic Zone unit on the basis of disclaimer from domestic tariff area unit:

Provided that where such goods have been procured by the Special Economic Zone unit against payment of foreign exchange, the Special Economic Zone unit shall not be liable to pay back the export benefits, taken by the domestic tariff unit from which such goods have been procured or, taken by the Special Economic Zone unit on the basis of disclaimer from such domestic tariff area unit, in case of destruction of such goods; and";

(F) for rule 14, the following shall be substituted namely:

"14. Submission of returns—Every Special Economic Zone unit shall endorse, a copy of the quarterly and annual return which it furnishes to the Development Commissioner, to the Assistant Commissioner of Customs or Deputy Commissioner of Customs, as the case may be, in a format as specified for such purpose in Appendix 14IF of the *Handbook of Procedures* (Vol. I), notified by the Director General of Foreign Trade, Government of India in the Ministry of Commerce and Industry under Public Notice No. 1 (RE-2003)/2002-07, dated the 31st march, 2003.

(G) in rule 18 for the words "Commissioner of Customs" the words "Deputy Commissioner of Customs or Assistant Commissioner of Customs, as the case may be," shall be substituted;

(H) for rule 19 the following rule shall be substituted, namely:

"19. Monitoring—The performance of a Special Economic Zone unit and a developer of the concerned Special Economic Zone shall be monitored by the Unit Approval Committee in which the Commissioner of Customs having jurisdiction over concerned Special Economic Zone or his nominee shall be a member";

(I) in rule 20, in clause (a),

(i) for the words "either exported or" the words "either exported or shall be transferred to another Special Economic Zone unit in other Special Economic Zone or to export-oriented undertaking or unit in electronic hardware technology park or software technology park without payment of duty or" shall be substituted;

(ii) after the proviso, the following proviso shall be inserted, namely:

"Provided further that in case the goods admitted into Special Economic Zone unit from domestic tariff area, on which benefit under duty exemption passbook scheme or duty drawback has been availed, are removed as such or after subjecting them to a process not amounting to manufacture, to an export-oriented undertaking or software technology park unit or electronic hardware technology park unit directly by the Special Economic Zone unit or through any unit in the same Special Economic Zone or another Special Economic Zone, the duty equal to benefit availed under duty exemption passbook scheme or duty drawback shall be liable to be paid."

Note: ...No. 58/2004-CUSTOMS (N.T.), dated the 30th April, 2004 [G.S.R 294(E), dated the 30th April, 2004].

NOTIFICATION NO. 62 /2004

In exercise of the powers conferred by sub-section (1) of section 157, read with sub-section (2) of section 76C of the Customs Act, 1962 (52 of 1962), the Board hereby makes the following regulations to further amend the Special Economic Zones (Customs Procedures) Regulations, 2003, namely:

1. (1) These regulations may be called the Special Economic Zones (Customs Procedures) (Fourth Amendment) Regulations, 2004.

(2) They have come into force from the day of their publication in the Official Gazette.

2. In the Special Economic Zones (Customs Procedures) Regulations, 2003,-

(A) in regulation 2,-

(i) In clause (f), for the words "permitted by the Commissioner of Customs" the words "approved by the Board of Approvals" shall be substituted;

(ii) After clause(n), the following clause shall be inserted, namely:

'(nn) "Unit Approval Committee", in respect of a Special Economic Zone means a committee set up for the Special Economic Zone as notified in the Official Gazette by the Central Government in the Ministry of Commerce and Industry';

(B) In regulation 3, for sub-regulation (3), the following sub-regulation shall be substituted, namely:

"(3) Each zone unit shall have separate establishment distinct and identifiable or distinct and partitioned, from other zone unit";

(C) For regulation 10, following regulation shall be substituted, namely:

....

(2) Notwithstanding anything contained in sub-regulation (1), where the goods are procured by a zone unit or developer from a domestic tariff area unit and where either the zone unit or the developer or the domestic tariff area unit do not claim duty drawback or duty entitlement passbook scheme credit or where such supplies from domestic tariff area unit to the zone unit or developer, as the case may be, are not against fulfillment of export obligation under any export promotion scheme or where no export benefits against such supplies are claimed either by the domestic unit supplying the goods or the zone unit or developer, as the case may be, then, the zone unit or the developer may procure any such goods from domestic tariff area for carrying out authorised operation subject to the following conditions, namely:

(i) zone unit or developer shall submit application to the proper officer of the zone for issuance of pre-authenticated Domestic Procurement Certificate and on the basis of such application, the proper officer of the zone or any other officer authorised by him in this regard shall issue to the zone unit or developer, as the case may be pre-authenticated Domestic Procurement Certificate in the Form specified in Annexure-I to these regulations;

(ii) the Superintendent of Central Excise having jurisdiction over the domestic tariff area unit shall, on the basis of Domestic Procurement Certificate issued under clause (i), allow the domestic tariff area unit to remove the goods under the cover of ARE-I;

(iii) the ARE-I shall contain complete description of goods such as model, make, serial number, technical specifications;

(iv) the goods allowed to be removed under clause (ii) may be allowed admission into the zone on the basis of ARE-I and a copy of ARE-I, with an endorsement that goods have been admitted in full into the zone, shall be forwarded to the Superintendent of Central Excise having jurisdiction over the domestic tariff area unit within a period of forty-five days from the date of removal of goods from the factory or warehouse in the domestic tariff area , failing which the proper officer in charge of zone unit shall raise demand of duty against such domestic tariff area unit;

(v) before allowing admission of such goods into the zone, the goods shall be examined by any officer of customs authorised in this behalf by the proper officer of the zone in respect of description, quantity, marks, model and other relevant particulars given in the ARE-I and invoice and packing list and also in accordance with the examination norms laid down in respect of export goods and instruction issued by the Board in this behalf from time to time;

(3) Nothing contained in sub-regulations (1) and (2) shall apply in cases where the duty paid goods are procured from domestic tariff area and no duty concession or export incentives are being claimed against such supplies by the domestic supplier or the zone unit or the developer, as the case may be, and such goods shall be allowed admission into the zone on the basis of invoice issued by the supplier of the goods and concerned transport documents, if any.

Explanation 1. For the purpose of this regulation, "export incentives" includes drawback, duty entitlement passbook scheme, rebate, advance license or counting of proceeds as export earnings or counting of proceeds as fulfilment of export obligation under any scheme.

Explanation 2. For the purposes of this regulation, "ARE-I" means Form ARE-I referred to in notification No 40/2001-Central Excise (N.T), dated the 26th June, 2001.

(D) In regulation 12, for the words " goods namely, capital goods or manufactured goods" the words " goods including capital goods or manufactured goods" shall be substituted;

(E) In regulation 15, in sub-regulation (1), in clause (i), the words "alongwith advance remittance certificate duly certified by the bank" shall be omitted;

(F) In regulation 20, the words "subject to condition that no wastage or manufacturing loss against such exchange of jewellery shall be permissible," shall be omitted;

(G) For regulation 21, the following regulation shall be substituted, namely:

....

(v) where goods admitted into zone unit from domestic tariff area, on which benefit under duty exemption passbook scheme or duty drawback has been availed, are removed as such or after subjecting it to a process not amounting to manufacture, to an export-oriented undertaking or software technology park unit or electronic hardware technology park unit directly by the zone unit or through any unit in the same zone or another zone, the duty equal to benefit availed under duty exemption passbook scheme or duty drawback shall be liable to be paid."

(H) In regulation 22,-

(i) in sub-regulation (4), for the word, bracket and figure "clause (4)" the word, bracket and figure "sub-regulation (3)" shall be substituted;

(ii) for sub-regulation (6), the following sub-regulation shall be substituted, namely:

....

Provided that in the case where such goods are supplied back to the domestic tariff area as it is and where the import duty on such goods is "Nil" and while procurement of such goods no export benefits were allowed against such goods, the zone unit may be allowed to supply back such goods to domestic tariff area on the basis of invoice only and filing of bill of entry in such cases shall not be required.

Explanation. "For the purpose of this regulation "export benefits" includes drawback, duty entitlement passbook scheme, rebate, advance license or counting of proceeds as export earnings or counting of proceeds as fulfilment of export obligation under any scheme";

(I) In regulation 24, for sub-regulation (5), the following sub-regulation shall be substituted, namely:

....

Provided that in case of failure of the zone unit to bring back the goods in the zone within the period as specified in this behalf by the proper officer, the zone unit shall pay the duty applicable on such goods under the provisions of clause (b) of section 76F of the Act."

(J) In regulation 25,-

(a) In sub-regulation (1),-

(i) in clause (iii), for the word "substantial" the word "entire" shall be substituted;

(ii) in clause (vii), for the proviso, the following proviso shall be substituted, namely:

....

(iii) in clause (viii), for the second proviso, the following proviso shall be substituted, namely:

"Provided further that no such bank guarantee shall be furnished by the status holder zone unit having an unblemished track record or a unit which has not come to the adverse notice of Customs authorities at least for a period of last two years;"

(b) in sub-regulation (2), for clause (iii) the following clause shall be substituted, namely:

"(iii) the facility of sub-contracting of production shall be allowed subject to the condition that the product is also being manufactured by the zone unit in the zone;"

(c) for sub-regulation (3), the following sub-regulation shall be substituted, namely:

"(3) Subject to permission of the proper officer, the zone unit shall be allowed to remove moulds, jigs, tools, fixtures, tackles, instruments, hangers, patterns and drawings to the jobworker's premises in the domestic tariff area without payment of duty and shall be allowed to keep such moulds, jigs, tools, fixtures, tackles, instruments, hangers, patterns and drawings in the job-worker's premises till the sub-contracting arrangement with job worker is in existence, subject to the following conditions, namely:

(i) the zone unit shall produce to the proper officer a verification report quarterly obtained from the jurisdictional Superintendent of Central Excise having jurisdiction over the of jobworker's unit to the effect that such moulds, jigs, tools, fixtures, tackles, instruments, hangers, patterns and drawings are lying in the jobworker's premises and are being used for production of goods for export on account of zone unit;

(ii) the zone unit shall bring back such goods to the unit immediately on expiry of such jobwork contract; and

(iii) such moulds, jigs, tools, fixtures, tackles, instruments, hangers, patterns and drawings shall be returned to the zone unit within a period of one year from the date of such removal where the jobworker's unit is not registered with Central Excise Department."

(d) for sub-regulation (6) the following sub-regulation shall be substituted, namely:

"(6). The waste or scrap or remnants generated during such processes at the jobworker's premises shall either be returned to the zone unit or shall be cleared on payment of duty as if the said waste or scrap or remnants have been cleared by the zone unit or may, where the job worker is a Central Excise Registrant, be destroyed at the jobworker's premises and such destruction shall be carried out under supervision of a central excise officer having jurisdiction over the job worker's unit and proof of such destruction duly certified by such Central Excise officer shall be submitted to the officer of the customs who is in charge of the zone."

(K) In regulation 28, for sub-regulation (2), the following sub-regulation shall be substituted, namely:

"(2) Where any goods procured from domestic tariff area under claim of duty drawback or duty entitlement passbook scheme credit or under any export promotion scheme are destroyed due to natural calamities, the zone unit shall be required to pay duty drawback or duty entitlement passbook scheme credit claimed on such goods: Provided that in case where the zone unit has procured the goods from domestic tariff area against payment of foreign exchange, the zone unit shall not be liable to pay back duty drawback or duty entitlement passbook scheme credit or any export incentive claimed on such goods";

(L) In the regulation 29,

(i) for sub-regulation (4), the following sub-regulation shall be substituted, namely:

"(4) The bond amount shall be equal to the twenty-five per cent of the duty leviable on the imported and indigenous capital goods plus duty forgone on raw materials to be held in stock for three months by the zone unit."

(ii) for sub-regulation (7), the following sub-regulation shall be substituted, namely:

"(7) Notwithstanding anything contained in sub-regulation (5), where the zone unit has a turnover of rupees one crore or above, or where the zone unit is in existence for more than a period of three years with an unblemished track record, such unit shall not be required to furnish surety or security."

(iii) for sub-regulation (9), the following sub-regulation shall be substituted, namely:

"(9) The bond shall be a running bond and shall be debited for an amount equal to duty forgone on the goods imported or procured by the zone unit, and credited for an amount equal to duty forgone on the raw materials used in the manufacture of finished products where such manufactured goods are either exported or cleared into domestic tariff area on payment of duty or for such imported or procured goods when exported as such or cleared into domestic tariff area on payment of duty as per the provisions of the Act or rules and regulations, made thereunder and such debiting and crediting of bond shall be done once at the end of every three months."

(M) For regulation 30, the following regulation shall be substituted, namely:

"30. Monitoring of performance—Performance of the zone unit shall be monitored by the Unit Approval Committee in which the Commissioner of Customs having jurisdiction over the zone or his nominee shall be a member."

(N) For regulation 33, the following regulation shall be substituted, namely:

"33. Import and procurement of goods by developer— (1) The developer shall be allowed to import or procure the goods from domestic tariff area without payment of duty for the purpose of development, operation and maintenance of the zone, subject to following conditions, namely:

(i) the activity of the developer shall be approved by the Board of Approvals;

(ii) the developer shall submit a list of machinery, equipments and the construction material required for development, operation and maintenance of the zone, duly certified by a chartered engineer;

(iii) the developer shall make an application to the concerned Development Commissioner for approval of the list of goods alongwith the certificate of the chartered engineer referred to in clause (ii), proposed to be imported or procured duty free for the purposes of the activity as approved by the Board of Approvals;

(iv) the developer shall submit to the Development Commissioner the proof of the ownership of concerned land, encumbrances certificate relating thereto, or in case the land is acquired on lease at least for a period of twenty years in his favour, the proof of such lease;

(v) on the basis of approval of the Development Commissioner, the proper officer having jurisdiction over the zone may allow the developer to import or procure goods without payment of duty;

(vi) the goods shall be stored in the premises appointed or licensed as public warehouse or private warehouse under section 57 or section 58 of the Act;

(vii) the developer shall maintain proper account of import or procurement, consumption and utilisation of the goods and submit quarterly return to the proper officer having jurisdiction over the zone in such form, as may be specified by such proper officer;

(viii) the developer shall execute a bond in Form II as annexed in the Special Economic Zone Rules, 2003 with the proper officer having jurisdiction over the zone, binding himself to utilise the goods within a period of six months or such period, as may be extended by such proper officer, and if the developer fails to do so, then the developer shall pay on demand an amount equal to the duty as leviable on the said goods alongwith interest at the rate of fifteen per cent per annum on the said duty from the date of import or procurement of said goods;

(ix) the developer shall not remove the goods from the zone except with the permission of the proper officer having jurisdiction over the said zone and on payment of duty applicable on such goods;

(x) no goods, other than which are required for the purposes of construction, development, operation, maintenance of the zone or for providing utilities in the zone, shall be allowed admission in the zone without payment of duty;

(xi) the developer shall produce, a certificate of utilisation of the goods from an independent chartered engineer other than who has given a certificate for the purpose of clause (ii), to the proper officer having jurisdiction over the zone on every six months of importation or procurement of the goods;

(xii) the procedure for import or procurement of goods as applicable to the zone unit shall apply *mutatis mutandis* in case of developer of the zone except that in case of developer, the goods imported or procured from domestic tariff area shall be allowed to be moved or utilised for the purposes of authorised operations in the non-processing area of the zone.

Explanation. For the purposes of this regulation, it is clarified that all approvals or permissions or extensions for utilisation to be given by or other functions to be discharged by the proper officer under this regulation shall be exercised by the Deputy

Commissioner of Customs or Deputy Commissioner of Central Excise or Assistant Commissioner of Customs or Assistant Commissioner of Central Excise, as the case may be, posted under the Commissioner of Customs or Commissioner of Central Excise, as the case may be, having jurisdiction over the zone during only such time when a regular Deputy Commissioner of Customs or Assistant Commissioner of Customs, as the case may be, is not posted in the zone."

Note: ...No. 59/2004-CUSTOMS (N.T.), dated the 30th April, 2004 [G.S.R.295 (E), dated the 30th April, 2004].

Ministry of Finance, Department of Revenue, Notification No. 53/ 2003 Dated 22nd July 2003

14

NOTIFICATION NO. 53/2003-CUSTOMS (N.T.)

G.S.R (E). In exercise of the powers conferred by sub-section (1) of section 157 read with sub-section (2) of section 76 C of the Customs Act, 1962 (52 of 1962), the Board hereby makes the following regulations, namely:

1. Short title, extent and commencement

(1) These regulations may be called the Special Economic Zones (Customs Procedures) Regulations, 2003.

(2) It extends to the whole of India.

(3) They shall come into force on the 15th day of August, 2003.

2. Definitions

In these regulations, unless the context otherwise requires:

(a) "Act" means the Customs Act, 1962 (52 of 1962);

(b) "Board" means the Board defined under clause (6) of section 2 of the Act;

(c) "Board of Approvals" means the combined Board of Approvals for export-oriented unit and Special Economic Zone units, as notified in the Official Gazette, from time to time, by the Government of India in the Ministry of Commerce and Industry;

(d) "custodian" means any person approved by the Commissioner of Customs under section 45 of the Act for the custody of imported goods unloaded in the customs area;

(e) "Development Commissioner" means the Development Commissioner of the concerned Special Economic Zone;

(f) "developer" means a person engaged in development, or operation, or maintenance of zone or in providing public utility services within the Special Economic Zone, duly permitted by the Commissioner of Customs and includes any other person authorised by the developer for such purpose;

(g) "Export and Import Policy" means the Export and Import Policy, notified from time to time, in the Official Gazette by the Government of India in the Ministry of Commerce and Industry under section 5 of the Foreign Trade (Development and Regulations) Act, 1992 (22 of 1992);

(h) "export-oriented undertaking" means an undertaking which has been approved as a hundred per cent export-oriented undertaking by the Board of Approvals;

(i) "Electronic Hardware Technology Park" means the "Electronic Hardware Technology Park Scheme notified by the Government of India in the Ministry of Commerce, and approved by the Inter-Ministerial Standing Committee appointed by notification of the Government of India in the Ministry of Industry (Department of Industrial Development);

(j) "Manufacturer Exporter" shall have the same meaning as defined in the Export and Import Policy;

(k) "Nominated Agencies" means the Metals and Minerals Trading Corporation Limited, the Handicraft and Handloom Export Corporation, the State Trading Corporation, the Projects and Equipment of India Limited and any other agency authorized by the Reserve Bank of India;

(l) "self certification" means the certification regarding sealing of container or package of goods under export given by the Zone unit and includes the certificate regarding contents and sealing of the container or package, given by the owner, the working partner, the Managing Director or Company Secretary of the said unit or any person, (holding a high position in such Zone unit, authorised by such owner, working partner or the Board of Directors of such unit (m), as the case may be, on the copies of shipping bill, which indicates that such package or container in respect of goods under export have been sealed in his presence;

(m) "Software Technology Park Scheme" means Software Technology Park Scheme notified by the Government of India in the Ministry of Commerce, and approved by the Inter-Ministerial Standing Committee appointed by notification of Government of India in the Ministry of Industry (Department of Industrial Development);

(n) "status holder" shall have the same meaning as defined in the Export and Import Policy;

(o) "Zone" means a Special Economic Zone specified by the Central Government under section 76 A of the Act;

(p) "Zone unit" means a Special Economic Zone unit of business establishment set up in the processing area of the zone for carrying out authorised operations only;

(q) Words and expressions used herein and not defined, but defined in the Act or Rules made thereunder, shall have the meanings respectively assigned to them in the Act or the rules.

3. Setting up of unit in the Zone

(1) A Zone unit may be set up for the purposes of carrying out authorised operations.

(2) The Letter of Permission for setting up of zone unit shall be issued by the Development Commissioner.

(3) Two or more Zone units shall not operate from the same premises.

4. Import of goods by the Zone unit

(1) The Zone unit may import goods required for carrying out its authorised operations or for the purposes of setting up the unit, through:

(a) ports or airports;

(b) land customs stations;

(c) inland container depots;

(d) foreign post offices;

(e) authorised courier;

(2) The goods may also be procured from public bonded warehouse or private bonded warehouse or international exhibition held in India.

(3) In case of software, imports shall also be allowed through data communication link, internet, e-mail or any other electronic mode.

(4) For clearance of imported goods at all ports, airports, land customs stations, inland container depots, the Zone unit or developer, as the case may be, shall be required to follow the procedures, namely:

(i) the Zone unit or developer, as the case may be, shall file a bill of entry for home consumption in quintuplicate giving therein, complete description, model, make, specifications, purpose of import of goods such as trading, manufacturing, nature of goods such as capital goods, raw materials, spares, consumables, with specially stamped endorsement as "Special Economic Zone cargo" alongwith bill of lading or airway bill, an invoice, packing list and purchase order or contract for noting of the bill of Entry in the Zone;

(ii) the bill of entry shall be assessed by the Custom officers in the Zone;

(iii) the assessed bill of entry shall be submitted to the Deputy Commissioner of Customs or Assistant Commissioner of Customs, as the case may be, (hereinafter referred to as proper officer) at the place of import such as port, airport, land customs station, inland container depot, and the same shall be treated as permission for transfer of goods to the Zone;

(iv) in case of sealed full container load (FCL) container, the goods shall be transferred to the Zone on the basis of assessed bill of entry after verification of the seal, without customs escorts;

(v) in case of other cargo, the goods shall be allowed to be transferred to the Zone on the basis of assessed bill of entry either under customs escort or under transshipment procedure, depending on the option made by the Zone unit; and for such transshipment, no separate documents shall be required to be filed and the transshipment permission shall be stamped on the fifth copy of the bill of entry;

(vi) on arrival of the goods in the Zone, the goods shall be subjected to verification of seal in case of full container load container or verification of marks and numbers of packages in other cases and after such verification, if in order, such goods received shall be allowed admission in the Zone;

(vii) the Zone unit shall submit fifth copy of bill of entry bearing endorsement of the Customs officers in the Zone that the goods have been received in the Zone, to the proper officer in charge of the airport, port, inland container depot, land customs station, post office, public or private bonded warehouse, as the case may be, within a period of forty-five days from the date of clearance of goods from such airport, port, inland container depot, land customs station, post office, public or private bonded warehouse, as the case may be, failing which the proper officer in charge of such airport, port, inland container depot, land customs station, post office, public or private bonded warehouse, as the case may be, shall write to the proper officer having jurisdiction over the Zone for raising demand of duty from the Zone unit;

(viii) the Zone unit shall be required to obtain notional out of charge of goods from the proper officer of the Zone on the same day if the goods are brought during the working hours or immediately on the next working day in case goods are brought beyond working hours;

(ix) where goods are imported by the Zone unit or developer through courier, customs officer in the Zone shall assess the goods as per the Courier Import and Export (Clearance) Regulations, 1998.

(5) The goods imported by the Zone unit or developer shall not be subject to detailed examination except in case of prior intelligence or information or to maintain an element of surprise.

(6) Where the goods have been imported by post, the Zone unit or the developer, following the procedure specified in sub-regulation (4), shall file the bill of entry with the Customs officers in the Zone marking clearly "Postal Imports" subject to following conditions, namely:

(i) for the purpose of bill of entry, the post office registration number as indicated in the intimation letter issued by the post office shall be taken as the import general manifest and item number, of the bill of entry;

(ii) copy of intimation letter received from the post office shall also be pasted on the reverse of the original bill of entry;

(iii) where the Zone is away from the foreign post office, the goods shall be moved to the Zone under customs escort from such post office or under control of the postal authorities.

5. Import of goods through personal carriage by gems and jewellery unit

(1) Notwithstanding anything contained in regulation 4, the Zone unit engaged in manufacture and export of gems and jewellery, shall be allowed to import precious goods, namely gold, silver, platinum, gems and jewellery through personal baggage, subject to the following procedure, namely:

(i) the passenger bringing the precious goods shall declare the goods with the customs authorities at the airport in the arrival hall in the declaration form as specified by Commissioner of Customs in charge of concerned airport alongwith a duly acknowledged copy of intimation submitted to the Customs officers in the Zone;

(ii) the passenger shall hand over the goods duly packed indicating name and address of the consignee Zone unit and accompanied by invoice and packing list to the Customs authorities for detention in the warehouse under the detention receipt;

(iii) the Customs officers shall detain the goods and issue detention receipt indicating full details such as weight, purity and number of bars, name of unit, passport number of the passenger and name of the supplier, etc.;

(iv) the Zone unit shall file the bill of entry in quintuplicate alongwith a copy of invoice, packing list, declaration with the Customs officers in the Zone and in such cases, the detention receipt number issued by the Customs at Airport at the time of arrival of the passenger shall be treated as Import General Manifest and item number;

(v) after assessments of bill of entry, original copy of the bill of entry shall be retained by the Custom officers in the Zone and the remaining copies shall be handed over to the representative of the Zone unit for presenting at the airport detention counter where goods shall be allowed clearance after receiving the original detention receipt, authorization from the Zone unit and making entries in the warehouse register, detention receipt register and obtaining signatures from the authorised representative of the Zone unit;

(vi) after release of the goods, the goods shall be moved to the Zone under customs escort and shall be allowed admission into the Zone unit after verification of marks and numbers of packages and notional "out of charge" by the Customs officers in the Zone;

(vii) the goods so detained at the airport may also be allowed to be transported by an authority or agency approved by the Commissioner of Customs having jurisdiction over the Zone.

6. Import through data communication or telecommunication link

(1) Where the Zone unit import computer software through data communication or telecommunication links, the Zone unit

shall file bill of entry within a period of twenty-four hours of such import alongwith invoice and other relevant documents and shall obtain notional 'out of charge' from the Customs officers in the Zone, subject to the following conditions, namely:

(i) the documents such as invoice, etc. in respect of such import of computer software shall be routed through banks;

(ii) the value of such software shall be verified by the Development Commissioner of the Zone;

(iii) instruction issued by the Reserve Bank of India, from time to time, if any, in this behalf shall be followed.

7. Procurement from warehouse

(1) Where goods are procured from the warehouse appointed or licensed under section 57 or section 58 of the Act, the Zone unit shall file bill of entry giving therein complete description of the goods such as model, make, serial number, specification, with the Customs officers in the Zone.

(2) The Zone unit shall submit the duly assessed bill of entry assessed by the Customs officers in the Zone to the proper officer in charge of the warehouse from where the Zone unit intends to procure the goods.

(3) The proper officer in charge of the warehouse shall allow clearance of the goods from the warehouse for supply to the Zone unit without payment of duty on the cover of ex-bond shipping bill and on the basis of bill of entry duly assessed by the customs officers in the Zone.

(4) Where the re-warehousing certificate by way of endorsement by the Customs officers in the Zone on the copy of ex-bond shipping bill is not received by the proper officer incharge of warehouse within the period of forty-five days from the date of clearance of the goods from the warehouse, the proper officer incharge of the warehouse shall proceed to demand of duty from the owner of such goods so supplied to the Zone unit.

(5) The Zone unit shall obtain notional "out of charge" of goods from the proper officer of the Zone on the same day if the

goods are brought during the working hours, or immediately on the next working day in case goods are brought beyond working hours.

8. Procurement of goods from international exhibition held in India

Subject to the procedure as specified in the regulation 7, the Zone unit shall be allowed to procure goods from international exhibitions held in India.

9. Re-import or replacement or re-export of goods

(1) The Zone unit shall be allowed to re-import the goods exported and found to be defective or damaged by the overseas buyer or in the case of failure of the buyer to take delivery of the goods, subject to the procedure as mentioned in regulation 4 and subject to the following conditions, namely:

(i) identity of goods is established at the time of re-import; and

(ii) goods are re-imported within a period of one year from the date of export.

(2) Where the goods imported by the Zone unit are found to be defective or damaged or found to be otherwise unfit for use and suppliers agree to replace such defective or damaged or unfit for use goods, then such goods received as free replacement shall be allowed admission in the Zone by way of import or replacement through the authorized dealer of the overseas supplier in India, subject to the following conditions, namely:

(i) the goods so found to be defective or damaged or otherwise unfit for use may be re-exported later on; or

(ii) where the overseas supplier of such goods does not insist for re-export of such goods, the re-export of the same shall not be insisted, provided such goods are either destroyed with the permission of proper officer, or shall be cleared into domestic tariff area on payment of duty as if cleared for home consumption.

10. Procurement of goods by Zone unit or developer from domestic tariff area

(1) The Zone unit or developer, as the case may be, may procure any goods from domestic tariff area for carrying out authorised operation subject to the following conditions, namely:

(i) the domestic tariff unit supplying the goods to the Zone unit or developer, or the Zone unit or developer on behalf of the domestic tariff area unit, as the case may be, shall file a bill of export giving therein complete description, model, make, specifications, nature of goods such as capital goods, raw materials, spares, consumables, with specially stamped endorsement as "Special Economic Zone cargo" alongwith invoice, packing list and purchase order for noting and assessment of the bill of export in the Zone;

(ii) the bill of export shall be assessed by the customs officer in the Zone;

(iii) the assessed bill of export shall be submitted to the proper officer having jurisdiction over the domestic tariff area unit and the same shall be treated as permission for transfer of goods to the Zone;

(iv) the domestic tariff area unit supplying goods to the Zone unit or the developer, as the case may be, shall be allowed to remove the goods on the cover of ARE-I and the assessed bill of export, giving therein complete description, model, make, serial number, specifications, etc.;

(v) the goods so brought to the Zone may be allowed admission into the Zone on the basis of assessement of bill of export and ARE-I and a copy of bill of export and ARE-I, with an endorsement that goods have been admitted in full into the Zone, shall be forwarded to the Central Excise Superintendent having jurisdiction over the domestic tariff area unit within forty-five days, failing which the Superintendent shall raise demand of duty against the domestic tariff area unit;

(vi) where domestic tariff area unit or Zone unit, on behalf of such domestic tariff area unit, has filed a bill of export under claim of duty drawback or duty entitlement passbook scheme and the domestic tariff area unit does not intend to claim duty drawback or duty entitlement passbook scheme credit, a disclaimer to this effect may be given to the Zone unit, and on the basis of such disclaimer given by the domestic tariff area unit, duty drawback or duty entitlement passbook scheme credit may be claimed by the Zone unit;

(vii) the proper officers in the Zone shall assess the bill of export in the same manner as it is assessed in the case of export of goods under claim of duty drawback or duty entitlement passbook scheme credit or no claim, as the case may be, and instruction issued under respective export promotion scheme shall apply *mutatis mutandis* in respect of these goods; and valuation of such goods shall be done in terms of section 14 of the Act;

(viii) before allowing admission of such goods into the Zone, the goods shall be examined by the Customs officer of the Zone in respect of description, quantity, marks, model, etc. given in the ARE-I and bill of export, invoice and packing list and also as per the examination norms laid down in respect of export goods and instruction issued by the Board in this behalf from time to time;

(ix) the duty drawback or duty entitlement passbook scheme credit against such supply of goods by domestic tariff area unit to the Zone unit or to the developer shall be admissible only when the payment for such supply of goods to the Zone unit is received in freely convertible foreign currency;

(x) a copy of the bill of export and ARE-I with endorsement of Zone Customs authorities on it to the effect that goods have been admitted in full in the Zone shall be treated as proof of export;

(xi) where the goods are intended to be procured by the Zone unit from a trader or merchant exporter, the procedure as stated hereinabove shall apply *mutatis mutandis*, including filing of bill of export except that the goods shall not be required to be brought to the Zone under the cover of ARE-I and assessed copy of bill of export shall not be required to be submitted to the jurisdictional Central Excise authority for removal of goods, from the premises of the trader or merchant exporter.

11. Procurement of goods from export-oriented undertaking or software technology park unit or electronic hardware park unit

(1) The Zone unit or the developer may also procure capital goods or manufactured goods from export-oriented undertaking or software technology park unit or electronic hardware technology park unit subject to following conditions, namely:

(i) subject to the procedure specified in regulation 7, the export-oriented undertaking or software technology park unit or electronic hardware technology park unit, as the case may be, may transfer capital goods imported or procured duty-free to the Zone unit or the developer, as the case may be;

(ii) subject to the procedure as specified in the regulation 10, the export-oriented undertaking or software technology park unit or electronic hardware technology park unit, as the case may be, may also transfer manufactured goods to the Zone unit or to the developer duty-free;

(iii) the goods procured by the Zone unit or developer under clauses (i) and (ii) shall be used by it for the purposes of carrying out authorised operations in the Zone only;

(iv) the capital goods or manufactured goods in export-oriented undertaking or software technology park unit or electronic hardware technology park unit so transferred under clauses (i) and (ii) to the Zone unit shall be considered as imported goods for Zone unit for all purposes.

12. Transfer of goods from one Zone unit to another Zone unit in the same Zone or different Zone

A Zone unit may procure goods, namely capital goods or manufactured goods from another Zone unit located in the same Zone or in another Zone, subject to following conditions, namely:

(i) the receiving Zone unit shall file bill of entry for home consumption in quintuplicate, giving therein, complete description, model, make, specifications, purpose of import of goods, nature of goods such as capital goods, raw materials, spares, consumables, alongwith an invoice, packing list with the Customs authorities in the Zone, having jurisdiction over such unit;

(ii) on the basis of such assessed bill of entry, the goods shall be allowed to be removed or transferred to the receiving Zone unit under transshipment permit;

(iii) there shall be no requirement to file any additional documents for the purpose of transshipment of goods and the transshipment permission shall be stamped on the bill of entry itself;

(iv) the supplying Zone unit shall submit the re-warehousing certificate to the proper officer having jurisdiction over the such supplying unit within a period of forty-five days, failing which the jurisdictional proper officer of the supplying Zone unit shall write to the jurisdictional proper officer of the receiving Zone unit for demand of duty from the receiving Zone unit;

(v) Notwithstanding anything contained in clause (1), in case where supplying and receiving Zone units are located in the same Zone, the movement of goods including raw materials shall be allowed subject to maintenance of accounts by both receiving and supplying Zone unit and no bill of entry shall be required to be filed with the customs authorities in the Zone.

13. Export of goods by Special Economic Zone unit

(1) Any goods manufactured, produced, reconditioned, re-engineered, imported or procured by the Zone unit, as the case may be, as per the terms and condition of letter of permission, may be exported out of India through airport or port or inland container depot, or land customs station or by post or courier or personal carriage, as the case may be, subject to the following conditions, namely:

(i) the Zone unit shall file shipping bill in quadruplicate with customs officers in the Zone, giving therein complete description of goods such as model, make, serial number, specification, alongwith relevant documents, namely, invoice, packing list, GR Form (in duplicate) for noting;

(ii) the shipping bill shall be assessed by the customs officers in the Zone in the manner and procedure as is followed in case of normal exports;

(iii) the goods shall not be examined in routine and Let Export Order may be given on the basis of self certification by the Zone unit;

(iv) notwithstanding anything contained in clause (iii), during the transit of goods from the Zone to the gateway port or at the gateway port, airport, or land Customs station itself, the goods may be examined by the Customs officers as per the norms prescribed by the Board from time to time;

(2) The Zone unit may export goods by post, subject to the normal procedure applicable to export through Foreign Post Office.

14. Export by software unit though data communication link or by providing on site services

(1) The Zone unit engaged in software sector may be permitted to export software or processed data or data analysed including call centre services via data link, internet, e-mail or through other electronic mode and Softex Form duly certified by the Development Commissioner of the Zone as per Foreign Exchange Management (Export of Goods and Services) Regulation, 2000, is submitted to the customs authorities in the Zone within a period of one month from the date of such exports.

(2) The Zone unit engaged in export of services including software may be permitted to provide consultancy services "on site" abroad subject to submission of details regarding the contract or purchase order, foreign exchange remitted and the persons deputed abroad, to the customs officers in the Zone.

(3) The consultancy fee received by the Zone unit for providing on site consultancy services in convertible foreign exchange shall be deemed to be export for the purposes of Net Foreign Exchange Earning.

15. Export by gems and jewellery through personal carriage

(1) Where the Zone unit is engaged in manufacture and export of gems and jewellery, the Zone unit may be allowed to export goods to be carried by the foreign bound passenger in their personal baggage, subject to the following conditions, namely:

(i) the Zone unit shall submit the shipping bill alongwith advance remittance certificate duly certified by the bank, invoice, GR-I with the customs officers in the Zone;

(ii) the shipping bill shall be assessed by the customs officers in the Zone in the same manner as is done in the case of normal exports;

(iii) the goods shall be transferred from the Zone to the airport under the cover of assessed shipping bill by the authorized agency approved by the Commissioner of Customs having jurisdiction over the Zone under customs escort of the Zone;

(iv) at the airport, the consignment shall be deposited with the warehouse in the airport against a "Detention Receipt" issued by the Customs officers at the airport;

(v) the consignment shall be handed over to the authorised passenger at the time of departure on submission of original Detention Receipt;

(vi) the Zone unit shall submit the proof of export issued by the Customs officer at the airport of export within a period of seven days from the date of removal of goods from the Zone to the customs in the Zone.

16. Export of goods by gems and jewellery unit through display and sale at showrooms at international airports

The Zone unit engaged in manufacture and export of gems and jewellery, shall be allowed to take gems and jewellery for display in the showrooms set up at Departure Lounge at International Airports in India for sale to passengers leaving India subject to such conditions and procedure as may be laid down by the Commissioner of Customs having jurisdiction over the Zone.

17. Export for participation in exhibition abroad

(1) The Zone unit shall be allowed to export goods including gems and jewellery for display or participating in exhibitions abroad in terms of the Export and Import Policy subject to following conditions, namely:

(i) the Zone unit shall obtain the permission of Development Commissioner of the Zone allowing the Zone unit to participate in the exhibition abroad;

(ii) shipping bill alongwith relevant documents shall be filed with the customs in the Zone in the same manner and following the same procedure as applicable to normal exports;

(iii) exports shall be allowed by the Customs officers in the Zone on provisional basis after examination of the goods;

(iv) the goods unsold in the exhibition shall be imported within such period as is stipulated in the Export and Import Policy;

(v) the Zone unit shall file bill of entry for unsold goods as required in case of normal imports and it shall be assessed in the same manner and subject to same procedure as applicable to normal imported goods;

(vi) the re-imported goods shall be allowed admission free of duty in the unit subject to establishment of identity of the goods with reference to the attested export documents and finalize the provisional assessment accordingly;

(vii) the Zone unit shall submit proof of inward remittance in respect of goods sold during exhibition abroad.

18. Export through courier

In cases where the Zone unit exports goods through couriers, such exports shall be allowed only through authorised courier, registered with the Commissioner of Customs having jurisdiction over the gateway airport and the procedure specified in the Courier Export and Import (Clearance) Regulations, 1998 shall be followed for this purpose.

19. Export of goods by the Zone unit through merchant exporter

The Zone unit may export goods through third party in accordance with the Export and Import Policy subject to the following conditions, namely:

(i) the goods shall be exported directly from the Zone;

(ii) export document shall contain the name of the merchant exporter and Zone unit;

(iii) merchant exporter at the time of assessment of shipping bill in the Zone shall submit a disclaimer that no export benefit is being or shall be availed by him.

20. Exchange of plain jewellery with unit in domestic tariff area

The Zone unit engaged in manufacture and export of gems and jewellery shall be permitted to receive plain gold or silver or platinum jewellery from domestic tariff area gems and jewellery unit in exchange of equivalent content of gold or silver or platinum contained in the said jewellery subject to condition that no wastage or manufacturing loss against such exchange of jewellery shall be permissible; and such exchange shall be allowed only after appraisement of the jewellery as well as precious metals by jewellery appraiser in the Zone.

21. Removal of goods manufactured or produced from a Zone unit to an export-oriented undertaking or software technology park unit or electronic hardware technology park unit

(1) The proper officer may permit a Zone unit to transfer capital goods or goods produced or manufactured by the Zone unit to an export-oriented undertaking or software technology park unit or electronic hardware technology park unit, as the case may be, without payment of duty for the purpose of manufacture and export, or for export or for use within the unit subject to the following conditions, namely:

(i) the Zone unit shall make such transfer against the procurement certificate issued by the proper officer in charge of receiving export-oriented undertaking or software technology park unit or electronic hardware technology park unit, as the case may be;

(ii) a warehousing bill of entry shall be filed by the export-oriented unit or software technology park unit or electronic hardware park unit or by the supplying Special Economic Zone unit on behalf of the receiving export-oriented unit or software technology park unit or electronic hardware park unit, as the case may be, with the customs officers in the Zone;

(iii) export-oriented undertaking or software technology park unit or electronic hardware technology park unit shall submit re-warehousing certificate duly signed by the proper officer, having jurisdiction over the receiving export-oriented undertaking or software technology park or electronic hardware technology park unit within a period of forty-five days from the date of clearance, to the Customs officers in the Zone;

(iv) where export-oriented undertaking or software technology park unit or electronic hardware technology park unit fails to submit the re-warehousing certificate within a period of forty-five days from the day of clearance of goods, Customs officers in the Zone shall take up the matter with the jurisdictional proper officer of the receiving unit, to initiate recovery proceeding against such export-oriented undertaking, software technology park unit or electronic hardware technology park unit, as the case may be.

22. Sale of goods by a Zone unit in domestic tariff area

(1) The Zone unit shall be allowed to sell goods manufactured or produced in the Zone unit including reject waste, scrap remnants and by-products arising out of such production, in the domestic tariff area on payment of customs duty in terms of clause (b) of section 76F of the Act.

(2) The Zone unit engaged in trading activities shall be allowed to sell imported or indigenously procured goods in domestic tariff area on payment of duty under clause (b) of section 76F of the Act subject to the condition that the Zone unit has achieved positive Net Foreign Exchange Earning cumulatively at the time of making sale in domestic tariff area and such sale of goods shall be allowed to the extent that Net Foreign Exchange Earning of the unit remain positive.

(3) Domestic tariff area unit intending to buy goods from the Zone unit shall be required to file bill of entry for home consumption giving therein complete description of the goods such as make, model number, serial number, specification, alongwith invoice and packing list with the customs officers in the Zone.

(4) Notwithstanding anything contained in clause (4), the bill of entry for home consumption may also be filed by the Zone unit on the basis of authorization by buyer located in domestic tariff area.

(5) The valuation of the goods cleared into domestic tariff area shall be determined in accordance with section 14 of the Act and rules made thereunder.

(6) Where the goods so procured from domestic tariff area by the Zone unit are supplied back to the domestic tariff area as it is or without substantial processing, such goods shall be treated as re-imported goods and shall be subject to such procedure and conditions as applicable in the case of normal re-import of goods from outside India.

(7) Where the Zone unit has surplus power generated in its captive power plant or diesel generating set, such surplus power may be allowed to be transferred to domestic tariff area on payment of duty on consumables and raw materials used for generation of power so sold on the basis of norms worked out for raw materials and consumables used, as may be approved by the Board of Approvals subject to the following conditions, namely:

(i) the proposal for sale of surplus power received in the office of the Development Commissioner shall be examined in consultation with the concerned State Government including State Electricity Board of that State;

(ii) the norms for production of unit of power that may be finalized shall be submitted to the Board of Approvals for consideration;

(iii) in case of sale of surplus goods to other unit in the same Zone or other Zone or to other export-oriented undertaking or to electronic hardware technology park unit or to other software technology park unit, as the case may be, the same shall be allowed without payment of duty:

Provided that the quantity of consumables and raw materials used for generation of power so transferred to another Special Economic Zone unit or export-oriented undertaking, electronic hardware technology park unit or software technology park unit, as the case may be, as quantified and approved by the Board of Approvals is accounted for by the supplying as well as receiving units for the calculation of Net Foreign Exchange Earning.

23. Removal of scrap or dust by gems and jewellery Zone unit

(1) The Zone unit engaged in the manufacture and export of gems and jewellery shall be allowed to send gold or silver or platinum scrap, dust or sweepings generated in such unit to the Government Mint or Private Mint for conversion into standard gold bars and return thereof to the Zone following the procedure laid down by the Customs officers in this regard.

(2) The gold or silver or platinum dust, scrap or sweepings may also be allowed to be cleared into domestic tariff area on payment of duty on the gold or silver or platinum content in the said scrap, dust or sweepings, in accordance with the provision of clause (b) of section 76F of the Act:

Provided that the samples of such gold or silver or platinum sweepings, scrap or dust shall be taken at the time of clearance and sent to Government Mint or Private Mint for assaying and assessment shall be finalised on the basis of reports received from the Government Mint or Private Mint, as the case may be.

24. Temporary removal of goods by a Zone unit into the domestic tariff area for specified purposes without payment of duty

(1) Subject to the grant of permission and fulfilment of such condition as may be imposed by the proper officer, the Zone unit shall be allowed to remove goods manufactured or produced including imported or procured capital goods to domestic tariff area temporarily without payment of duty for the purpose of test or repairs or calibration or re-engineering or re-conditioning in the domestic tariff area:

Provided that the identification marks such as make, model, seal number, specification of the goods received back after such test, repair, calibration or re-engineering or re-conditioning matches those mentioned in the repair challan prepared and countersigned by the Customs officers in the Zone at the time of taking capital goods into domestic tariff area:

Provided further that goods shall be brought back to the Zone within a period of forty-five days from the date of taking the goods out of the Zone:

Provided also that the proper officer of the Zone may, if he thinks proper, extend the said period of forty-five days upto further period of two months.

(2) In case of failure of the Zone unit to bring back the goods in the Zone within the period specified in sub-regulation (1), the Zone unit shall pay the duty applicable on such goods in terms of provision of clause (b) of section 76F of the Act.

(3) Subject to the provisions in sub-regulations (1) and (2), the Zone unit shall be allowed to take goods including capital goods to another unit in the same Zone or in another Zone, or export-oriented undertaking unit or electronic hardware technology park or software technology park unit, as the case may be, for the purpose of test or repairs or calibration or re-engineering or re-conditioning.

(4) The Zone Unit, engaged in development of software or otherwise, shall be allowed by the proper officer to take laptop computers and video projection system out of the Zone temporarily for use by the authorised employees of such unit subject to the following procedure, namely:

(i) the Zone unit shall account for the laptop computers or video projection system in their inventory after import or local procurement;

(ii) the Zone unit shall issue a certificate authorising the employee by name and giving the full specification, such as serial number, model number, make, etc. of the laptop computers and video projection system intended to be taken outside the bonded area temporarily and a copy of the certificate shall be endorsed to the proper officer and acknowledgement received by the unit;

(iii) the Zone unit shall be required to maintain a record of such certificate of authorization issued under clause (ii) for temporarily taking out or bringing in such unit the laptop computer or video projection system and the same shall be made available at the time of inspection by the customs officers having jurisdiction over the Zone.

(5) Subject to such conditions as the proper officer may specify and subject to such procedure, as may be laid down by the Commissioner of Customs of the Zone from time to time, the Zone unit shall be allowed to take limited quantities of goods manufactured or produced into domestic tariff area without payment of duty for the purpose of display, market promotion, export promotion, exhibition and return thereof within the period of time as specified by such proper officer or as the case may be, the Commissioner of Customs:

Provided that in case of failure of the Zone unit to bring back the goods in the Zone within the period as specified in this behalf by the proper officer, the Zone unit shall pay the duty applicable on such goods under the provisions of clause (b) of section 76F of the Act.

25. Subcontracting of production or production process in domestic tariff area or abroad by the Zone unit

(1) The Zone unit shall be permitted to take goods including inputs, semi-finished or semi-processed goods to the jobworker's premises into domestic tariff area without payment of duty for further processing of the goods or to carry out a production, subject to the following conditions, namely:

(i) the Zone unit shall file an application containing the name and address of the jobworker, Central Excise registration number of the jobworker, if registered with the Central Excise Department, processing capacity of the jobworker, details of the processes to be carried out by the jobworker, justification for processing of goods outside the bonded premises and any other relevant information before the proper officer for further processing of the goods or to carry out production;

(ii) the proper officer may, after examining the application and after satisfying himself about the bonafide requirement of the Zone unit, grant permission for jobwork and such permission shall normally be valid for a period of one year. However, considering the sensitive nature of the commodities to be sent out for jobwork and past record of the Zone unit, such permission may be less than said period of one year;

Provided that in case of Zone unit engaged in manufacture and export of gems and jewellery, no cut and polished diamonds, precious stones and semi-precious stones shall be allowed to be taken out of the Zone;

(iii) while considering the application of the Zone unit, the entire processing activity in relation to the manufacture of the export products by the said units may be studied, and the proper officer may ensure that there is no attempt to parcel out the substantial manufacturing operations outside the bonded premises;

(iv) in respect of activities permitted to be carried out on jobwork basis outside the premises of the Zone unit, identity of finished products received after jobwork shall be established with the raw materials or components or partially processed goods sent out to ensure that the finished products are manufactured out of raw materials imported or procured duty-free by the units or admitted under claim of duty drawback or duty entitlement passbook scheme credit into the Zone unit and there is no substitution or diversion of such goods in the domestic tariff area:

Provided that in case of Zone unit engaged in manufacture and export of gems and jewellery, there shall be no requirement of taking out the samples or retaining the same if such goods have been appraised by jewellery appraiser at the time of both taking out of such goods from the Zone or receiving back of goods in the Zone after completion of jobwork:

Provided further that where the precious metal in bullion form, having marking regarding fineness, purity, make, serial number, is being taken out of the Zone for the purpose of jobwork, appraisement by jewellery appraiser shall not be mandatory;

(v) the Zone unit sending out goods for jobwork in domestic tariff area shall be required to give an intimation to the proper officer and a sample of the goods being sent out for jobwork shall be drawn and retained in the office of the proper Officer in the Zone;

(vi) on receipt of the goods in the Zone unit after jobwork, the Customs officers of the Zone shall establish the identity of the goods so returned with reference to the sample retained by him at the time of removal and a sample of the processed goods so returned to the Zone shall be retained for the purpose of record for a period of six months and both the samples shall be returned to the Zone unit after obtaining an acknowledgement from the Zone unit;

(vii) the Zone unit sending out imported or domestically procured raw materials, components, etc. as it is, i.e. without any processing in the unit for jobwork in the domestic tariff area, shall furnish bank guarantee to cover the duty forgone on such duty-free materials being taken out, to the proper officer:

Provided that no such bank guarantee shall be required in case of status holder unit having an unblemished track record;

(viii) the Zone unit removing semi-processed goods for jobwork in domestic tariff area shall furnish bank guarantee equivalent to fifty per cent of the duty payable on the goods being taken out for jobwork:

Provided that no fresh or additional bank guarantee shall be insisted upon if the Zone unit has furnished a bank guarantee as security along with bond in Form-I, and the same is sufficient to cover the duty payable on such goods being taken out:

Provided further that no bank guarantee shall be furnished by the status holder Zone units having unblemished track record;

(ix) in all cases of jobwork in domestic tariff area, the goods sent out for jobwork shall be required to be returned to the Zone unit within a period of ninety days or such period as may be extended by the proper officer for reasons to be recorded in writing for granting such extension, from the date of removal and in case of failure to receipt of goods within the said period, action shall be taken by the proper officer to recover duty such as encashment of the bank guarantee given at the time of removal of goods into domestic tariff area for jobwork;

(x) the proper officer shall carry out the checks expeditiously to verify the premises of the jobworker, processing capacity of the jobworker, existence of facility for carrying out the declared process in the jobworker's premises within a period of one month from the date of granting permission for jobwork by either visiting the premises of the jobworker by himself or the officer authorised by him in this behalf or by letters or fax or E-Mail to the concerned Range officer having jurisdiction over jobworker's premises and getting report in writing;

(2) The Zone unit shall be allowed to subcontract production in domestic tariff area subject to the following conditions, namely:

(i) the proper officer shall satisfy himself regarding the bonafide necessity of such subcontracting of production in domestic tariff area and shall not allow such permission in routine manner to the Zone unit;

(ii) while giving permission for subcontracting of production in domestic tariff area or in other export-oriented undertaking or software technology park unit or electronic hardware technology park unit or Zone unit, the proper officer may verify the past antecedents of the Zone unit as well as jobworking units, and in case of any misuse of serious nature noticed by him in the past or due to any other reasons, where it is satisfied that there is no justification for such permission or there are high chances of abuse of such facility, such permission may be denied with the approval of Commissioner of Customs having jurisdiction over the Zone;

(iii) the facility of subcontracting of production shall only be limited to the extent of fifty per cent of the free on board value of physical export made in the previous year subject to the condition that the product is also being manufactured in the Zone;

(iv) in case of Zone unit engaged in manufacture and export of gems and jewellery, no cut and polished diamonds, precious stones and semi-precious stones shall be allowed to be taken out of the Zone;

(v) other conditions as stipulated in sub-regulation (1) except clause (viii), shall apply *mutatis mutandis* in case of subcontracting of production in domestic tariff area.

(3) Subject to permission of the proper officer, the Zone unit shall be allowed to remove moulds, jigs, tools, fixtures, tackles, instruments, hangers, patterns and drawings to the jobworker's premises in the domestic tariff area without payment of duty, subject to the condition that such unit shall bring back such goods to the unit on completion of such subcontracting within a period of six months from the date of such removal.

(4) The Zone unit shall be allowed to subcontract part of the production process abroad, that is outside India following the provisions of Export and Import Policy in this regard, and after such processing abroad, the goods shall either be returned to the Zone unit for carrying out further processing or may be sold to buyers in that country or any third country:

Provided that the scrap or waste or remnants generated at the subcontractor's premises abroad may either be returned to the Zone unit; or may be disposed of abroad itself:

Provided further that in case of sale of goods processed abroad or scrap, waste or remnants arising during the processing of goods abroad, directly from the jobworker's premises abroad, the unit shall take permission from the Reserve Bank of India.

(5) The proper officer may permit the Zone unit to export the finished goods directly from the jobworker's premises subject to the following conditions, namely:

(i) the jobworker should be registered with the Central Excise Department;

(ii) export of finished goods from the jobworker's premises shall not be allowed through third party;

(iii) sample of goods exported from the jobworker's premises shall be sent to the proper officer in the Zone for establishing the identity of the goods exported with the sample drawn at the time of taking out of the goods to the jobworker;

(iv) in case of such exports, the shipping bill for duty-free goods shall be processed at the port of export as in the case of normal export and shipping bill shall be filed in the name of the Zone unit;

(v) the goods for such export shall be removed from the jobworker's premises under bond.

(6) The waste or scrap or remnants generated during such processes at the jobworker's premises shall either be returned to the Zone unit or shall be cleared on payment of duty as if the said waste or scrap or remnants have been cleared by the Zone unit.

(7) The Zone unit engaged in trading shall not be allowed the facility of subcontracting of production or production process in domestic tariff area.

26. Subcontracting of production process for domestic tariff area unit in the Zone unit for export

The Zone unit shall be allowed to undertake jobwork for export on behalf of domestic tariff area unit, subject to the following conditions, namely:

(i) the semi-finished goods or raw materials shall be supplied by domestic tariff area unit to the Zone unit;

(ii) no export benefit shall be claimed by the domestic tariff area unit on such semi-finished goods or raw materials supplied to the Zone unit for jobworking;

(iii) the finished goods shall be exported directly from the Zone unit on behalf of domestic tariff area unit;

(iv) the export document shall be in the name of domestic tariff area unit;

(v) the value of such goods shall not be counted towards achievement of Net Foreign Exchange Earning of the Zone unit; and

(vi) the unit in domestic tariff area shall not be eligible for all industry rate of drawback or duty entitlement passbook scheme credit.

27. Removals of samples from the Zone unit

(1) Subject to the provisions of Export and Import Policy, the Zone unit shall be allowed to take out the samples of the goods manufactured or produced by it into domestic tariff area for the purposes of display or market promotion on payment of duty as per the provision clause (b) of section 76F of the Act or for the purposes of export without payment of duty.

(2) Where samples of the goods manufactured or produced are to be taken into domestic tariff area on payment of duty, the procedure as laid down in regulation 21, shall apply except that the bill of entry shall be filed by the Zone unit.

28. Destruction of goods imported including capital goods or goods manufactured or produced by the Zone unit

(1) Subject to the procedure specified in regulation 22, where any scrap, waste or remnants arise out of destruction of

goods in terms of rule 12 of the Special Economic Zone Rules, 2003, the Zone unit shall be permitted to take the same into domestic tariff area on payment of duty applicable to such scrap and remnants as per the provision of clause (b) of section 76F of the Act.

(2) Where any goods procured from domestic tariff area under claim of duty drawback or duty entitlement passbook scheme credit or under any export promotion scheme are destroyed due of natural calamities, the Zone unit shall be required to pay duty drawback or duty entitlement passbook scheme credit claimed on such goods.

29. Security

(1) On the basis of the Letter of Permission issued by the Development Commissioner of the Zone, the Zone unit shall execute a bond with the proper officer, in the Form I as annexed to the Special Economic Zone Rules, 2003 and such surety or security shall be given as per procedure specified hereinafter in this regulation.

(2) The bond, in respect of a limited company, shall be executed by the Managing Director of the company or the Director(s) who have been duly authorised for this purpose by a resolution of the Board of Directors of the Company and shall be affixed with the common seal of the company.

(3) Where the unit is a partnership firm, the bond shall be executed by all the partners of the unit.

(4) The bond amount shall be equal to the duty leviable on the goods but for the goods admitted duty-free in the Zone unit, the value of the goods shall be taken as per declared value on the bill of entry at the time of admission of goods in the Zone.

(5) The Zone unit shall furnish surety for the bond amount or furnish five per cent of the bond amount as bank guarantee or any other security as approved by the Central Government and in case of surety, the solvency of sureties shall be certified by any Chartered Accountant or the Banker of the Surety, as the case may be.

(6) The Directors or Members of the limited company may stand as surety in their personal capacity for the company, and

other corporate bodies, including limited companies may also stand as surety for the unit.

(7) Notwithstanding anything contained in sub-regulation (5), where the Zone unit have a turnover of rupees one crore or above, such unit shall not be required to furnish surety or security.

(8) Where the value of the bond executed with the custom officers is initially worked out on the projected value of goods imported and the value of such bond falls short of duty forgone on goods admitted duty-free in the unit, then the unit shall be required to submit a revised bond and furnish additional security or surety, as the case may be, and in case of subcontracting of production process or production in domestic tariff area, if the security given with the bond is not sufficient to cover duty leviable on goods being taken into domestic tariff area, the unit shall be required to give additional security.

(9) The bond shall be a running bond and shall be debited whenever there is fresh admission of duty-free goods in the unit. The value debited from the bond amount in respect of raw materials shall be credited again when the raw material is used in the manufacture of finished products and such manufactured goods are either exported or cleared into domestic tariff area on payment of duty as per the provisions of Act or rules and regulations, as the case may be, made thereunder.

(10) In respect of the capital goods or infrastructured materials, surety or security shall not stand discharged on arrival of the capital goods or infrastructure materials within the unit and the surety or security shall not be discharged as long as the capital goods are in the Zone unit or the capital goods of the unit are not debonded.

(11) The duty for debiting the bond amount in respect of capital goods or infrastructure materials or raw materials shall be as per the duty forgone amount given in the bill of entry or shipping bill, as the case may be.

(12) After execution of the bond, the proper officer shall retain the original copy of the bond and provide a certified copy to the unit for its record.

(13) Notwithstanding anything to the contrary, in case the Zone unit is engaged in manufacture and export of gems and jewellery, the effective rate of duty as specified in notification No 80/97-Customs of the Government of India in the Ministry of Finance (Department of Revenue), dated 21st October, 1997, shall be taken instead of tariff rate of duty, for the purpose of calculation of bond amount in case of import of gold or silver.

30. Monitoring of Performance

Performance of the Zone unit shall be monitored by the Commissioner of Customs having jurisdiction over the Zone.

31. Disposal of obsolete or surplus goods

(1) The Zone unit shall be allowed to dispose of obsolete or unusable capital goods, spares and other goods in the domestic tariff area on payment of customs duty as per provisions of clause (b) of section 76F of Act following the conditions mentioned in the Export and Import Policy and the provisions of ITC(HS) Classification of Export and Import Items Book as applicable in case of goods imported into India.

(2) In case of used capital goods, depreciation shall be allowed in terms of sub-rule (1) of rule 9 of the Special Economic Zone Rules, 2003.

32. Co-relation of import consignment with corresponding export consignment

The Zone unit using homogenous material may be allowed to adopt 'First-in-First-Out' arrangement and a consignment which has been received first, may be deemed to have been utilised first for this purpose, and in such cases, co-relation of every import consignment with the corresponding export consignment may not be required.

33. Import and procurement of goods by developer

(1) The developer shall be allowed to import or procure the goods from domestic tariff area without payment of duty for the purpose of development, operation and maintenance of the Zone, subject to following conditions, namely:

(i) the developer shall make an application to the concerned Development Commissioner for approval of the list of goods proposed to be imported or procured duty-free;

(ii) the developer shall submit the application accompanied with the proof of ownership of land, encumbrances certificate, or in case the land is acquired on lease at least for a period of twenty years in his favour, the proof of such lease;

(iii) the developer shall submit a list of machinery, equipments and the construction material required for development, operation and maintenance of the Zone, duly certified by a Chartered Engineer;

(iv) the goods shall be stored in the premises appointed or licensed as public warehouse or private warehouse under section 57 or section 58 of the Act;

(v) the developer shall maintain proper account of import or procurement, consumption and utilisation of the goods and submit quarterly return to the Deputy Commissioner of Customs or Deputy Commissioner of Central Excise, as the case may be, having jurisdiction over the Zone in such form, as may be specified by him;

(vi) the developer shall execute a bond in Form II as annexed in the Special Economic Zone Rules, 2003 with the Commissioner of Customs having jurisdiction over the Zone, binding himself to utilise the goods within a period of six months or such period, as may be extended by him, and if the developer fails to do so, then the developer shall pay on demand an amount equal to the duty as leviable on the said goods alongwith interest at the rate of fifteen per cent per annum on the said duty from the date of import or procurement of said goods;

(vii) the developer shall not remove the goods from the Zone except with the permission of the proper officer having jurisdiction over the said Zone and on payment of duty applicable on such goods;

(viii) no goods, other than which are required for the purposes of construction, development, operation, maintenance of the Zone or for providing utilities in the Zone, shall be allowed admission in the Zone without payment of duty.

(2) The application mentioned in clause of sub-regulation (1) shall be submitted by the developer to the concerned Development Commissioner of the Zone and the Development Commissioner after processing of the application, shall forward such application alongwith relevant documents to the Committee of Approval, for consideration.

(3) The approval for duty-free import or procurement shall be given to the developer only in respect of such goods which are required for construction, maintenance and operation of the Zone.

(4) When an application is submitted for approval of additional items, the Committee of Approval shall determine such additional requirement taking into account quarterly statement submitted by the developer.

(5) The Committee of Approval shall fix the time schedule for commencement and completion of the construction of the Zone and in case of delay in the completion of the project, the developer of the Zone shall explain the reasons of such delay to the Committee of Approval.

(6) The Committee of Approval may direct the developer to get the account audited by a Cost Accountant as nominated by Committee of Approval in this behalf.

(7) The procedure for import or procurement of goods as applicable to the Zone unit shall apply *mutatis mutandis* in case of developer of the Zone except that in case of developer, the goods imported or procured from domestic tariff area shall be allowed to be moved or utilised for the purposes of authorised operations in the non-processing area of the Zone.

Explanation. For the purposes of this regulation, the Committee of Approval shall consist of following persons, namely:

(i) Commissioner of Customs or Commissioner of Central Excise, as the case may be, having jurisdiction over the Zone—Chairman.

(ii) Development Commissioner of the Zone—Member.

(iii) Joint Director General of Foreign Trade—Member.

(iv) The Chief Engineer of Central Public Works Department—Member.

(v) Jurisdictional Deputy Commissioner of Customs or Assistant Commissioner of Customs having jurisdiction over the Zone—Member.

Ministry of Commerce and Industry, Department of Commerce, Public Notice No. 17 (RE-03)/2002-07 Dated 16th July 2003

15

In exercise of powers conferred under paragraph 2.4 of the Export and Import Policy, 2002-07, the Director General of Foreign Trade hereby makes the following amendment in the *Handbook of Procedures* (Vol. 1):

1. The following rows are added in S.No (3) of Appendix 4A pertaining to the "Format of Registration Cum Membership Certificate.

(3) *(i)* *Address of Registered/ Head office:*

(ii) *Address of Branch office(s):*

(iii) *Address of Factory (s):*

2. The following amendments are made in Appendix 14.I pertaining to the "Export Oriented Units, Electronic Hardware Technology Parks and Software Technology Parks Scheme":

(a) The last sentence of para 4.6 is amended as under:

However, proposals approved prior to 01.04.2002 shall be considered on a case to case basis by BOA for extension of validity of LOP beyond six years.

(b) The words and expression "8.9" shall be corrected to read as "4.9" in para 4.11.

(c) The following is added at the end of sub para (b) of para 12.1 as under:

Within the entitlement of DTA sale, the unit may sell in DTA its products and services. Entitlement will be determined in totality and not with reference to specific items.

(d) The first sentence of para 13.1 of Appendix 14.I is amended as under:

The following supplies effected in DTA by EOU/ EHTP/ STP units will be counted for the purpose of fulfilment of positive NFE:

(e) The second sentence of para 14.3 is amended as under:

The procedure for submission of application for grant of Replenishment Licence as contained in the relevant chapter of the Handbook of Procedures (Vol. 1) shall be applicable.

(f) A heading is added to para 20.2 as under:

Sale through showrooms/ retail outlets at International Airports

(g) The words and expression "units" is deleted in para 21.1

(h) Para 25.1 is amended as under:

In case an EOU/EHTP/STP unit is unable, for valid reasons, to utilize the goods and services, imported or procured from DTA, it may be transferred to other EOU/SEZ/EHTP/STP units or disposed off in the DTA with the approval of the Development Commissioner on payment of applicable duties and submission of import license by DTA unit, wherever applicable or exported. Such transfer of imported goods and services from EOU/EHTP/STP unit to another such unit would be treated as import for the receiving unit.

3. The following amendments are made in Appendix 14.IA pertaining to "Application for setting up EOUs or units in Special Economic Zones,"

(a) The following column is added at S.No. I:

The name and address of each of the Director/ Partner.

(b) The following sub serial no (d) is added to S.No. IX pertaining to "INVESTMENT" as under:

(d) *details of source(s) of finance, (both Indian as well as foreign) for the above investments.*

4. The following amendments are made in Appendix 14.I F pertaining to "Form of Legal Agreement for EOU/ SEZ units".

(a) Para 12 of the agreement is amended as under:

Any changes in the Board of Directors/ Partners, telephone number, E-mail address, Website, Passport No., Bank Address and Factory address shall be duly intimated by the unit within a fortnight

(b) The following columns are added in S.No. 3 of Annexure III and S.No. 8 of Annexure IV to this appendix as under:

Details of production figures

Quantity (MT/ pieces) *Value (Rs. Lakhs)*

5. The following amendments are made in Appendix 14.II pertaining to "Special Economic Zones Scheme:"

(a) The second sentence of para 10.1 is amended as under:

However, if any permission is required for import under any other law, the same shall be allowed with the approval of the BOA.

(b) Para 15.2 is amended as under:

DTA sale by service/trading unit shall be subject to achievement of positive NFE cumulatively upto the last financial year. Similarly for units undertaking manufacturing and services/ trading activities against a single LOP, DTA sale shall be subject to achievement of NFE cumulatively upto the last financial year.

(c) Para 15.3 is amended as under:

Scrap/ wastes/ remnants/ rejects arising out of production process or in connection herewith may be sold in the DTA on payment of applicable duty.

(d) Para 17.2 is amended as under:

Notwithstanding the above, SEZ units/SEZ Developer shall, on production of a suitable disclaimer from the

DTA supplier, be eligible for obtaining the entitlement of Drawback or DEPB in lieu of Drawback.

(e) Para 20.8 is amended as under:

Export value of goods, software and services by SEZ units may be realised and repatriated to India as per the RBI instructions in the matter.

6. Amendments are made in Appendix 15 pertaining to the "Agri Export Zones" as under:

S.No.	Product	State	Districts covered
20	Lychee, Vegetables and Honey	Bihar	Muzaffarpur, Samastipur, Hajipur, Vaishali, East and West Champaran, Bhagalpur, Begu Sarai, Khagaria, Sitamarhi, Saran and Gopalganj
46	Value Added Onion	Gujarat	Bhavnagar, Surendranagar, Amreli, Rajkot, Junagadh and Jamnagar
48	Pomegranate	Maharashtra	Sholapur, Sangli, Ahmednagar, Pune, Nasik, Osmanabad and Latur

7. The following amendment is made in Appendix 27 pertaining to the "List of Export Promotion Councils/ Commodity Board" as under:

S.No.	Name of Export Promotion Council	Address of the Regd. Office of the Council	Address of the Regional Office (s) of the Council
1	2	3	4
31	Export Promotion Council for Export-Oriented Units and SEZ Units	705, Bhikaji Cama Bhavan, Bhikaji Cama Place, New Delhi 110066 Tel: 011-26165508/ 7042/ 6185 Fax: 011- 26165538 *E-mail*: epces@vanl.com	

8. S.No. 4 in the declaration given in Appendix-36B is amended to read as under:

"The imports made under the Duty-free Credit Entitlement number..........are those of spares, office equipment and furniture, professional equipment and consumables which are freely importable and which are required in my/our line of business."

9. Para 4.21 is amended to read as under:

"In respect of an Advance License, the licensing authority concerned (as per their financial powers) may consider a request for enhancement/ reduction in the CIF value of the license, provided the value addition after such enhancement does not fall below the stipulated minimum value addition and provided there is no change in the input-output norms and the Policy under which the license was issued. However, Advance Licenses issued under Para 4.7 shall be enhanced upto 100% of their original value only."

Ministry of Commerce and Industry, Department of Commerce, Directorate General of Foreign Trade, Notification No. 9 (RE-2003)/2002-2007 Dated 30th September 2002

16

To

All Licensing Authorities

All Commissioners of Customs

Sub: Imports of approved & unapproved drugs under the Advance Licensing Scheme—Exemption from Registration procedure.

Attention is invited to Notification No.2(RE-2003)/2002-2007 dated 31.3.2003 vide which certain types of drugs & pharmaceuticals have been placed under free category and their imports have been subjected to the registration and other requirements administered by the Drugs Controller General of India under the provisions of Drugs & Cosmetics Act.

2. Subsequent to the above Notification, representations have been received from various Drug Manufacturers' Associations requesting for exemption from registration requirements of the Drugs & Cosmetics Act for imports under the Advance Licensing Scheme. The requests have been considered and it has been decided that import of approved & unapproved drugs under the Advance Licensing Scheme will not be subjected to the Registration procedure and the imports will be permitted subject to the following conditions:

(i) Import license will only be given against an existing valid export order and to the extent raw material is required as per that order.

(ii) The Drug Controller would be a member of the Advance Licensing Committee. A copy of the license would be endorsed to the Drug Controller and the concerned State Drug Controller.

(iii) Drug Controller along with the State Drug Controller would make random checks.

(iv) Any violation is punishable under the Foreign Trade Development and Regulation Act and the Customs Act. The Drug Controller could also make provisions for penalizing the Drug Manufacturing Units in terms of suspension or cancelling of his license.

(v) Pre-import condition will have to be fulfilled.

(vi) Export obligation will be fulfilled within a period of six months from the date of issuance of the license.

3. Similarly, 100% EOUs/EPZs & SEZs would also be exempted from the condition of registration. However, if they make supplies to the domestic market, they will have to follow the formalities of registration as under the Drugs & Cosmetics Act.

4. Representations have also been received regarding issuance of Form-10 under the Drugs & Cosmetics Act for manufacturers. It is clarified that Form-9 issued by the registered manufacturers should also be accepted for the purpose of issuing Form-10 license under the Drugs & Cosmetics Act.

5. In addition, as far as imports of drugs/raw materials for purposes of (i) clinical trials & (ii) for formulation development is concerned, it is clarified that exemption in such cases will be permitted on case-to-case basis.

This issues with the approval of the DGFT.

Ministry of Commerce and Industry, Department of Commerce, Notification P. 2(1) 2002—EPZ Dated 23rd May 2002

17

To

All Development Commissioners, EPZs/SEZs

Sub: Sub-contracting by EOUs/EPZ/SEZ units—regarding

1. Several representations were received from the trade as well as Office of the Development Commissioners in respect to the new restrictions on subcontracting by EOU/EPZ/SEZ units imposed w.e.f. 01.04.2002. Issue was deliberated upon in the meeting held on 17.05.2002 under the Chairmanship of Shri D.K. Acharya, Member (Customs), CBEC. During the discussions, it was felt unanimously that the new restrictions are seriously affecting the working of EOU/EOZ/SEZ units and that the same need to be relaxed. Accordingly, it was decided that the following guidelines would be enforced in respect of subcontracting by EOU/EPZ/SEZ units:

(i) In case an EOU wants to send the imported or domestically procured raw material as it is, i.e. without being subjected to any processing in the unit, for jobwork in the Domestic Tariff Area (DTA), then the unit would be required to furnish 100% bank guarantee to cover the duty foregone on such duty-free material being taken out for jobwork. The bank guarantee shall be required to be furnished to the jurisdictional Range Officer of Central Excise or the Jurisdictional Superintendent of Customs, as the case may be. However, the status holder EOUs having unblemished track record shall be exempt from the requirement of furnishing bank guarantee.

(ii) In case an EOU wants to remove the semi-processed goods for jobwork in DTA for carrying out further process(es), then it would be required to furnish bank guarantee equivalent to 50% of the duty payable on the goods being taken out for jobwork. However, in case the unit has furnished a bank guarantee as security along with B-17 bond, and the same is sufficient to cover the duty payable on such goods being taken out, then no fresh or additional bank guarantee would be insisted upon. But, in cases, where only surety is given at the time of execution of B-17 bond or the security given along with B-17 bond is not sufficient to cover the duty payable on such goods being taken out for jobwork in DTA, then the unit would be required to furnish bank guarantee equal to 50% of the duty payable on goods being sent for jobwork. The status holders' EOUs having unblemished track records shall be exempt from the requirement of furnishing bank guarantee.

(iii) An EOU sending out goods for jobwork in DTA, shall be required to give an intimation to the jurisdictional Bond Officer and a sample of the goods being sent out for jobwork would be drawn and retained in the Range Office. On receipt of the goods in the unit after jobwork, the Bond Officer would establish the identity of goods so returned with reference to the sample retained by him at the time of removal. He would also retain sample of the processed good so returned for the purpose of record. On expiry of six months, both the samples would be returned to the unit after taking due acknowledgement from the unit.

(iv) In all cases of jobwork in DTA, the goods sent for jobwork shall be required to be returned to the unit within a period of 30 days from the date of removal. Further, extension of time may be considered by the Jurisdictional Assistant Commissioner only in deserving cases. In case of non-receipt of goods within the stipulated period, the Range Officer may take appropriate measures to recover duty, such as, encashment of the bank guarantee given at the time of removal of goods into DTA for jobwork.

(v) The Range Officer in charge of EOU would carry out the checks to verify the premises of jobworker, processing capacity of the jobworker, existence of facility for carrying out the declared processes in the jobworker's premises. Such verification should necessarily be carried out within a period of one month from the date of granting permission for jobwork. The verification may be carried out either by visiting the premises of the jobworker or by sending letters/FAX/E-mail to the jurisdictional Range Officer of jobworker's premises and getting confirmation in writing.

(vi) The requirements prescribed in the *Handbook of Procedure* (Vol. I) such as jobworker being a Central Excise Registrant, compulsory carrying out first processing in the unit before sending the goods for jobwork, and forwarding the sample to the Range Officer in charge of jobworker's shall not be applicable henceforth.

(vii) The above-mentioned conditions shall also apply *mutatis mutandis* to units located in Export Processing Zones, Special Economic Zones and to the STP and EHTP units. However, in case the jobwork is done through another unit in the same EPZ/SEZ the above condition will not apply

2. You are requested to permit sub-contracting as per the above guidelines. Changes in the Exim Policy made w.e.f. 01.04.2002 would be deemed to have been amended accordingly.

Appendix 14-IB—Criteria to be Adopted for Automatic Approval of Units Under EOU/SEZ Scheme

18

Approval of New Units

Proposals for setting up units under EOU/SEZ scheme under automatic route shall be considered by the Unit Approval Committee taking into account the following:

(i) Residence proof in respect of individual/partnership firms of all Directors/Partners. (Passport/ration card/ driving licence/voter identity card or any other proof to the satisfaction of Development Commissioner;

(ii) Income Tax return of all the promoters for the last three years;

(iii) Experience of the promoters;

(iv) Marketing tie-ups;

(v) In case of EOUs, inspection of the project site by an Officer;

(vi) A report from other DCs as to whether any case under SEZ/EOU Scheme in regard to diversion of goods, etc. is pending.

Wherever necessary, the above may be verified through personal interview with the promoters of the project. In the event of the promoters being a well-established entity, the procedure of personal interview may be dispensed with.

The Unit Approval Committee shall meet on Monday, every week. In case of the absence of Development Commissioner, the meeting will be held by the next senior officer in the Zone. The unit shall intimate the problems being faced by them in advance. In the meetings, apart from the promoters, the other concerned agency with which difficulties are being faced by the unit, may also be called.

Recycling of ferrous and non-ferrous metal proposals will be considered only if the unit has ingots making facility and proposes to achieve value addition.

Sensitive Sectors

Care shall be taken by the Development Commissioner while approving projects in sensitive sectors such as yarn texturising unit, textile processing, pharmaceuticals/drugs formulations/re-cycling of ferrous and non-ferrous metal scraps, etc. Projects for setting up units in sensitive sectors under EOU scheme shall be approved by the Development Commissioner after personal verification of the Directors and inspection of the factory site before signing LUT. Verification could also be carried out through General Manager, District Industries centre or jurisdictional DY/ Assitant Commissioner of Customs/Excise.

Appendix 14-IC—Sector Specific Requirements for EOU/SEZ Units

19

(1) Coffee

Export of imported coffee shall be subject to approval from Coffee Board under relevant Act.

(2) High Grade Iron Ore

Proposals for export of high-grade, i.e. 64% Fe Iron Ore and above, except iron ore of Goa origin and Redi origin are presently canalized through MMTC and its exports would be subject to annual quantity allocation by the BOA.

(3) Polyester Yarn

(i) No jobwork with EOU/SEZ/DTA unit shall be permitted. However, this shall not be applicable to units which intend to send the fabric (made out of Polyester (or) texturised yarn within the unit) for job-work to EOU/SEZ/DTA unit for dyeing of the fabric;

(ii) None of the units making polyester yarn—existing or new—shall be permitted to do exports through third party and they have to export directly;

(iii) These restrictions shall not apply to units in the same SEZ.

(4) Sale of Surplus Power

The following procedure shall apply in regard to sale of surplus power by EOU/SEZ units:

(i) Henceforth, whenever the Development Commissioner receives proposals for sale of surplus power, it would be examined in consultation with the State Government, including State Electricity Board. This shall, however, not apply to sale of power within the SEZ. The Development Commissioner will report the norms of raw materials and consumables required for generation of a unit of power for consideration and approval by the Board of Approvals.

(ii) No duty shall be required to be paid on sale of surplus power from an EOU/SEZ unit to another EOU/ SEZ unit. Development Commissioner of SEZ concerned would be informed in writing of such supply and proper account of the consumption of raw material would be maintained by the supplying unit. The value of imported inputs and consumables shall be taken into account for NFE calculations of the supplying unit.

(iii) The unit will obtain permission of the Assistant Commissioner of Customs/ Central Excise for sale of surplus power in the DTA, after obtaining permission from the SEBs under the relevant statute. Duty on sale of power to the DTA shall be as per the Notification of the Department of Revenue in this regard.

(iv) Due care shall be taken by the Development Commissioner/Board of Approval while approving the power plants by EOU/SEZ units vis-a-vis their actual requirement.

5. Guidelines for the Existing Plastic Units

The following shall be guidelines for the existing plastic units under EOU/SEZ scheme:

(i) Extension of LOP of the existing units under EOU/ SEZ Scheme may be granted based on the terms & conditions of earlier LOP.

(ii) No enhancement of the production capacity be allowed.

(iii) Relocation of the existing units from one Zone to another will be approved on case-to-case basis.

(iv) EOU/SEZ units be exempted from the purview of Public Notice No. 392 dated 1-1-1997 regarding restrictions on physical forms & sizes and inspection would be done by Zone. However, for any supply into DTA, all conditions of public notice will apply.

(6) Non-ITA-I Items that May be Sold in DTA

Following non-ITA-I items may be sold in the DTA in terms of para 13.1(f) of the EOU Scheme and 16(f) of the SEZ Scheme:

(i) Colour Display Tubes (CDT) for monitors

(ii) Deflection components for colour monitors.

Appendix 14-IG—Guidelines for Monitoring the Performance of EOU/SEZ/STP/EHTP Units

20

The annual review of performance of each operational unit and its compliance with the conditions of approval shall be undertaken by the Development Commissioner before the end of the first quarter of the following financial year;

A summary of annual performance review will be sent by each Development Commissioner to the Ministry of Commerce for information under the three formats indicated below, latest by 30th September every year:

Proforma I: Comparative statement of performance and monitoring as compared to previous year;

Proforma II: Summary of annual performance of the EOU/SEZ units, sectorwise with sectoral sub-totals.

Proforma III: Unitwise statement on NFE showing the result of review.

PART (A)

1. Criteria for Annual Monitoring

The criteria for keeping the unit under watch or initiating penal action in respect of EOU/SEZ units would be as follows:

(i) Watch—If there is shortfall in achieving the NFE as per norms in EOU/SEZ Scheme at the end of 1st and IInd year;

(ii) Issue of show cause notice—At the end of 3rd or subsequent year if positive NFE is not achieved as per EOU/SEZ Scheme, show cause notice will be issued.

After the completion of first five years, if it is noted that the unit has not achieved positive NFE, as per EOU/SEZ Scheme the Development Commissioner would initiate penal action under the F T (D&R) Act, 1992;

(iii) No action to be initiated if the Development Commissioner, on the receipt of reply from the unit, is satisfied that the shortfall has been on account of genuine reasons.

2. Method of Monitoring

(i) In all cases of exit from the Scheme where the unit has imported inputs and failed to fulfil the conditions of LOP with regard to NFE, appropriate steps are to be taken for penal action after issuing Show Cause Notice to the unit. Steps may also be initiated for cancellation of LOP/LOA of unit, which is not operating for more than a year;

(ii) NFE is to be calculated as per Para 9.1 to 9.4 of EOU Scheme and Para 12.1 to 12.4 of SEZ Scheme. For purpose of uniformity, guidelines for calculation of NFE is given in EOU/SEZ Scheme may be followed.

3. Monitoring Period

Units which have not completed one year from the date of commencement of commercial production, will not be monitored. In case a unit has completed less than five years from the date of commencement of commercial production it will be monitored for the number of completed years. Annual monitoring in the cases of old units which have completed more than five years will be undertaken for only such number of years which fall in the second block of five years.

4. Other Conditions

Development Commissioner will monitor Foreign Exchange realization/remittance of EOU/SEZ units in coordination with the concerned General Manager of RBI as per instructions issued on the subject vide RBI circular No. COEXD. 3109/05.62.05/ 99-2000 dated 21.2.2000.

PART B: SCHEME SPECIFIC CONDITIONS

5. Concurrent Joint Monitoring of EOU Units

(a) The performance of EOUs would be jointly reviewed by the Development Commissioners of SEZs and concerned Customs/Central Excise Officers on six monthly basis, i.e. April-September each year to be completed in the following quarter on the basis of QPRs/APR to be furnished by the EOUs. The formats of QPR/APR have been prescribed in the LUT at Appendix-14-IF.

(b) Joint review of NFE of the EOUs would be conducted by the DC/JDC and jurisdictional Deputy Commissioner/Asstt. Commissioner of Customs and Central Excise in the office of Commissioner of Customs/Central Excise where representatives of units would also be invited. This will help them to understand the scheme and clear the doubts about operation. The Development Commissioners are advised to identify the number of Customs and Excise Commissioners, where the meetings are to be held and work out a schedule for visiting each of these places. It is suggested that at least two places should be visited each month, so that all places are covered within a period of three months. Some places may be covered by JDC and in the next six months, these could be interchanged between JDC and DC.

(c) For publicising the scheme, advertisement in the local papers may be arranged before the date of such meetings. Promotion programmes may be organised in collaboration with local industry, Association or any other organisation, which has good presence in the area. General Manager of District Industries Center may be associated.

(d) For each existing unit, review should be done at length to understand their problems and their possible resolution. Efforts should be made to identify the reasons for shortfall / poor performance, and unitwise action plan should be prepared for removal of bottlenecks. It should be ensured that the unit should have an export promotion strategy as well tentative targets for next few years, so that it has an idea as to what is to be achieved by them. Effective action should be taken against erring units to discourage any misuse of the scheme.

(e) For units under implementation, separate review be held so that their issues could be resolved.

(f) At such places, if any infrastructure gaps are noticed, District Administration may be advised to prepare projects which can be routed through State Government to the Ministry for approval under Scheme for Central Assistance for Developing Export Infrastructure and Other Allied Activities (ASIDE).

(g) Based on the joint review, Development Commissioner concerned would prepare a report for information of the Department of Commerce and CBEC and suggest corrective measures to enable the defaulting units to fulfill their obligation as per EOU Scheme / Customs Notifications.

6. Quarterly and Annual Monitoring of Sez Units

(a) The performance of the SEZ units shall be monitored by a Committee as provided for in the SEZ Scheme.

(b) The performance of the SEZ units to be monitored each quarter period on the basis of reports received on formats prescribed in SEZ Scheme.

(c) Annual monitoring would be undertaken on the basis of APR prescribed in Annexure IV of Appendix-14-IF. However, penal action is to be initiated only if NFE achieved is negative at the end of first five years.

(d) During the joint review, efforts should be made to identify the reasons for shortfall/poor performance, and unit-wise action plan should be prepared for removal of bottlenecks through such a review.

(e) Based on the joint review, Development Commissioner concerned would prepare a report for the information of the Department of Commerce and CBEC and suggest corrective measures to enable the defaulting units to fulfil their obligations as per SEZ Scheme/ Customs Notifications.

ANNEXURE I: CALCULATION OF NFE

1. While calculating NFE achieved, following basic components are to be taken into consideration:

(i) Amortised value of capital goods and technical know-how fee.

(ii) Value of import of R.M. (which is consumed during the year and consumables, spares, etc.).

(iii) Other outflow of foreign exchange towards royalty, interest on external commercial borrowings, etc.

(iv) Value of physical exports effected excluding DTA sales but including supplies made under para 13.1 of the EOU Scheme and para 16.1 to 16.2 of the SEZ Scheme.

2. Amortised Value of Capital Goods: For this purpose as much value of CG is taken into account as indicated in para 9.4 of the EOU Scheme and para 12.4 of the SEZ Scheme. The CG imported prior to the 10 years period is not taken into consideration for the purposes of NFE if the value of said CG is fully amortized. If any capital goods imported duty-free are leased from a leasing company or are taken in loan, the CIF value of the capital goods shall be included under the imported inputs. However, on return of such CG, its unamortized portion of value would be excluded from the calculation formula.

3. Import of raw material, consumables and spares, etc.: Whatever RM Consumables and spares are imported during the year are taken into account. However, it should be noted that whatever RM is in balance at the end of the previous year is added while the RM at the end of the current year is deducted which will give the amount of RM consumed during the year. RM purchased as inter-unit transfer is also included.

4. Other outflow of foreign exchange: All the foreign exchange outflow on account of royalty, dividends, commission on exports, interest on external commercial borrowing, etc. during the particular year has to be accounted for while calculating value addition. However, outflow on account of know-how fee would be apportioned during a period of ten years as applicable.

5. Value of exports: While calculating value of exports, DTA sales made during the year are not to be accounted for. However, supplies made in accordance with the para 13.1 of the EOU Scheme and para 16.1 to 16.2 of the SEZ Scheme will be taken into consideration for calculation of NFE.

Appendix 14-IH —Guidelines for Sale of Goods in the Domestic Tariff Area (DTA) by EOU/EHTP/ STP Units

21

I. DTA Sale Entitlement for EOU Units

Paragraph 12 of the EOU Scheme provides for sale in DTA by EOU/EHTP/STP units. Such sales in the DTA will be governed by the following guidelines:

(a) The sale of goods in DTA will be subject to the payment of applicable duties as notified from time to time by the Department of Revenue, Ministry of Finance, Government of India. DTA sale includes clearance to any other unit within India under para 12.

(b) DTA sale entitlement will be applicable only to those goods and services, which are permissible as per EOU Scheme. No DTA sale will be permissible if such sale is specifically prohibited in the EOU Scheme or the Letter of Permission/Letter of Intent.

(c) Units may opt for DTA sales on a quarterly, half-yearly or annual basis by intimation to the concerned Development Commissioner of the SEZ.

(d) The DTA sales entitlement shall be availed of within three years of the accrual of entitlement.

(e) An application for sale of goods in DTA as per EOU Scheme by the EOUs shall be submitted to the Development Commissioner concerned in the form given at Annexure-A. The application shall be certified by an independent Cost/Chartered/Cost and Works

Accountant and endorsed by the Bond Officer of Customs/Central Excise having jurisdiction over the unit. The Development Commissioner concerned will determine the extent of the DTA sale admissible and issue authorization in terms of value.

(f) Advance DTA sale permission not exceeding the entitlement accruable on the exports envisaged in the first year shall be permitted and such sale shall be adjusted against the subsequent entitlements in a maximum period of two years. However, drugs and pharmaceuticals units can make advance DTA sale of the production on the exports envisaged in the first two years adjustable against subsequent entitlements within a maximum period of three years from the date of commencement of production by the unit. The Unit shall be required to execute a bond with the Assistant Commissioner Customs/Central Excise concerned to cover the difference between the amount of duties paid on the advance DTA sale and the full duties applicable on such goods.

(g) Advance DTA sales permission would also be admissible in cases of capacity expansion/product diversification. In such cases, the unit would be entitled to advance DTA sales linked to the exports envisaged from the expansion or new production streams or through product diversification. However, no advance DTA sale would be admissible to a DTA unit converted into EOU except in respect of new production stream as a result of change of technology.

(h) The DTA sale entitlement would accrue only if the unit has achieved positive NFE on cumulative basis.

(i) EOUs engaged in the manufacture of perishable items like floriculture, horticulture, pisciculture can also avail the facility of simultaneous sale in DTA of such perishable items on quarterly basis, while earning DTA entitlement on exports made during the said quarter. Such permission can be granted in advance by the DC concerned, subject to the condition that the unit has achieved positive NFE cumulatively up to the previous quarter.

(j) Units in the service sector can also avail DTA sale as per procedure mentioned above.

(k) DTA sale of instant tea will be allowed up to 20% of FOB value of exports in the form of tea bags or bulk.

II. Sale of Gem & Jewellery Products

DTA sale of Gem & Jewellery items will be permitted on annual basis by the Development Commissioners up to 10% of FOB value of exports during the preceding year subject to following conditions:

(a) The application by an EOU will be submitted to DC concerned on yearly basis (licensing year) giving the details of production and exports made during the preceding licensing year duly certified by a Chartered Accountant and endorsed by the jurisdictional Custom Authority.

(b) The DTA sale of plain jewellery shall be permitted on payment of concessional rate of duty in Indian Rupees as applicable to sale from nominated agencies. In respect of studded jewellery, duty shall be payable in Indian Rupees as notified by Customs.

(c) Advance DTA sale permission not exceeding the entitlement accruable on the exports envisaged in the first year shall be permitted and such sale shall be adjusted against the subsequent entitlements in a maximum period of two years. The Unit shall be required to execute a bond with the Assistant Commissioner Customs/Central Excise concerned to cover the difference between the amount of duties paid on the advance DTA sale and the full duties applicable on such goods.

III. Other Supplies in DTA

(i) Sale under para 13.1 of the EOU Scheme.

The following guidelines shall apply to the sale of goods in the DTA in respect of supplies specified in paragraph 13.1 of the EOU Scheme:

(a) The unit shall, at the time of application, indicate the quantity and value of goods sought to be supplied in the DTA. If the sale is effected against an import license held by the DTA purchaser, the Customs/ Central Excise Officer concerned will allow such sales after making a suitable entry on the license of the quantity and value of such sales. The Import license shall cease to be valid for further imports to the extent of such supplies effected by units.

(b) If, the goods proposed to be sold by the units do not require an import license, the Customs/Central Excise Officer concerned will allow such supplies from the unit to the DTA.

(c) (i) Goods supplied under (a) and (b) above will be taken into account for the purposes of achievement of NFE. The unit will file a quarterly statement to the Development Commissioner giving details of the goods cleared in the DTA category-wise. (ii) Sale under para 12.4 & 12.5 of the EOU Scheme shall be considered by the Development Commissioner on quarterly basis. While considering the domestic sales, the Development Commissioner will keep the circumstances of the case to ensure that the export orientation of the scheme is maintained.

IV. Sale of Rejects

Sale of rejects is also permitted in the DTA, as provided for in para 12.1(a) of the EOU Scheme.

V. Sale of By-products

The sale of by-products in the DTA is also permitted as per provision of para 12.7 of the EOU Scheme after inclusion of the item in LOP/LOI.

VI. No DTA sale will be granted to compacting/micronization units